The Metaphysics
of Sound in
Wallace Stevens

THE METAPHYSICS
OF SOUND IN
WALLACE STEVENS

Anca Rosu

The University of Alabama Press

Tuscaloosa and London

Copyright © 1995
The University of Alabama Press
Tuscaloosa, Alabama 35487–0380

∞

The paper on which this book is printed meets the minimum requirements of
American National Standard for Information Science-Permanence of Paper for
Printed Library Materials, ANSI Z39.48–1984.

Library of Congress Cataloging-in-Publication Data

Rosu, Anca, 1947–
The metaphysics of sound in Wallace Stevens / Anca Rosu.
p. cm.
Includes bibliographical references and index.
ISBN 0-8173-0797-4
1. Stevens, Wallace, 1879–1955—Criticism and interpretation.
2. Sound poetry—History and criticism. 3. Metaphysics in
literature. 4. Music and literature. 5. Sound in literature.
6. Poetics. I. Title.
PS3537.T4753Z7625 1995
811'.52—dc20 94-43107

British Library Cataloguing-in-Publication Data available

For Ernesto

Contents

Preface

Harmonium, Wallace Stevens's choice of title for his first volume of verse, introduces his poetry with a subtle elegance. It invites speculation and a search for its significance and origins. I do not wish, however, to speculate about its meaning or its relation to the poems. I would like to consider it before I read the poems, to ponder what it has to tell about a book not yet opened. Without extended speculation about the word's possible meanings, I can read the title as a metaphor, since it implies the analogy between poetry and a musical instrument, and if I want to go into further detail, between the keys of the musical instrument and the individual poems.[1] I could "see" the volume as a musical instrument. This visual suggestion is not, however, the first to come to mind when I read this title, because *Harmonium* rings closer to something more familiar: harmony. The word "harmonium" thus speaks to the uninitiated reader in at least two ways: through its reference, on the one hand, and through its sound, on the other, and the difficulty is that the two are inextricable. The evocation of the object, which usually plays the primary role in the perception of meaning, is, in this instance, secondary, as the old, or perhaps exotic, instrument refuses to take shape in a reading process hard to detach from mental hearing. Nonetheless, with its familiar ring, the word is reminiscent of harmony, therefore music, and its sense, which has been dominated by the sound, emerges again in a process related to both understanding and audibility. A new vitality raises the mere word to the rank of a rhetorical figure.

And the figure is not a simple one, since it involves a doubled understanding determined by both the silent reading experience and its sound in the audial imagination. As a result of that process, the musical instrument comes to stand for music in general: not only for a particular contraption that produces sound but for the aspiration toward harmony that produced the contraption in the first place. Because of its sound, which relates it to other words and other contexts, the word does not merely represent the object but rises to new powers of meaning and transcends its (arbitrary) ties with the physical world. The title is, I think, exemplary of the complex ways in which the sounds of words, whether taken individually or in patterns, come to be involved in the perception of meaning in Wallace Stevens's poetry.

The present study is not an attempt to *look* at Stevens from the *point of view* of sound. Such visual metaphors, used habitually to describe poetry, would defeat the purpose of the enterprise. What is needed, I think, is a way to listen to poetry and to Stevens's poetry in particular. The traditional view of prosody as an ornamental device proves insufficient for Stevens, whose usage of sound goes beyond mere contrivance and is intimately related to the content of his poetry. My thesis is simply that the way Stevens uses sound in his poems serves to prove that language functions to establish rapport between people more often and more powerfully than it does to communicate ideas. Stevens tried to make this point in his essays in an expository manner, but words seem to have betrayed him. He tried to make it rhetorically in his poems, but somehow they can always be interpreted in different ways. For exposition relies on what language can make us see, and rhetoric is only partly a relation between speaker and listener or poet and reader. And only sound (whether voiced or silent) can be understood on the basis of shared familiarity, which is the foundation for rapport.

In many ways, I face the same difficult task here that Stevens himself did when writing his essays: I must somehow conceptualize the ephemeral effects of the sound. And since I cannot write poetry as he did, I have elected to read for effect rather than for ideas, to follow the poems' action rather than their argument. Reading for effect may seem secondary to the task of understanding the sense, but Stevens's poems demand such a reading as a complement to the more usual kind. This kind of reading appears the more necessary if one agrees with Richard Poirier that "barriers to clarity can in themselves be modes of communication, expressions of human bonding."[2] My readings will, therefore, be an attempt not to clarify but to deal with obscurity.

I have tried to read Stevens from inside out, starting with the text of his poems and building my argument on what they exhibit as performance. What I hope to show is that the poems not only speak but act and that their action is meaningful. My argument should not be taken for a series of interpretations in the strict sense of the word, for it is nothing of the sort. I do not seek to compete with the often brilliant interpretations of other critics. My interest lies rather in the way sound works to dissolve meaning as we usually conceive of it and then reveals it again on another plane. Any attempts at interpretation, which may often appear at the start of my analyses, are exercises meant to show the need for a departure from a decoding to a listening mode. It is my contention that such a change is necessary for a full understanding of any of Stevens's poems. What I, in fact, want to interpret are the poetic gestures, and with my emphasis on sound, I aim to supplement rather than replace the previous critical work on Stevens. Thus my readings of various poems are only steps in an argument concerned with Stevens's view of language and the uses to which it can be put. They also touch on the main questions related to Stevens's poetics that are often debated in criticism.

I started from the premise that the way we conceive of language determines the way we use it and is determined, in turn, by the way we conceive of reality, knowledge, or truth and ourselves in the world. Several assumptions current in Stevens's time have inspired the stages of my argument, which ultimately proves that Stevens works against these assumptions. In his time, it was generally assumed (and the assumption still persists today) that language is a reflection of reality; that reality is made up of objects whose existence cannot be doubted; that knowledge means a thorough assessment of this world of objects; and that the self is perfectly centered and poised within reality and able to know it. This is not to say that there weren't many thinkers who contested such ideas, but the assumptions remained current in the climate where Stevens developed intellectually. Inspired by his mentors at Harvard, William James and George Santayana, Stevens dedicated his poetry to challenging such ideas by using his language to conjure rather than to reflect reality, by putting the fictional before the real, by proclaiming knowledge beyond reality, and by conceiving of self as a fluid entity liable to be recreated in sound. These qualities have often been noticed by his critics. My argument is that, to achieve this purpose, Stevens made language into a sort of music that is meaningful not only through its semantics but also through its patterns and its appeals to our sense of being connected to other fellow human beings. I think that ultimately Stevens's message is that a world swarming with others should appeal not to the eye, which would transform it into a collection of objects, but to the ear, which can receive and appropriate the others' voices.

The poet's use of sound is thus an integral part of his poetics. For Stevens, the question about poetry, or the question of poetry, is actually a question about and of language, about its status as a means of representing reality, as well as about the excess of meaning always attending the attempt to produce a representation in words. And such excess has to do with musicality as much as it has to do with language's condition as dialogue between real or virtual speakers. Beyond what the words have to express, all details of grammar, choices of diction, or patterns of sound are meaningful to the reader. Such elements become, in Stevens, more than stylistic devices, since they are made to play a role in the poetry's drama of self-definition, a drama that brings language not only to self-awareness but also to the point of self-transcendence. I would like to show here the dynamic through which Stevens's poems aspire to and eventually transform into a language rendered fluid by its pattern, a language in which meaning circulates between poet and reader through what I shall call images of sound. And this language, where meaning dissolves before being regenerated in the words' sound, gives Stevens's poetry its philosophical value without ever letting it turn into philosophy, as such language alone has the capacity to transcend its own condition.

Stevens's use of sound ranges from the traditional to the experimental to the parodic, and its overwhelming importance lies in the fact that it does not simply "follow sense" but participates in creating meaning. Sound patterns result from an exploration within the possibilities of language, an experimentation with discourses and their combination, whose ultimate outcome consists of new conceptions regarding language, reality, truth, and the self. I will thus direct my attention to the implications of sound manipulation in Stevens's poems, implications extending to changes in the assumptions on which the usage of language is based. Because the poems challenge many assumptions at once, and because the discursive transformations that take place in them are of a complex nature, I have tried to group the poems in chapters according to their most salient discursive features, on which the discussion is focused, so that the full impact of Stevens's experiment may be perceived gradually.

In the first chapter, I follow a theoretical itinerary that may seem idiosyncratic but that actually establishes an approach to the question of sound in language and in poetry as it has been suggested to me by various theorists and philosophers. Sound can be regarded as a meaningful feature of language only within a theory of meaning based on more than a correspondence between "reality" and its representation in language. Linguistic theories gathered under the name of pragmatics make it possible to see language as a dialogue between speakers and draw particular attention to the cultural and social conditions under which meaning is generated. Such theories are nicely supplemented by theories of meaning in music and folkloric productions, where sense is also produced in the interaction between a player/singer and a listener. I contend that the relation between the partners in the dialogue persists even after language has been written and that listening is possible even in the absence of speakers. If my contention is true, it is possible to approach the pattern of sound as a meaningful feature of language.

A similar theory on the importance of sound emerges in the second chapter, where I consider how the topic of sound was treated by modern poets like Frost and Stevens. My theoretical framework is thus consonant with the poet's own ideas about sound.

In chapter 3, I start my exploration of Stevens's poetic with the challenge he presents to the assumption that language is secondary to reality. In a number of poems that coincidentally belong to Stevens's early career, the poet experiments with patterns of sound so powerful that many have subsequently accused him of writing nonsense. The repetitions, as well as a special use of parodic effects, detach the words from their habitual meaning and make their materiality evident. Insofar as the words become significant simply as material presences, their effect is similar to that of charms and incantations, in the sense that they do not evoke but rather conjure up realities. Verbal magic is an interesting equivalent for and metaphor of Stevens's discourse, because, like his verse, it operates on the assumption—contrary to the one on which the commonsense use of language is based—that language is the primary element and reality follows as its consequence.

By changing the basic assumption about the relation between reality and language, we challenge the very notion of reality, an idea that I explore in the fourth chapter. To think of reality as secondary, as a consequence of language, implies that it depends on human understanding, whereas the commonsense notion would have reality independent and outstanding. But as William James repeatedly pointed out, an independent, outstanding reality is of no consequence to human affairs unless it has been integrated into human experience. Human action is practically guided by that which has been founded as real in human experience. What counts as reality is thus a construct, a negotiated product of human action. Stevens makes poetry a terrain upon which the notion of the real is constantly negotiated, while the distinction between real and fictional is eventually dissolved. Failing to render the outstanding "real," language returns to its own foundations in form and pattern and lets reality emerge as a human creation.

The negotiation of the real normally raises questions about the nature and purpose of knowledge, on which I focus in the fifth chapter. Because they fail to represent a reality independent of human activity, Stevens's poems seem to lead to an epistemological breakdown signaled by a dominance of repetitions, which block both the intelligibility of language and the cognitive effort directed at the reality beyond it. The configurations of sound resulting from repetitions produce, however, a different kind of intelligibility based on the perception of pattern. Such perception satisfies a basic desire for knowledge, and repetition thus acquires a cognitive value.

This new epistemological basis creates the need for a new ontology also based on repetition, which becomes evident in the sixth chapter. Stevens's poems considered here act as verbal rituals, the result of which is a coming into being, a founding of the self. Repetition is a way of interacting with and appropriating the collective way of being and speaking. The process of differentiation accompanying every act of repetition—one never repeats identically unless the repetition is mechanical—makes it possible that individuality might emerge in the very act of appropriating the collective manner of being/speaking. In Stevens's poems, this coming into being of the self becomes possible through the repetition and appropriation of a collective discourse, which eventually gives the individual speaker the authority of a collective voice.

The changes that Stevens's stylistic maneuvers effect at the level of the assumptions underlying language usage produce not only a change of discourse but also the reversal of a view of the world that originated in Platonic philosophy and subsequently dominated Western thought. The poems considered in the seventh chapter show that Stevens creates a new type of discourse that may be called poetic but not in any traditional sense. The main characteristic of Stevens's poetic discourse is its transitional quality. Constituted as a mutation of the realistic, narrative, or analytical discourse into a sound-dominated discourse, Stevens's poetic language is recognizable by its fluidity and by its mobility. Sense is not arrested in formulation but rather transcends itself permanently, residing basically in the language's movement. The worldview that this fluid, sound-dominated discourse promotes is radically different from the traditional one, in which the working of the mind is likened to the function of the eye. To Plato's metaphysics of sight Stevens responds with a metaphysics of sound.

The ultimate purpose for Stevens is not, I think, to replace philosophy with poetry but to enhance the poetic and endow it with philosophical import. At its best, his language is at once abstract and capable of producing emotion. The most relevant illustration of such achievement is "The Comedian as the Letter C," which I discuss at some length in the eighth chapter and in which the "musicality" of language plays the starring role, for the quality of the diction, the syntactic variation, the carefully managed repetitions, produce a meaning analogous to that of music. Becoming musical, in this particular way, language loses transparency, but it deploys an action whose main result is a special kind of meaning, which, like that of music, is indistinguishable from emotion. At the same time, abstract ideas, which linguistic representation would not be able to express, are reached through language's own self-transcendence.

After having considered the challenge that Stevens's poetry poses to philosophy, in the final chapter, I take a closer look at his philosophical affiliations proper. Although none of his poems is genuinely philosophical in the sense of being systematic and conceptual, Stevens claims poetry as a way of thinking and of reaching for the knowledge usually associated with philosophy. The unstated claim that poetry is a way to think—actually the only way to think and a better alternative than philosophy—brings Stevens close to the thought of Martin Heidegger. The notable difference is that while Heidegger's passion for poetry threatens his profession—philosophy, as it has traditionally been understood—with its end, Stevens, being a poet, can only triumph in the triumph of poetry. Yet the similarities with Heidegger are limited and actually have their origin in the earlier and more powerful influence exerted on Stevens by American philosophers like William James and George Santayana, who themselves challenged the tenets of traditional philosophy by stressing the cultural construction of such notions as reality, truth, and knowledge. Both William James and George Santayana, whose ideas became familiar to Stevens while he was studying at Harvard, can be said to have been experimental philosophers in the way that Stevens was an experimental poet. Their distrust of the standing notions of truth, reality, and knowledge and the special attention they give to language constitute a subversion of philosophy from the inside that validates the poet's attack on it from the standpoint of poetry. Stevens's experimentation with sound is thus not only essential to his poetics but also profoundly related to the pragmatist ideas that informed his way of thinking.

Acknowledgments

I THANK THE PEOPLE who helped me as I shaped this book: James Guetti, who introduced me to the philosophy of Wittgenstein, made me obsess over word/music, and generally guided every step of the project; Andrew Welsh, who read the manuscript attentively and encouraged me to bring the book to its present form; Carol Smith, who fostered my interest in modern poetry and made me believe in myself; William Dowling, who showed me how to endow my writing with authority; and last but not least Stefan Stoenescu, who first introduced me to Stevens.

Part of the chapter entitled "The Image of Sound" has previously been published as an article in the *Wallace Stevens Journal,* Fall 1992, and is reproduced here by permission of the Wallace Stevens Society.

The poems and excerpts of poems, prose, or letters from *Collected Poems* by Wallace Stevens Copyright 1954 by Wallace Stevens; from *Opus Posthumous* by Wallace Stevens Copyright © 1957 by Elsie Stevens; from *Letters of Wallace Stevens* by Wallace Stevens Copyright © 1966 by Holly Stevens; and from *The Necessary Angel* by Wallace Stevens Copyright 1951 by Wallace Stevens are reprinted by permission of Alfred A. Knopf Inc.

*The Metaphysics
of Sound in
Wallace Stevens*

1

Sound and Language

A BOOK-LENGTH STUDY on sound in the work of a single author may seem excessively narrow if not downright paradoxical. Normally, we consider sound in small fragments of prose or verse, and seldom do we feel inclined to follow its implications in a full piece, let alone a large part of a writer's work. Sound is usually of secondary interest, a poetic device among others that only rarely, and with some difficulty, can be said to determine the meaning of a literary work. "Prosodic study justifies itself only as an *adjunct* to criticism," declares Paul Fussell in his study *Poetic Meter and Poetic Form*.[1] In spite of such prejudice, a full study on the subject is imperative for Wallace Stevens, since in his poetry sound is not merely a prosodic element, or a stylistic device of limited significance, but an integral part of a distinctive poetics. For this reason, defining the role of sound in his verse must be not an isolated task but an enterprise derived from and contributing to an understanding of his entire poetic achievement.

That Stevens uses sound in very special ways is a well-known fact, and his innovative prosody has attracted no small amount of attention. There are a number of approaches to sound reflecting diverse ways of interpreting oral/aural effects. Some studies concentrate on the significance of onomatopoeias, which abound in Stevens's work. Although departing from the naive belief that the sound of a word can coincide with its meaning, critics find that Stevens can employ sound symbolic words as metaphors[2] or use onomatopoeia to contrast highly intellectualized language with the preverbal.[3] Prosodic studies proper emphasize either an unusual discordance between the pattern of sound and meaning[4] or the innovative manner in which Stevens uses traditional prosody.[5] There have also been interesting attempts to read Stevens as a "musical" poet either by following the development of musical themes in his poetry[6] or by arguing that the sound of poetry produces noncognitive images in the way music does.[7] Sound as a thematic element has also attracted attention, although attempts to show the significance of different types of sounds have met with some difficulty in detaching sound as theme or trope from the sound effects themselves.[8] The quality of Stevens's diction is sometimes considered to be an aural feature, since through its foreign[9] or Latin origins[10] it may appeal first to the ear and only second to the imagination.

These discussions on the subject—most of them in articles or sections of books dedicated to sound in poetry in general—follow a predictable movement from observations about prosody to an evaluation of the relation between sound devices and the poem's meaning. That relation is found, also predictably, to be one of harmony, unless it is discovered to be quite the reverse.[11] The wealth of innovations revealed by these prosodic studies suggests, however, that beyond enhancing the work of interpretation, the relation between sound and meaning may be more intimate than a simple concordance or discordance. In addition, the complex theories that underlie the mainstream criticism on Stevens's poetry show that the very notion of meaning is problematic in his poems. The question of meaning, however, has rarely been related to that of sound.[12] This may not seem surprising, since, as Kevin Barry notes, "It has become, since Jacques Derrida's *Of Grammatology,* an accepted idiom in theories of literature to value writing and to devalue speech. Writing is thought of as the play of difference and of the material sign. However, it is clear that the materiality, diversity and uncertainty of language can also be thought of in terms of its sound."[13]

The purpose of this study is to discuss precisely the "materiality, diversity and uncertainty" of Stevens's language in terms of its sound. But before proceeding in this direction, I would like to establish something like a theoretical framework in which the proper relevance of sound in the perception of meaning may become apparent. To do so, I will have to consider theories of meaning related to both language and music. Through an examination of both, I hope to establish some axioms that will constitute the starting points of my exploration of Stevens: (1) that language is by nature dialogic, and distinctive discursive styles can coexist in the same utterance; (2) that meaning is generated in the interaction between speakers, and sound understood as pattern plays an important role in this interaction; (3) that the meaning of sound pattern in language can be described by analogy with the meaning of music.

More than any other modernist, Stevens practiced a poetic art that disarms the traditional methods of critical reading. The abundance of criticism on his poetry, especially in the aftermath of structuralism and deconstruction, signals, not only the rise of the poet to posthumous glory, but also a need for a new way to read his work. Such need is generated by the poems themselves, and if it was not felt by his early critics, the reason was that criticism itself had still to progress toward a certain flexibility regarding the ways of reading. For Stevens's most important innovations reside, as has often been suggested, in the way he manipulates language, and before New Criticism, language itself was not the main concern of critical approaches.

The question of a new way to read also stems from a quality of Stevens's poetry often noticed by his critics, especially by Joseph Riddel, namely its self-reflexivity, which draws attention to language as such.[14] Speaking of poetry in poetry is less a matter of direct statement than a matter of letting language play and of making its own materiality relevant. Performance is thus one of the most interesting features of Stevens's poetry, and although it has been noticed and explored as such, most critics still search for the poet's ideas in his direct statements. To my mind, the implications of Stevens's linguistic performance exceed even the import of his direct statements about poetry, for not only does he use language poetically, in a traditional sense, but he also aims to discover where the roots of the poetic as an essence lie.

Stevens's own engagement with questions about the nature of language makes it possible, if not necessary, that the discussion of his poems should be integrated within a linguistic theory. In fact, the later critical works of Joseph Riddel and J. Hillis Miller, as well as Paul Bové's[15] alignment of Stevens with Heidegger's "destructive poetics," have responded to this need that continues to be felt even in recent years, when a more historical and cultural perspective has been directed on Stevens, especially by Frank Lentricchia.[16] Whether integrated in his cultural and historical context or not, Stevens has to be seen as an experimenter with language, simply because such experimentation is the main feature of that very context.

Yet a mechanical application of a linguistic theory in interpretation may well prove insufficient for an understanding of the poet's achievement. In her book *Stevens and Simile: A Theory of Language,*[17] Jacqueline Brogan makes use not only of certain concepts developed by deconstruction but also of more traditional theories of language, and her enterprise proves that only by taking them all a step further can one evolve a theory of language suited to Stevens's poems. According to Brogan, both "a unitive/realist/or logocentric conception, in which the work is regarded as naming at the source of being, and a disjunctive/nominalist/even deconstructive conception of language in which the word is regarded as a deferral of being and even of meaning"[18] are inscribed in Stevens's work. The two tendencies of language—one to unite the signifier to the object/reality, and the other to fragment, to distance language from reality—compete in Stevens's poetry, but they are kept in balance by the use of simile. Brogan is not the first to find inspiration in deconstruction for an interpretation of Stevens's poetry, as the works of Riddel, Miller, and Bové testify, but her aims are higher. Not only does she use deconstructive concepts to analyze Stevens, but she brings an important amendment to the theory as well. The balance of the two tendencies of language in Stevens—to unite and to fragment—demonstrates that a unilateral theory is insufficient. Moreover, there is here the suggestion that the usage of language in one direction or the other is the decision of the speaker/writer. Thus Brogan allows the speaker much more control over language than orthodox deconstructionists would. And whereas the aversion to logos demonstrated by deconstruction does not invite any probing into the question of sound, Brogan's amendments are quite germane to the kind of theory I would like to develop here. I shall return to her later.

As Brogan's effort demonstrates, the main difficulty confronting any attempt to interpret Stevens with the aid of theory relates to the complexity of Stevens's poetic language, which, although often forbidding because of its intellectualism and sophisticated diction (qualities usually attributed to abstract discourse), has the vitality of everyday speech and disarms systematic approaches. In fact, dealing with Stevens's poetry is as difficult as dealing with complex language in action. And as Gerald Bruns points out, "Language in the world is structured like a conversation rather than like a grammar. It is the many-layered discourse of contrary voices in diverse tongues, each expressing its own 'socioideological' outlook, its own temporal horizon, its own special history. It is not, as logic, linguistics, and the philosophy of language would have it, a system that makes possible the endless creative production of sentences."[19] The problem is thus not to find, among the existing theories, the one most adequate for Stevens's poetry but to discover the very principles informing the making of that poetry, that is, to find a reading mode demanded by the poems themselves.

It would reduce the impact of Stevens's poems to read them in light of a single language theory, because language varies with speakers, genres, and occasions, and Stevens uses, indeed, a wide variety of all three. Competing linguistic theories, on the other hand, tend to seize upon one single kind of usage, which they take to exemplify language in general. Rather than rely on a single theory, it is more useful, I think, to combine several such theories and let them illuminate the complexity of Stevens's verse as they interact with each other. Roughly put, the main conflict—reflected also in the critical works on Stevens—has been between the positivist or realist view of language, which emphasizes the relation between language and reality, and the Saussurian theory, later modified by deconstruction, which places the main stress on the internal relations present in the system of language. According to the positivist orientation, an extralinguistic reality is primary, and what constitutes meaning in language is a representation of it. One should note here that positivism, which according to Richard Rorty[20] extends from Hobbes to Carnap, may be of a materialistic or idealistic orientation. The former considers objective reality as primary, whereas the latter takes the world of ideas as point of reference. In both cases, however, the meaning of language is determined by a correspondence to something external to language (either things or ideas), whereas deconstruction would contend that meaning is constructed (and therefore liable to be deconstructed) within the system of language and that it depends solely upon the differences between linguistic signs. Deconstruction is not, however, the first theory to have opposed positivism. As Thomas Grey notes in his study on Stevens and law, "Against the Lockean approach to language and the scientific world view, there has of course always been an opposition party. In ancient times and during the Renaissance, it consisted of the teachers and practitioners of the classical art of rhetoric; but since the nineteenth century, rhetoric has been supplanted by literature."[21] Stevens himself, as I shall show in the next chapter, found positivism rather distasteful, but such an aversion does not automatically place him in the camp of deconstruction.

Both positivism and deconstruction find themselves in a new rivalry with a number of related theories about language—from the philosophy of the later Wittgenstein to speech act theory as represented by Austin and Searle, from the work of Paul Grice to the neopragmatism of Richard Rorty—that can be gathered under the name of pragmatics.[22] The designation, only loosely related to pragmatic philosophy, is used by Steven Levinson[23] to describe those aspects of meaning that go beyond semantics, as they result from what Wittgenstein called "human customs and institutions." Besides a correct decoding of semantic units and of the syntax that holds them together, the process of understanding an utterance depends on sharing the same culture and on being aware of the circumstances under which a word is used. The pragmatics of language does not replace semantics (or syntax) but rather explains the excess of meaning that cannot be classified under any systematic heading. Nevertheless, Wittgenstein's definition of meaning as the "use" of the word in a situation that he calls a "language game" enables pragmatics to become an overall theory of meaning in language.

Although the focus of Wittgenstein, and many of those inspired by him, has been on one-on-one communication situations, the theory can easily be extrapolated to a more complex cultural context. Within such an extended theory, language should be considered in its action, and meaning should be defined as the function of the utterance within a certain social and cultural circumstance. In a way, pragmatics may be considered rather a complement than a rival of Saussurian theory, since it can explain how the differences between signs are achieved and how they work—a point on which Saussure remained vague. Such an approach to language also seems ideally suited to complement the study of Stevens's poetry, especially if one aims at discovering the role of sound in the creation and perception of its meaning.

A finer point needs to be made in relation to pragmatics, however, especially if one is to use it to approach literature. If one accepts the idea that meaning in language is determined by its social and cultural context, one has to take into account all the constraints (deriving from that context) that govern the functioning of language. But as Dominick LaCapra points out, any context is, in its own turn, a text also subject to contextualization.[24] One of the constraints governing language use is thus the speaker's own conception about the function and role of language. What speakers think of language—thought that either generates or is generated by dominant linguistic theories—determines their use of it, the choice of the language game in Wittgenstein's terms.

Indeed, one can see striking differences between a usage informed by the positivist idea that language should build representations of things/ideas and another usage whose purpose is immediate communication according to custom—the difference between a scientific paper and an exchange of greetings, for instance. Neither usage is exempt from the significance of the situation, but whereas the speakers participating in an exchange of greetings are aware that semantics is marginal, the intention one can infer in a paper is to make sense in purely semantic terms, in terms independent of all circumstantial factors. The meaning of the paper also depends on its own condition as a paper and on our complicity in recognizing its intention, but such dependence is perceived as some kind of embarrassment. For the paper is supposed to convey concepts and ideas—this is why it relies heavily upon semantics—whereas the exchange of greetings is allowed to be meaningful only because of usage and situation. Actually, the degree to which an utterance relies on semantics places it in a certain "language game," or a certain variety of what Michel Foucault has called "discourse."

The notion of "discourse"—a linguistic practice with its own rules and regularities characteristic of a certain domain of human activity—was developed by Michel Foucault in order to make some distinctions between the different uses to which language was put during what he calls the "classical age." At first, Foucault uses the term "discourse" to characterize a transformation of language produced by the need to express a new form of knowledge appearing in the seventeenth century: science. Scientific discoveries demanded a new kind of language, a new way of describing things, one more explicit, more precise and consistent, more capable of generalizations. The change in the way one conceived of knowledge profoundly affected language: "The men of the seventeenth and eighteenth centuries do not think of wealth, nature, or languages in terms that had been bequeathed to them by preceding ages or in forms that presaged what was soon to be discovered; they think of them in terms of a general arrangement that not only prescribes their concepts and methods, but also, more fundamentally, defines a certain mode of being for language, natural individuals, and the objects of need and desire; this mode of being is that of representation."[25]

In defining the "new mode of being" Foucault historicizes the concept of language as representation, and his gesture demonstrates that the positivist theories about language—starting with those of Locke and Leibniz in the eighteenth century and continuing, in a slightly different vein, with the work of Bertrand Russell in the twentieth—are not necessarily wrong. Yet they apply only to a certain variety of discourse conditioned by specific historical circumstances. The development of structuralist and poststructuralist theories, on the other hand, reflects a change in the Western culture's attitude toward language determined by yet other historical conditions. Timothy J. Reiss aptly describes the new situation as "the uncertainty of analysis."[26] Reiss's book, of the same title, reveals the linguistic changes produced by a weakening of the confidence in scientific methodology and in the certainty of knowledge in the twentieth century. And as Thomas Grey points out, the challenge to positivism is not limited to the field of language: "In our time, . . . phenomenological, hermeneutic, and pragmatic approaches to social and legal theory have emphasized intuition, insight into meaning (*Verstehen*), and tacit belief as alternatives or supplements to the standard scientific account of the knowledge of human social life."[27]

Such changes in the attitude toward language need not touch literature, if we define it, with Foucault, as the form of language that "breaks with the whole definition of genres as forms adapted to an order of representations, and becomes merely a manifestation of a language which has no other law than that of affirming—in opposition to all other forms of discourse—its own precipitous existence."[28] But in spite of the attractiveness of Foucault's definition, we must admit that literature is not exempt from the influence of the dominant forms of discourse. The development of such trends as realism, naturalism, and some varieties of modernism has to do with an adjustment of "literary" language to a certain discursive climate, an adjustment determined by its capacity to compete with other forms of discourse and accompanied by the slightly contradictory aspiration to differentiate itself from them. In the twentieth century, the weakening of the authority once bestowed upon representational language encourages a stronger self-assertion of the literary discourse, and in literary modernism we find a powerful emphasis on nonrepresentational forms of expression.

Within the historical and literary context where Stevens belongs, one can legitimately question critical methods that reduce language to its representational function and search for a new approach that would consider the pragmatics of language as well. A study of literature informed by pragmatics will thus have to take into account the complex situation of the literary phenomenon in society and culture, and it will imply a detailed analysis of linguistic and social conventions incorporated in meaning along with the literary conventions. It will have to follow the formation and transformation of discursive genres, their confluence as well as their disparity, their cooperation as well as their competition within an utterance that presents itself as a literary work.

The copresence of different discourses within the same utterance is amply demonstrated by Mikhail Bakhtin in his essays on the "dialogic imagination." Although his theory is built around the novel, its relevance for language in general is quite obvious. Bakhtin starts from the observation that the novel, as a genre, is characterized by a multiplicity of styles specific to the speech types that the narrator wants to imitate. This stylistic diversity has its source in the social condition of language. Language, as we speak it, is stratified, containing numerous stylistic levels determined by the speakers' social positions and by their interaction. Those linguistic theories according to which language is an abstract system of rules are contradicted by the social reality, where there exists not a single, unitary language but a multiplicity of "languages": "At any given moment of its evolution, language is stratified not only into linguistic dialects in the strict sense of the word (according to formal linguistic markers, especially phonetic), but also—and for us this is the essential point—into languages that are socio-ideological: languages of social groups, 'professional' and 'generic' languages, languages of generations and so forth."[29]

A "language" represents, according to Bakhtin, a worldview reflecting, in its stylistic markers, a certain ideological position. As worldviews may be different, even within the same culture, there are many "languages" or rather strata of a language. What Bakhtin means by "language" within a language, as it were, corresponds ideally to Michel Foucault's notion of discourse. Stratified in "discourses," language is a dialogic affair, in the sense that different discourses may appear, whether at odds or in harmony, within the speech of the same person. Dialogue is thus for Bakhtin an inner quality of language that sustains different ideological positions that may interact with each other within the same utterance.

But there is also another kind of dialogue: between the speaker's ideology and that of the listener s/he implicitly addresses. Even utterances that are not specifically rhetorical address an ideal listener, whose anticipated resistance may motivate the speaker's strategies. For in actual speech situations, understanding is never passive and should be conceived rather as a response, an active confrontation of one conceptual system with another. The speaker can only try to anticipate this response, and in doing so, s/he constructs an ideologically split utterance. This produces an effect similar but not identical to that of the presence of two or more different discourses within the same utterance. The two kinds of dialogue may, at times, be indistinguishable: "Although they differ in their essentials and give rise to varying stylistic effects in discourse, the dialogic relationship toward an alien word within the object and the relationship toward an alien word in the anticipated answer of the listener can, nevertheless, be very tightly interwoven with each other, becoming almost indistinguishable in stylistic analysis."[30]

A dialogic quality is pervasive in Stevens's poems, both in the first sense and in the second. For by confronting different discourses the poet addresses the reader's expectations, which he may (or may not) satisfy by favoring a kind of discourse against another. This quality, which I perceive as the coexistence of two different kinds of discourses, is noted by many of Stevens's critics but is described in a different manner. As mentioned above, Jacqueline Brogan talks about two theories of language that are both inscribed in his poetry. She attributes the coexistence of the two views on language to Stevens's continuous preoccupation with the relation between reality and the imagination, which has been debated extensively by many other critics. Margaret Peterson, on the other hand, finds the root of the disjunction in Stevens's essays in the form of a dichotomy between science and art, which is naturally reflected by two styles that compete with each other in his poetry.[31] Thomas Grey argues that Stevens demonstrates an awareness of the differences between the language of law—which follows the injunctions of logical positivism—and the language of poetry, which is, in many respects, its opposite.[32] All critics share the feeling that Stevens's poems exhibit a kind of duality that I see as best explained by an inner dialogue sustained by his language.

Yet because of their rather conventional beginnings, Stevens's poems can (and have been) read as (poetic) representations, and their discursive fluctuations may easily pass unnoticed. But far from being unimportant stylistic diversions, the changes from one discourse to another place the poems' meaning in a dispute between different modes of interpretation, and their value transcends that of a mere representation. In fact, the struggle between competitive discourses is apparent in most of his poems. "The Glass of Water," for instance, starts as a lecture using some principles of physics to explain metaphysics. The language is clearly marked as explanatory and logical:

alternative examples are considered, for the obvious purpose of a demonstration, and the conclusion is emphasized. Such markers determine that this utterance should be perceived as an analytical discourse, specific to science or philosophy. Probably for this reason Thomas Hines thinks that Stevens here "continues his interest in . . . philosophical speculations and returns to a consideration of the different aspects of the act of perception."[33]

> That the glass would melt in heat,
> That the water would freeze in cold,
> Shows that this object is merely a state,
> One of many, between two poles. So,
> In the metaphysical, there are these poles.[34]

The diction itself indicates a discourse of a philosophical or scientific nature: words like "object," "state," "poles," or "the metaphysical" belong in the vocabulary of lectures addressed to an audience interestèd, perhaps, in popular science or philosophy. The presence of an audience can be guessed from the little details by which the speaker betrays his purpose: the syntactic repetition, the use of a qualifier like "merely" or of an adverbial like "so" to produce emphasis. Such fine indications of an audience's presence—the speaker would not use them were he writing a book—adulterate the analytical quality of the discourse and actually constitute its weakness, because they go contrary to the purpose of representation. The supplementary connectives are determined by the speaker's relation to his audience and bring about an excess of meaning that foreshadows the disintegration of the analysis the poem ostensibly performs. And indeed the analytical stance cannot be sustained beyond the first line of the second stanza:

> Here in the centre stands the glass. Light
> Is the lion that comes down to drink. There
> And in that state, the glass is a pool.
> Ruddy are his eyes and ruddy are his claws
> When light comes down to wet his frothy jaws
>
> And in the water winding weeds move round.
> And there and in another state—the refractions,
> The *metaphysica*, the plastic parts of poems
> Crash in the mind—
>   [CP 197]

Although we can, with Hines, see in metaphor an extension of the philosophical speculation, the discursive ambivalence of the first line of the second stanza, which might be part of a textbook as well as of a poem, constitutes a transition to a different kind of discourse recognizable as poetic. Such recognition is determined not by the presence but by the quality of the metaphors. The difference between the two discourses is not based on a crude identification of poetry with metaphoric language. Instead, it relies on the possibilities of the metaphor, which, while it is being used to represent, pushes representation beyond its analytical purposes. "Light is a lion" is not a simple metaphor—a term replacing another by analogy—but a sort of metamorphosis. It cannot easily be explicated or literalized.[35] Unlike metaphors currently used for scientific representation, Stevens's does not finalize the image but rather expands the possibilities of interpretation indefinitely. As a result, the former logical frame has a totally different outcome.

The logic of the argument sketched in the first stanza would require that the various states of water should be detailed here, and indeed they are, but in another verbal register. If the discourse of the first stanza betrays some analytical purpose and aims at narrowing down the possibilities of interpretation, the discourse of the second prompts the imagination toward various proliferating interpretations. The whole change from one discursive mode to another has been made possible by the sudden introduction of the metaphor, but it is supported by a kind of logic: if light is a lion, then the water must be in a pool, not in a glass; if there is a pool, there must be vegetation around it, and so on. Following this logic, language escapes the constraints of analysis and creates an imaginative space where something like a story may develop. In the process, it does not modulate itself to represent another state of the water but changes its own state, for being too well followed, the logic of the representation is undone. Thus, "Light is a lion that comes down to drink," although logically (and analogically) connected with the discourse about the glass of water, transmutes that discourse into another, where imagination is not expelled in favor of reality but rather called upon to complement it.

The objective, analytical representation fails, or rather fades, even beyond its transformation into an indeterminate metaphorical speech. For not only does metaphor insinuate itself in the description, but it also introduces a number of possible associations of the word "water" as we use it. Lost in such associations, "water" ceases to be the focus of the description and is displaced by the ferocious image of the lion that had been invented for the occasion. By contrast to the semantic uncertainty surrounding the word "water," the image of this lion is clear, leaving no doubt about its animal violence. Significantly, as the metaphor opens new possibilities of connection derived from the usage of the word in language, the speaker invents himself an interlocutor, and the poem becomes, literally, a dialogue.

> But, fat Jocundus, worrying
> About what stands here in the centre, not the glass,
> But in the centre of our lives, this time, this day,
> It is a state . . .
>   [CP 197–98]

Even before it becomes an actual conversation, the poem presents itself as a dialogue between two different types of discourse, two languages based on different ideologies: one of the scientist, the other of the poet. But the poem also functions as a dialogue with its implied reader, since it can stage its dissolution in figurative ambivalence only through an appeal to our sense of objective representation. Without the expectation for an objective, analytical account created in the first stanza, the second one would not appear unsuccessful. In addition there is the more direct appeal of a sound pattern, which develops first in syntactic symmetry ("Ruddy are his eyes and ruddy are his claws"), follows up with a rhyme (claws/jaws), and culminates in alliteration (water winding weeds). The repetition distances language from its representational function and, at the same time, it appeals to the reader simply as sound pattern.

That this pattern should be able to gather sense depends on the reader's cooperation. Should the reader be deaf to the different registers of this language, the poem would need the reader's cooperation in another way: in supplying a context or translating the metaphors. But the language of the poem is best regarded as mainly conversational rather than representational. Stevens carries on a conversation with his implied reader through a rhetoric that elicits the reconsideration of the premises according to which the poem is perceived and understood. And as the prosody of the poem suggests, sound has a role to play in this process.

This language, which escapes from the constraints of analytical discourse, may seem to lose its grip on reality, in the limited sense that science gives to the word. But we find a more complex reality in the process, one that engages the mind in its movement. The curious thing about the imaginative conception of the real is that it is closer to our ordinary experience of reality than the description provided by science. The excess of meaning generated by the metaphor, which analysis would brush away, proves useful eventually on a superior plane, where "one would continue to contend with one's ideas." Becoming imaginative, the discourse has been enriched not only in beauty but in depth as well, for it liberates meanings that an analytical discourse would try to contain.

What I hope to have established so far is that a theory of language, if it is to be employed in reading Stevens, should embrace not only purely linguistic structures but also the interaction between speakers that normally takes place in a social and cultural environment. Such interaction is also implied in the verbal gesture that we call a poem. In a poem as well as in a novel, stylistic markers of various types of discourse representing various ideologies are recognizable even as they coexist within the same utterance. Later I will contend that Stevens makes deliberate use of the inner dialogism of language in order to favor, as he does in the poem analyzed above, a type of discourse against another. The distinction between various types of discourse is important in the study of sound, because sound pattern can be the mark of a certain type, that is, the very characteristic that distinguishes one type from others. In addition, meaning as defined by pragmatics bears many similarities to the meaning of music.

The question of musical meaning has its own complexities, deriving from the apparent contradiction between the condition of music as expression and its nonrepresentational quality, especially in its instrumental variety. Theorists of musical meaning have long recognized the importance of the cultural context, although some, such as Leonard Meyer and Wilson Coker,[36] place a greater emphasis on the internal relations between sounds, which stimulate the listener's response. It should be noted that this emphasis is not purely formal. Wilson Coker distinguishes between extrageneric and congeneric meaning, the former being determined by the expectations a listener brings to the piece and the latter by the expectations formed at the time of listening and determined by the formal relations of the sounds within the piece itself. Congeneric meaning is, according to both Meyer and Coker, dominant in instrumental music, and musical significance is achieved through an internal reference, which is actually repetition. In order to achieve meaning, sounds have to refer to (repeat) other sounds.[37] Repetition, combined with variation, forms a pattern that creates expectations that, in turn, either may be fulfilled and give satisfaction or may be frustrated and create suspense. Meyer considers such moments of satisfaction or suspense emotional states, and he argues that the meaning of the piece thus produced by its pattern is indistinguishable from this kind of (intellectual) emotion.[38]

The return, in more recent studies of meaning in music, to an emphasis on the cultural context has been prompted by new analogies between music and language. For instance, Lawrence Kramer[39] uses the speech acts theory to substantiate the claim that music has some semantic structure, but the notion of meaning as a result of symbolic action cancels that claim, since the very notion of semantics depends upon a view of language as representation, not as action. The analogy is more profitable, I think, seen the other way around, since Meyer's and Coker's "formal" analysis reveals important implications concerning the relation between form and the cultural context. The stress on the expectations of the listener is crucial and actually brings the musical theory quite close to pragmatics.

The two categories of expectations—extrageneric and congeneric—described by Coker are part of a dialectic in which meaning is created in a cultural context. "For without a set of gestures common to the social group," says Meyer, "and without common habit responses to those gestures, no communication whatsoever would be possible. Communication depends upon, presupposes, and arises out of the universe of discourse which in the aesthetics of music is called style."[40] The expectations that the listener brings to the piece belong to a certain cultural sensibility, and the formal structures that stimulate the other kind of expectations—the ones formed during listening—are addressed to that very sensibility. Congeneric and extrageneric meaning are thus interdependent. In fact, the whole concept of genre is culturally constituted. To search for a musical meaning in poetry thus complements a pragmatical treatment of meaning. Renouncing a certain crude notion of reference to a standing reality, the consideration of musical meaning implies placing the poem in its cultural matrix. And although such a notion of meaning obliges one to consider formal elements quite closely, the resulting reading exceeds the scope of a purely formal analysis.

The challenge that musical theories may present to epistemology has been noticed and discussed by Kevin Barry in *Language, Music, and the Sign,* a study of eighteenth-century poetics. The main linguistic theories of the time, like those of Locke and Leibniz, were opposed by arguments that defined meaning by using an analogy between language and music rather than the more common equation of language with painting. The representational theory of the sign was thus contradicted and subverted by ideas about music that seemed to threaten the very notion of meaning. According to Locke's view of the sign, music should be completely void of significance, but its enjoyment by the public is proof to the contrary. It is obviously meaningful to the people who respond to it, although what the signs of music stand for would be hard to assess.

Music is thus an "empty sign," in which the notion of meaning becomes free and undefined. "The meaning of music depends upon the enigmatic character of its signs which, instead of replacing a source which they would imitate or express, turn the listener's attention to his own inventive subjectivity."[41] This enigmatic character of the sign/sound accounts for the resistance to analytical annihilation of the musical text, and it determines the change of the interpretive activity into a creative one. For turning to his/her own subjectivity, the listener must invent an interpretation starting from the text rather than search for its source outside the text.

As Barry notes, this way of conceiving of the relation between poetry and music is totally different from symbolist aesthetics, "For the process of ideas about music has a quite different perspective. Wherever these ideas emerge in discussions about the origin of language, about linguistic structure, about poetry, or about passional speech, they tend towards a theory of response and of interpretation as relatively uncertain and free. It is this activity of response as opposed to notions of description or specific naming, which ideas about music and about 'empty' signs are used to analyse."[42] Therefore the musical model of language reorients the concerns of the reader or critic who, instead of being engaged in the decoding of the text, is moved to respond. The emphasis is placed no longer on the thing behind the sign but rather on the effect of the sign. The shift may seem to block interpretation, but it actually makes response more imaginative.

In the conclusion of his book, Barry emphasizes the delicate relationship between formal elements, effect, response, and the cultural context, which are central for an understanding of the music of poetry: "The argument concentrates itself around, not the expressive source of music, but the relationship between the music and the listener; the argument also concentrates itself around the question of the texture of sound itself. In the discourses of language, be they philosophy, poetics, aesthetics, rhetoric, or the poem, these arguments are reflected in a questioning of the relationship between reader and text and in a questioning of the 'poematic' qualities of the sounds of words."[43] As poetry becomes a kind of music, language suffers a subtle transmutation, in which semantic meaning is doubled, and at times even displaced, by the "musical" one. Semantics is thus not the only path toward understanding language.

The enigmatic character of the musical sign may lead to the idea that music, and more generally sound, have to do with the dark, irrational, and emotional side of the human psyche. In fact, insofar as they address the question, some poststructuralist critics tend to assign sound a function related either to bodily participation[44] or to prelinguistic states of consciousness.[45] In his recent study on sound, Garrett Stewart relies on the notion that such ideas also involve a sense—inspired by Derrida's sophisticated wordplays—that sound can produce accidental meaning.[46] Although Stewart's book makes the valid point that the reading (or the reader) has a major role in the production of meaning, his concentration on the accidental or contrived coincidences of sound, which may generate alternative meanings, leads away from a proper understanding of the relationship between reader and text. For such a relation must be conceptualized within a social/cultural context, in what Kristeva calls symbolic order, where the accidents of meaning are checked by the necessity of consensus.

By assigning sound an accidental, irrational, or prerational function, poststructuralist theory actually upholds the conception of language as exclusively representational. In the poststructuralists' view, because it is excluded from representation, sound must be excluded from normal social interaction. Yet under quite normal (conscious and social) circumstances, language speaking and understanding usually include the however ineffable impression that the sound of language leaves on the mind. The empty sign functions in all kinds of contexts, and it is part of our contact with language and with each other. In fact, Barthes's own discriminations between meaning and *signifiance* in "The Grain of the Voice" tend to show the importance of such interaction, which explains his personal response to the techniques of different singers. Sound does indeed create emotion but an intellectual emotion of the kind Meyer describes, which, although hard to put in representational terms, belongs nonetheless in a social/cultural context. Music (or sound) must thus be regarded as another dimension of language not less important than syntax and semantics, although it is usually underestimated because we are accustomed to viewing sound as a conventional, material carrier of meaning.

The importance of pattern and musical effect in general is, with the exception of discussions on prosody, rarely touched upon in connection with literature proper, but it appears quite frequently in discussions related to folkloric productions. Such discussions may provide another connection between musical theories of meaning and pragmatics. Like the studies on music, folkloric theories focus on formal elements and on the effect of form on the audience. Folkloric productions such as narratives, ballads, or shorter genres like charms and incantations are usually repetitive, rhythmical, and approach the state of a song, even when they are not actually accompanied by one. The repetitiveness of folkloric productions is sometimes considered to have mnemonic purposes, for the oral poet faces an audience that must periodically be reminded of the story's main events. There is, however, Milman Parry's[47] alternative theory of production (later developed by Albert Lord),[48] which stresses the fact that the composition of a folkloric piece takes place in performance. Parry's research proved that folkloric singers do not repeat their performances identically but practically create a new version of the narrative every time they perform. Repetitiveness is due to the singer's need to produce the narration from a schematic memory of its plot, which he fleshes out by using stock formulas in front of an audience. The formal characteristics of such productions are thus directly related to the social situation that generates them.

The role of the audience is crucial in shaping the story's form, since many times singers adjust their stories to the audience's response. The audience of a folkloric performance displays an interest in the telling of the story, in the singer's manner, that is stronger than the interest in the action, since the plot may well be known in advance. Whatever representation of events is offered in such a story, its significance becomes secondary to the relation that the performer develops with his public. The main function of the language, in this case, is to establish and consolidate the relationship.

Although such language is profoundly different from the language of representation described by Foucault, one cannot call it "literary," because too many features distinguish it from written poetry or prose. W. J. Ong describes the language of folkloric productions as "oral," a kind of language whose characteristics are determined by the absence of writing in society.[49] The development of writing, he points out, produced a revolution in human way of thinking and of perceiving the world: "Writing, in this ordinary sense, was and is the most momentous of all human technological inventions. It is not a mere appendage to speech. Because it moves speech from the oral-aural to a new sensory world, that of vision, it transforms speech and thought as well."[50] The formal aspect of language, whether oral or written, with its precise characteristics reflects, as the quotation above indicates, not only a different view of its function determining a particular use but also a whole different conception of the nature of reality and knowledge. A different use of language actually reflects a different epistemology as well as a different ontology. This correlation between the use of the language and the ideas dominant in a culture will become apparent in the analysis of Stevens's poems, where philosophical ideas are not only expressed but also enacted in a sound pattern.

2

Sound and Poetry

A N APPROACH DESIGNED to identify types of discourses in Wallace Stevens permits, besides a fresh understanding of his poems, a reconsideration of the role played by sound in both the production and the perception of meaning. Such a reconsideration seems the more necessary, as sound is virtually set aside not only by positivist approaches to language but by structuralism and deconstruction as well. For what most linguistic theories share is a view of language as a code functioning beyond the intervention of its speakers. Language is mainly studied in its written form, and by analogy with writing it is seen either as a transcription of reality or of itself. This is perhaps normal in a philosophical tradition that views the world as divided between subjects and objects, a division that deconstruction proposes to subvert but cannot ignore.

A different view of language emerges if we consider its poetic use, where sound is of primary importance. For although the flourishing of vers libre during modernism coincided with the rejection of prosody as a cumbersome traditional device, the theorists of modernism in America—Pound and Eliot—did not totally discard sound as an important element in poetry. Less appreciated as theorists, Frost and Stevens are remarkable for the attention they give to aural effects. Their position is not conservative, however, and it is interesting to consider the implications of their scattered remarks about sound, because these poets form part of a more important opposition to the dominant philosophical position of their day. Sound is normally supposed to be only the carrier of meaning, and to consider sound meaningful in itself is implicitly to attack epistemology and an entire philosophical and linguistic tradition.

Saussure's dictum about the arbitrariness of the sign agrees with a view of sound as a material carrier, practically without meaning. Derrida's deconstruction of Saussure's argument actually reveals an attitude inherent in the Western culture: whereas sound is glorified because it suggests presence, the gist of linguistic theory—as well as the basis of common language use—lies in attributing to sound a codifying purpose, a function ultimately similar to that of writing.[1] Saussure's analysis, as it is deconstructed by Derrida, therefore appears to assimilate the spoken language with the written one. As far as meaning is concerned, sounds seem to play a minimal role, since they function only as material symbols, whereas meaning is generated by the differences between such symbols. Saussure's theory dismisses, quite convincingly, the attempt to find a connection between sound and meaning on the model of onomato-poeia.

There is, however, another aspect of sound that is rather overlooked by linguistic theories that confine meaning either to a representational function or to the relations established within the system of language itself. This aspect consists of the rhythm of the utterance, its unity as a sound pattern, which may impress the participants in a dialogue either by its familiarity or by its strangeness. As Richard Poirier put it, "One virtue of [this] kind of sound . . . is . . . that it can create spaces or gaps in ascertained structures of meaning and that it can do so in such a way as simultaneously to create trust and reassurance instead of human separation. The sounds invite us to live with others in a space of expectation rather than deferral."[2]

Questions about rhythm have naturally been raised in literary discussions, especially those dedicated to prosody. The debates around the role of sound pattern range from the time-honored opinion that the meter parallels the feeling expressed by the verse to the more sophisticated idea that literary themes or motifs can be handled in the same way that themes and motifs are handled in music. The classic prejudice persists, however, that sound is secondary to meaning.

The prejudice has been challenged by John Hollander, who, seeking to show the relation between sound and poetic meaning, discovers that sound pattern can play the role of an allegory or metaphor of the poem's content.[3] In spite of the fact that he maintains there is a parallel between sound and sense—and thereby implies that these two elements of language act separately—Hollander's analysis strongly suggests that sound plays a greater role in semantics than any linguistic theory would admit. In fact, the role of sound in language becomes clear only when expression becomes artistic, so that language exceeds its purely representational function. This function remains, however, and it is hard to ignore. Critical interpretations are most often directed not at language but beyond it, at what language, whether in prose or poetry, has to represent.

The question of critical interpretation pertains to language only in part, and its difficulty arises from its epistemological implications. Is a text knowable after all? The common assumption that language reflects or represents reality precludes any questions about the epistemological availability of the text as such. For according to such an assumption, what we want to know is outside the text; it is actually what the text reflects. And if we want to ask whether the text itself is knowable, all current assumptions of epistemology must fail. What does it mean to "know" a text, when actually, in order to understand it, one has to make it vanish in order to lay bare the reality (whether things, events, feelings, emotions, ideas, or thoughts) that stands behind it?

Texts resist such annihilation, and this resistance, as well as the failure of analysis, leads to the inference that there is something more to language than mere reflective power, something having less to do with its systematic nature, and more with its functioning, or its pragmatics. For the resistance to analysis derives precisely from the ex-

cess of meaning, which does not fit in the system and which is generated by the relation a text establishes between writer and reader. Language does not mean only in a
static way; it means through its movement and through the pattern of that movement—in other words, it means when it happens. As Foucault advises, "We should not
restrict meaning to the cognitive core that lies at the heart of a knowable object; rather,
we should allow it to reestablish its flux at the limit of words and things, as what is said
of a thing (not its attribute or the thing itself) and as something that happens (not its
process or its state)."[4]

In fact, meaning hardly exists without that movement of the language from one
speaker to another. "Words exist in the mouth not books," exclaims Robert Frost in a
letter to his disciple, John T. Bartlett.[5] I discuss Frost here not just because he is the
friendly rival of Stevens, but because he brings up, unwittingly, of course, the same
question that Derrida's deconstruction of Saussure's *Course* obliquely recognizes.
Why is the linguist treating language as an abstract code similar to writing rather than
studying speech? Why is *langue* the object of analysis and study, whereas *parole* is left
to the vagaries of circumstance? We should not be misled by Frost's reference to books.
The distinction between spoken and written language is not, in either Saussure or
Frost, to be taken literally. The difference between their theories is rather the difference
between recognizing the existence of a second party, of the other of the dialogue, or
suppressing it in order to reduce language to an analyzable system.

Frost's meditations do more than spontaneously reveal some problems in Saussure's theory. Like Stevens's insistence that "poetry is words; and that words, above
everything else, are, in poetry, sounds,"[6] they rather hint at the importance of sound,
of those aspects of language that are rarely and only secondarily discussed by the
theorists of meaning. The neglect should not be surprising, since communication itself,
as it usually takes place, demands that sound be set aside so that information may be
conveyed quickly and efficiently. We speak to communicate, but we rarely listen to
the sounds of language, unless they are strange or literally foreign. The child of Mexi-
can parents living in America, caught between two languages, Richard Rodriguez describes his truly exceptional experience of sounds: "I lived in a world magically compounded of sounds. I remained a child longer than most; I lingered too long, poised at
the edge of language—often frightened by the sounds of *los gringos,* delighted by the
sounds of Spanish at home."[7] But the magic world of sound vanishes as soon as he
masters English: "Conversations became content-full. Transparent. Hearing someone's
tone of voice—angry or questioning or sarcastic or happy or sad—I didn't distinguish
it from the words it expressed."[8] Richard Poirier has the same kind of sounds in mind
as he comments: "We all hear these sounds every day, in the flow of familiar, sometimes scarcely audible phrases and words. They call little attention to themselves; they
belong so naturally to the rhythm of human speech that everyone takes them for
granted. . . . But in letting them pass unnoticed, it is likely that in our exchanges with
one another we unintentionally suppress large areas of feeling and thinking."[9]

The neglect of sound is thus due to the assumption, underlying our use of language that words are transparent, the media of a cognitive activity thoroughly assimilated to seeing. And it is against such an assumption that Frost formulates his objections. "We value the seeing eye already. Time we said something about the hearing ear—the ear that calls up vivid sentence forms."[10] Frost's invocation of the senses places his discussion within the traditional model of cognition, in which the "eye" suggests the capacity to understand, whereas the "ear" is evocative of relations between the self and the other. But Frost recalls, at the same time, the "form" of the sentence that the ear calls up. The ear is thus the receptacle not only of the voice of the other but of a form, of something culturally constituted and already agreed upon as intelligible.

The "sentence form" is important to Frost, because it is implicitly familiar to speakers. In fact, it is the very familiarity of the sound that renders the sentence transparent, since it is recognizable to the point where one does not have to think about the sense of the individual words in order to understand the whole: "I give you a new definition of a sentence: A sentence is a sound in itself on which other sounds called words have been strung."[11] Frost's definition of the sentence is quite close to the thought of the later Wittgenstein. In *Philosophical Investigations,* Wittgenstein arrives at a point where he considers the understanding of a sentence similar to the understanding of a musical theme: "Understanding a sentence is much more akin to understanding a theme in music than one may think. What I mean is that understanding a sentence lies nearer than one thinks to what is ordinarily called understanding a musical theme."[12] In the process of understanding language, a sentence functions thus as a unit, a "sound," which is perceived as a totality and is understood because it is recognized as meaningful. For both Frost and Wittgenstein, sound is actually a formal element, neither a physical (phonic) presence nor a "sum of distinctive features" but a certain pattern that, through the phenomenon of understanding—a mental hearing in the sense in which thinking is a mental seeing—can easily circulate between speakers of the same language.

Frost's nearly metaphorical description of the "sentence sound" has a number of implications. First, he is talking about the "perception" of language, not about a decoding or an analysis, as do the structuralist or other linguistic theorists. The utterance of one speaker is perceived by the other, who reacts according to this perception. Understanding thus implies neither an analysis nor the annihilation of the communicative medium but rather the interaction of speakers with the help of the medium. For the sentence sound can be meaningful only if it is recognized as such by both participants in the dialogue. Under the aspect of sound, language does not reveal knowledge, but it is meaningful precisely because what it says is already known. Knowledge is, in this case, a matter of agreement, of a common bond that the speakers of the language share. Frost is of course the inspiration for Poirier's view on the matter in *Poetry in Pragmatism.*

The implications, for epistemology, of focusing on the perception of language rather than on the reality beyond it become clear here. As Gerald Bruns notices, in connection with the poetry of Wallace Stevens, the whole relation between knowledge and language changes when language is viewed as a bond between speakers: "This is not a problem of knowledge or of language (that is, it is not a problem of how language links up with reality); rather it is a problem of dialogue, of speech that presupposes and even engages the discourse of other people."[13] Under the conditions of dialogue, the very aim of cognition is no longer to reveal (objective) reality but rather to establish a relation between partners: to know means to be able to read each other, know what "we" are about. Therefore epistemology, if understood as the way "mind links up with reality," collapses in this perspective on language.

The concept of sound as pattern endowed with significance by its very usage in discourse points to the possibility of dialogue beyond the physical presence of the speakers. Heidegger had already opened the door to a discussion about the dialogic nature of language in relation to sound: "We can make clear the connection of discourse with understanding and intelligibility by considering an existential possibility which belongs to talking itself—hearing. If we have not heard 'aright', it is not by accident that we say we have not 'understood'. Hearing is constitutive for discourse. And just as linguistic utterance is based on discourse, so is acoustic perception on hearing. Listening to . . . is Dasein's existential way of Being-open as Being-with for Others."[14] But hearing and listening are not pure phenomena, as Heidegger points out; they are determined by a previous familiarity with the world or the other. Listening or "hearkening" is conditioned by a certain intimacy between speaker and listener, which prepares the latter for understanding.

This kind of intimacy between speakers demonstrates that language is a dialogic affair even when the speakers are not present, that is, even when one reads or writes. Although Heidegger is not very explicit on this point, what he calls "the existential possibility of speaking and hearing" would seem to function even in the speakers' absence. Frost may be more helpful here, as he speaks of readers who must modulate their "voices" according to the sound of the sentences. Clearly, the "voice" is not the reader's vocal and physical presence but the process of understanding that takes place in the reader's mind.

The sounds of the utterance are patterned and thus remain audible even in the speakers' absence, when the speech has become text. If such is the case, then reader and listener are interchangeable, and the writer or speaker may equally convey the meaning through the sentence sounds. Frost's "sentence sounds" may seem, since understanding is based on their recognition, like a new type of code not too different from, if a little more complex than, Saussure's system. But codification is barred in this case, since, unlike the elements of a code, the sentence sounds are subject to change and growth. The sound of sense springs from the inexhaustible reservoir of language in action, since sentences belong to the speakers: "Many of them are already familiar to us in books. I think no writer invents them. The most original writer only catches them fresh from talk, where they grow spontaneously."[15]

The fact that such spontaneous growth takes place in "talk"—that is, in the interaction between speakers—imposes certain constraints on the range of sentence sounds that can "grow." For a sentence sound "to grow," it must not only be invented and launched by a speaker but also be accepted and used again by other speakers. Sentence sounds cannot have meaning unless they are not only intended (by the speaker) but also recognized as intentional and therefore meaningful (by the listener). They develop very much in what Wittgenstein calls a "language game," where intention is bound by certain rules: "An intention is embedded in its situation, in human customs and institutions. If the technique of the game of chess did not exist, I could not intend to play a game of chess."[16]

The question then arises whether Frost's recommendations to Bartlett to "listen to the sentence sounds" and use them in his writing may limit expression and poetic invention. Their tie to "human customs and institutions" ensures that they are familiar and easily accepted, but it may also restrict the possibilities for using the language in a new way. Frost is aware that a mechanical use of the "sound of sense" would not lift poetry beyond ordinary expression: "But remember," he says, "we are still talking merely of the raw material of poetry."[17] And his definition of poetry surprises with its simplicity: "Verse in which there is nothing but the beat of the metre furnished by the accents of polysyllabic words we call doggerel. Verse is not that. Neither is the sound of sense alone. It is a resultant from those two."[18] His own verse largely conforms to this definition, as he can achieve what he calls "abstraction," with all its intricacies and subtleties, through a seductive verbal simplicity. Margerie Sabin gives its best description when she observes that, "The sound is initially like 'talk,' but almost immediately it rises into a more elaborate syntax, a more songlike rhythm. The talking syntax remains one of the sounds in the sentence, but is from the start crossed with other, more 'poetic' sounds."[19] The bond of the speakers, if not ignored, allows thus for personal assertion, and it becomes in fact the means by which the self finds its (poetic) expression.

In the hands of Stevens, however, the "sound of sense" becomes the norm from which poetry must necessarily depart. Although he shares with Frost the capacity to awaken dead metaphors and to make etymology significant,[20] Stevens does not try to evoke the sound of popular wisdom, and his poems strike the reader with strangeness rather than familiarity. As William Pritchard remarks, the sound Stevens produces in his poems, and sometimes even talks about, is "not 'the sound of sense,' not the pleasing and preaching simultaneously recommended by Alexander Pope, but a purer and stranger satisfying of the ear, and of the mind as it gives itself up to the desolate or delightful music."[21] Yet Stevens also appeals to the familiar as he relies on a (quasi-parodic) enactment of particular kinds of discourse that are immediately recognizable and that range from the academic, scientific, and philosophic to the literary or poetic and even the folkloric.

The recognition of these different kinds of discourse by the reader is essential for the kind of subversion that Stevens's verse ultimately enacts in transforming them into a kind of language that may be called poetic. Academic discourse, for instance, is evoked in the title of "Academic Discourse at Havana" and is pursued in the poem but not without a parodic undertone. In true academic fashion, the poem explicates a proposition about "life"; yet the proposition itself, "Life is an old casino in the park," is too metaphorical for the purpose, and the extension of the metaphor takes so many turns in the poem that its academic stance becomes doubtful.

The same kind of discourse appears in the tone of an art historical expertise, which turns to parody in "So-and-So Reclining on Her Couch": "On her side, reclining on her elbow. / This mechanism, this apparition, / Suppose we call it projection A" (*CP* 295). In spite of its didactic fastidiousness (there is a projection B, followed by projection C), the poem does not really demonstrate anything. In other poems, didactic overtones appear in what sounds like a scientific demonstration that is subverted from the outset: "Let the place of the solitaires / Be a place of perpetual undulation" (*CP* 60). What a geometrician would postulate as a center or point of reference, Stevens's speaker establishes as "a place of perpetual undulation," an image of motion and relativity.

The parodic treatment of sound is even more subtle when the poem assumes the guise of philosophical or literary discourse. But parody itself becomes ambiguous, and there is an evident tension between sense and the sound of it. The final section of "Peter Quince at the Clavier," for instance, reverses parodically but not without a special twist, a philosophical cliché concerning eternal beauty: "Beauty is momentary in the mind— / The fitful tracing of a portal; / But in the flesh it is immortal" (*CP* 91). The sound of "philosophy" is so powerful here that it makes many readers and critics meditate on the truth of such statement and ignore the possibility of pure parody. To the same effect, the invocation of the muse reminiscent of a Renaissance sonnet muffles the ironies of that address in "To the One of Fictive Music":

Sister and mother and diviner love,
And of the sisterhood of the living dead
Most near, most clear, and of the clearest bloom,
And of the fragrant mothers the most dear
And queen, and of diviner love the day
And flame and summer and sweet fire, no thread
Of cloudy silver sprinkles in your gown
Its venom of renown, and on your head
No crown is simpler than the simple hair.
     [*CP* 87]

Manipulated in this way, sound comes to have a direct bearing on meaning, which results from an interplay between the reader's expectations and their satisfaction or betrayal by the speaker of the poem. Meaning thus accumulates in Stevens's verbal action, beyond or apart from representation. At his best, Stevens attains the same "abstract vitality of speech" that Frost attributes to the sound of sense, because he relies on the appeal to the same inner "ear" of understanding that the strangeness of his diction and the peculiarity of his grammar impress as strongly and as mysteriously as music.

This discussion would not be complete without an evocation of Stevens's own ideas about sound. I shall limit my references to his essays, since an incursion into the poems would generate the need to explore sound and music as a tropes, a topic too extensive to treat in this book, which aims to foreground only the effects of sound in the poetry of Stevens. In the course of the following survey of Stevens's opinions about sound and its relation to language and poetry, many complicated notions regarding his poetic will surface and will be treated more fully in the chapters that follow. The survey itself must be seen, therefore, only as a sketch.

Stevens's treatment of sound must be placed within the context of modernism. The new ideas about form promoted by the modern poets, especially by Ezra Pound, called into question the traditional identification of poetry with prosodic text, and Stevens's position on the subject does not differ in any essential ways from those of Pound and Eliot (at the start of his career). Like them, he thinks that prosody should not be discarded but should develop into the "music of poetry," that is, a poet should innovate in the use of sound rather than letting his poetry be constrained by classical meters. The similarity between Stevens's ideas and Eliot's is reinforced by the example Stevens uses to make his point—a poem by Eliot himself, which demonstrates the latter's innovative and musical use of language. Stevens's comment on that poem might appear banal and inconsequential if it did not end with an unexpected description of the change brought about by the music of poetry: "It is like the change from Haydn to a voice intoning. It is like the voice of an actor reciting or declaiming or of some other figure concealed, so that we cannot identify him, who speaks with a measured voice which is often disturbed by his feeling for what he says. There is no accompaniment. . . . Instead of a musician we have an orator whose speech sometimes resembles music."[22]

This description complicates, at once, the concept of music in poetry and the role of sound in language in general. The name of Haydn is suggestive of highly formal instrumental music whose beauty resides in the indirectness of its relation to its human creator. The change that the poetry of Eliot is thus making, according to Stevens, is to give up the pure, almost instrumental formalism of prosody in favor of a more personal kind of music: a voice intoning. Yet the personal touch is not to be confused with romantic emotionalism, for in no way does Stevens misread Eliot as a "personal" poet.

His image here rather does justice to Eliot's injunction that the poet should speak through a mask. The voice intoning the poetry is not that of the poet but that of an actor or of somebody hidden from view, and his emotion is simply directed toward the words of poetry.

Here, as on other occasions, Stevens's theorizing touches, although his emphases are slightly different, on the same problems as Eliot's. Both are interested in defining the role of the poet in society, and the questions related to the poet's personality and emotions are, for both, raised in that context. In "The Irrational Element in Poetry," Stevens declares without hesitation that "poetry is the medium of [the poet's] personal sensibility."[23] The statement is qualified by the whole argument of the essay, however, which, in explaining the irrational element of poetry, turns toward poetic phenomena that escape the poet's will.

Although the very term "irrational" and the rhetoric of the essay might suggest a metaphysical poetics, it turns out that, in Stevens's view, the element that the poet cannot himself control has to do with his relation to the reader.[24] And at its crucial point, the argument turns to sound again: "The slightest sound matters. The most momentary rhythm matters. You can do as you please, yet everything matters. You are free, but your freedom must be consonant with the freedom of others."[25] This "consonance" is reminiscent of the insistence, pervading Frost's argument about sound, that the poet should always go back to the spoken language for the raw material of poetry. And although Stevens's notoriously extravagant use of diction would indicate a major departure from Frost's precepts, sound is, for him, involved in the most crucial questions regarding both the nature of poetry and the role of the poet in society. The poet is free to innovate in form, but innovation has limits imposed by the reader's willingness to accept and understand the new form.

Without calling the poet a catalyst, Stevens shares Eliot's idea that the poet's personality can become expressive of a shared, collective feeling. As an individual, the poet matters only insofar as his personality is inclusive of all other individualities. An Emersonian concept of individuality makes its way in Stevens's meditations but not without certain alterations: "We are talking," he explains, "about something a good deal more comprehensive than the temperament of the artist as that is usually spoken of. We are concerned with the whole personality and, in effect, we are saying that the poet who writes the heroic poem that will satisfy all there is of us and all of us in time to come, will accomplish it by the power of his reason, the force of his imagination and, in addition, the effortless and inescapable process of his own individuality."[26]

The concept of "process" is crucial to an understanding of Stevens's theories about the nature of poetry. He uses the word quite frequently not only in connection with the personality of the poet, which makes possible the "process" of poetry itself,[27] but also to describe imagination, which, "like the personality of the poet in the act of creating, is no more than a process."[28] This notion of process, recalling Frost's description of a poem's creation, which "begins in delight and ends in wisdom," serves, in Stevens, as a solvent of the dichotomies that he frequently evokes in order to establish the ways in which poetry differs from other ways of speaking: reality and the imagination, reason and imagination, the rational and the irrational, and so on.

His insistence upon such dichotomies may often obscure his purpose of dissolving them, but such a purpose is always apparent. The debate around the pair of opposites reality/imagination in his essays, for instance, results in nothing else but a refutation of the notion that imagination can be contrary to or radically different from reality. Stevens conceives of the imagination from a point of view that is much less aesthetic than that of his romantic predecessors. Margaret Peterson[29] points out that Stevens inherits the notion from Coleridge, but as she does not fail to mention, Stevens also read I. A. Richards on Coleridge, and the influence of the former is quite obvious, as J. B. Leggett[30] has made abundantly clear.

Richards's psychologism becomes apparent when Stevens names imagination a "faculty" and describes it in terms that could easily be traced to a psychology textbook, as in "The Relations Between Poetry and Painting": "This is the typical function of the imagination which always makes use of the familiar to produce the unfamiliar."[31] In that context, the relation between reality and the imagination becomes, quite literally, a transformation of the former into the latter, a process that is creative only insofar as it rearranges, recomposes, and recombines. The dependence of imagination upon reality is thus much more literal than one would be inclined to think when applying the two notions exclusively to art.

The fact that the imagination is secondary, in the sense that it feeds upon reality and could never profitably leave its range, does not prevent it from being essential. Stevens stresses the role of the imagination in what he calls "our lives," in the being of a society: "Reality is life and life is society and the imagination and reality; that is to say, the imagination and society are inseparable."[32] Here the usage of the word enhances its sense, for if imagination is defined only as a mental faculty that literally processes reality into art, its inseparability from society indicates that the process is neither particularly artistic nor exclusively individual. The whole of what we call culture appears in Stevens's essays as the cumulative effect of individual imaginations at work. "[Imagination] enables us to live our own lives. We have it because we do not have enough without it. This may not be true as to each one of us, for certainly there are those for whom reality and the reason are enough: It is true of us as a race."[33] The reality we live in is thus, at least in part, the product of our imagination.

The same dissolution of an opposition appears whenever Stevens attempts to define one term in relation to another. In "A Collect of Philosophy," poetry itself is defined by opposition with philosophy. Yet the very start of the argument underscores the similarity more than the difference between the two activities: "It is often the case that concepts of philosophy are poetic."[34] Eventually poetry and philosophy appear to be distinct only in purpose, for whereas the philosopher aims to discover, the poet's end is to celebrate.[35] The untenability of a distinction between poetry and philosophy is the more important in Stevens's poetic as it finally results in an assertion of poetry's dominance among the manifestations of the human spirit. Based on the imagination, which Stevens has established elsewhere as an essential faculty of the mind, poetry represents the ultimate stage of philosophy itself: "Does not philosophy carry us to a point at which there is nothing left except the imagination?"[36] And although Stevens seeks, at every turn of the argument, to stress the equality of his terms—reason acts in concert with the imagination, poetry and philosophy use the same world and the same means for different purposes—the essay ends up by giving the upper hand to poetry: "It is as if in the study of modern man we predicated the greatness of poetry as the final measure of his stature, as if his willingness to believe beyond belief was what had made him modern and was always certain to keep him so."[37]

As the quotation above makes abundantly clear, the dissolution of the oppositions by means of which poetry is defined has as its purpose the establishment of its dominance. Poetry, as well as its presiding faculty—the imagination—abandons its marginal role in society and becomes the very predicate of modernity. But the privileging of what may habitually be considered secondary appears to be the rule any time Stevens sets up a pair of opposites. "The Irrational Element in Poetry" is such an occasion. In it Stevens explains at length how essential the irrational, the unconscious, or the mystery is to our lives. Similarly, in language, modernity is characterized, according to him, by a dominance of the connotative,[38] which is inextricably connected with the imagination. Imagination is also related to metaphor, analogy, and sound—all areas of meaning that may appear as marginal and to which Stevens awards a role equal to, if not greater than, that of denotation. Stevens's view of language and his theories of meaning constitute the context in which one must consider his view of sound in poetry.

Richard Poirier thinks that Stevens gives sound a more philosophical treatment than Frost: "When he gets round to discussing sound in poetry, it is with a rhetoric that magnifies its importance and its implications far beyond anything allowed by Frost with his 'sound of sense' or by James with his desire to 'reinstate' the vague, the inarticulate, the nameless 'to their proper place in our mental life.' Sound for Stevens becomes a supreme fiction, one that by implication has maintained its power more than have gods no longer with us."[39] In many ways, however, Stevens's view is similar to Frost's. The sound of poetry is an imaginative variation on the sound of language in general. Even more emphatically than Frost, Stevens relates sound with the coherence of society, with the very existence of a culture.

Sound is the aspect of language that constitutes the single presence and physical bond to which all members of a society or culture can feel related. There are not many references to sound in Stevens's essays, but whenever sound is mentioned, the discussion extends beyond aesthetic matters to social ones. His pronouncement about the music of poetry in "The Noble Rider and the Sound of Words" deserves particular attention, as it makes at once the most explicit and the most intricate reference to sound in language. Its explicitness renders it quotable, but its intricacy demands that it be contextualized with other of Stevens's theoretical notions regarding language and poetry. Given its importance, this quotation will have to be extensive:

> I do not know of anything that will appear to have suffered more from the passage of time than the music of poetry and that has suffered less. The deepening need for words to express our thoughts and feelings which, we are sure, are all the truth that we shall ever experience, having no illusions, makes us listen to words when we hear them, loving them and feeling them, makes us search the sound of them, for a finality, a perfection, an unalterable vibration, which it is only within the power of the acutest poet to give them. Those of us who may have been thinking of the path of poetry, those who understand that words are thoughts and not only our own thoughts but the thoughts of men and women ignorant of what it is that they are thinking, must be conscious of this: that, above everything else, poetry is words; and that words, above everything else, are, in poetry, sounds.[40]

This passage stresses once again the importance Stevens places on the reader as a controlling presence in the process of writing as well as the relation between reader and writer. The poet, according to him, definitely fulfills an essential mission, that of giving the thoughts of men and women their best expression that can be shared by all. Given that such thoughts are otherwise not expressed, the social presence of the poet is more than desirable: it is necessary.

What is more intriguing, however, is the idea that, as a reader, one would be emotionally affected not by the thoughts that the poet expresses but by the words in which he expresses them and by their sound even more than by the words. Why would sound, normally a meaningless feature of language, suddenly acquire this overwhelming importance? It is true, as Stevens often hints, and Frost also did, that as a physical presence sound is the most obviously shared element of language. Speaking and at the same time hearing can be the most of sharing that humans do. For Stevens, however, there is more to the sound of words than their sharable presence. He sees us feeling and loving the words—not the things or other people—and searching for their sound. Sound seems indeed the only meaningful feature of the words or of language.

A question of what is meaningful, of what actually constitutes meaning in language makes its way to the surface of this passage apparently concerned only with the music of poetry. What exactly does Stevens find meaningful? It is time to remember at this juncture that Stevens has the same background as the other American poets I have mentioned above. Like them, he inherits a positivist outlook on language, a tradition that the modernists, beginning with Pound, found inimical. More specifically than Pound, Eliot, or Frost, Stevens discusses logical positivism, quoting Ayers when he writes about the imagination. Neither can one ignore the fact that Stevens was not only informed about positivism but also instructed against it by his Harvard education. He is able to quote William James at critical junctures in his essays in order to refute positivist arguments. The kind of scholarship Stevens enlists as his aid to make his theoretical points suggests that his poetics may extend beyond aesthetics into the realm of epistemology.

Returning to the question of meaning, one cannot help but detect Stevens's antipositivist bias. In the argument he advances in "Imagination as Value," he remarks ironically: "We feel, without being particularly intelligent about it, that the imagination as metaphysics will survive logical positivism unscathed."[41] He launches his basic attack against the truth value of "reality" as promoted by Ayers and against the exclusion or marginalization of the imagination on that account. Much of what Stevens perceives as meaning develops from what he calls imagination and is, in many ways, the opposite of the basic notion of truth as a correspondence with reality that dominates positivism. On more than one occasion, he defines meaning as something that the words generate rather than something to which they refer: "A poet's words are of things that do not exist without the words"[42] or "Poetry is a revelation in words by means of words."[43] In "The Relations Between Poetry and Painting," he remarks that the words' "referential importance is slight, for the importance of the action to which they refer is not in the action itself, but in the meaning; and that meaning is borne by the words."[44]

The suggestion that meaning resides exclusively in the words, having little or no connection with the extralinguistic reality, could place Stevens in the camp of deconstruction, and it may explain why he has indeed often been seen as a deconstructionist avant la lettre. Following the logic of Derrida, the notion of meaning advanced by Stevens should lead to a view of language based on an analogy with writing. Stevens immediately evokes sound, however: "above everything else, poetry is words; and . . . words, above everything else, are, in poetry, sounds."[45] Even for those who are not partisans of Derrida's views, the evocation of sound may seem paradoxical, as we are quite aware, and Stevens must have been too, that poetry was, in his day, written. But the discussion here has pivoted on "our thoughts and feelings, which we are sure, are all the truth we shall ever experience."[46] That truth is predicated on the sharing of those thoughts, and the sharing is possible only in the virtues of sound: "a finality, a perfection, an unalterable vibration."[47] We read this statement with the suspicion that the subject is not exactly the physical sound but a combination of sound understood as voice and sound understood as music, perhaps "a voice intoning." Sound is thus treated as a meaningful feature of language communicating the interpersonal bond involved in language itself and heightened by poetry.

This conception of meaning is directly related to Stevens's aesthetic concerns, which he often debates, as I have noted above, in the form of pairs of opposites. The crucial question in the context is not whether art is related to reality in a more or less direct way but whether faculties like the imagination, areas of mental activity such as the irrational, linguistic possibilities such as the connotative, have any role in what he calls "our life." The answer to this question will, naturally, determine the role of poetry and of the poet in society, but in the case of Stevens the route toward establishing that importance seems to me more interesting than its destination.

His attention seems to be drawn toward activities and capabilities that are habitually considered marginal or even abnormal and undesirable: the imagination, the irrational, the connotative, the metaphor, the sound of language. These peripheral areas are not his own inventions or findings but notions circulating in the intellectual climate of the time. If one were to take into account only the popularity of Freud's concepts of the conscious and the unconscious, or Marx's notions of basis and superstructure, one could understand the propensity of Stevens's age for establishing what was the dominant feature by revealing the dominated one. This dichotomic kind of thinking persists even as late as structuralism. But as I have shown above, against such influential trends, Stevens places the emphasis on the secondary element rather than on the main one. That emphasis is achieved by dissolving the opposition or rather making one pole of it merge with the other until the distinction becomes insignificant.

The popularity of the pairs of opposites leaves its imprint on Stevens's efforts to define the poetic, which itself is, on one occasion, placed in direct opposition to philosophy and most of the time is evoked in the other pairs of opposites: imagination and reality, denotative and connotative, irrational and rational. But such oppositions are dissolved, as I have shown above, in a subtle process. The purpose of these distillations and transitional movements is no other than to permit the author to show the importance of the marginal or the secondary, of which poetry itself is considered to be a part.[48]

Stevens succeeds, however, in doing more than just privileging activities that are habitually considered secondary, for this privilege forces a radical transformation of a whole system of thought. More than a change of the values involved, this is a change of the axis along which such values are being perceived. The dominance of the imagination over reality, paralleled by the dominance of sound over denotative meaning, implies different concepts of reality and language that may be seen in relation not to their correspondence to each other but to the roles they perform in human life. Once the center of the debate moves from "reality" to "our lives," reality and imagination become equal, and indeed the latter may dominate the former. I shall return to this point in chapter 4, where I will discuss it fully in connection with the poems.

The reversal of what had been promoted as the natural order of things suggests that Stevens's poetics sought deeper changes than those advanced by his fellow modernists. His quarrel was not simply with traditional forms of poetry but with epistemology, a dominant trend of thought in his time, which ultimately determined the way one conceived of language and consequently of poetry. In his timely article about Stevens's use of sound in poetry, Gerald Bruns proposes to read Stevens "without epistemology." Stevens's opposition to epistemology will be more fully explored in chapter 5.

The emphasis upon the role played by sound in the relations between people appears clearly when Stevens speaks about the individuality of the poet. His designation of the imagination as the moving force of society may lead to the idea that a culture is the product of collective imagination. But such a totalizing view of culture would exclude the individual process and product that belong to him as creator.

Individual creativity is threatened here, but Stevens does not have to give up the notion as long as he holds onto his Emersonian view of individuality. Such a view seems to be shared by the other modernists, especially by Eliot, whose image of the poet as catalyst is meant to explain the relation between a poet and his society. The main difference between Emerson and Stevens, as well as between Eliot and Stevens, has to do with the way in which the question of individuality or personality is defined. Unlike the others, Stevens considers the relation from the reader's end. What is important is not that the poet should express his public's feeling but that his feeling should find acceptance with his readers: "I think that his function is to make his imagination theirs and that he fulfills himself only as he sees his imagination become the light in the minds of others. His role in short is to help people live their lives."[49]

Stevens's awareness of the readers' needs, to which the mission of the poet is inextricably connected, informs his view of the sound of language. The importance of his meditations on sound appears clearly when we consider the depth of the poetic innovation that he is proposing. The brilliance of his verbal performance in his poetry reveals its full meaning only when seen in the light of this poetics, which, whether his emphasis allows it or not, turns on the idea of sound. Stevens's poetic does indeed attack the tenets of Western philosophical tradition. In the spirit of Stevens's inclination to dissolve oppositions, one may observe, however, that his path may have been cut by the pragmatic philosophy that was fashionable at Harvard during his undergraduate years. The same spiritual presence may explain Frost's inclination to see in sound the symbol and embodiment of interpersonal relations.

As I have shown in chapter 1, a certain view (and use) of language develops in relation to a certain view of knowledge, of reality or the world, and of the self. Hence the importance of Stevens's verbal performance (mainly but not exclusively through sound), which I see as the symptom of a restlessness concerning the nature of reality and the origins of the self characteristic of his time. His intense concern with sound pattern stems from more than a desire to embellish language or to maintain a certain sense of tradition. It grows from a distinctive sensibility that his position as a modernist and his identity as (American) poet conspired to create. In his poetry, sound is not purely a formal element but a way of interacting with a certain conception of language as representation, which was still dominant in his day although on its way to being subverted and discredited. His particular use of sound is the poet's way of connecting with this emerging sensibility and of joining in its creation.

3

Sense, Nonsense, and the Magic Word

THE EARLIEST COMMENTS on Wallace Stevens relate sound to nonsense in arguments that either directly compare him to Lewis Carroll[1] or attempt to demonstrate that nonsense is only an unfulfilled possibility, a matter of flirtation.[2] Some time later, Stevens's flirtation with nonsense and his way of associating words on the basis of sound similarity began to be perceived as an unsuccessful effort to make language coincide with reality. Situated in the context of modernism, where imagist theories prevailed, Stevens's poetic performance appeared to some as one more attempt to make language do the impossible. J. Hillis Miller's initial appraisal of the poet's work is characteristic of that trend:

> A poem may start coherently enough, but as it progresses the poet becomes more and more exasperated with the distance between words and things. The language finally dissolves into incoherence and the reader faces words that are nonwords, a thick linguistic paste, like the splotches of paint on an expressionist canvas. By draining all referential meaning out of words Stevens hopes that they will become the thing they represent, or, even more radically, beyond onomatopoeia, that only the sound and appearance of the words will remain.[3]

Hillis Miller's haste to declare the poet's attempt a failure is motivated by his own skepticism about any poet's power to make words stand up as things, which is, in turn, rooted in the idea that language functions primarily as a means of representing reality. But this positivist view of language (Stevens sometimes calls it "realist") is precisely what comes under attack in Stevens's poetic performance, where not language but the conception that it is a reflection of the real is put to such a severe test that it naturally fails.

Yet this apparent failure need not lead to the conclusion that Stevens is inviting us to contemplate a collapse of communication. More recent criticism on Stevens has been probing his own views on language in order to explain the enigmatic character of his writing, the significance of his wordplay, or the sense of his resort to nonsense. J. B. Leggett, for instance, describes the poems in a manner not very different from Hillis Miller's, but he discerns a purpose behind Stevens's notorious obscurity:

Frequently the poems establish antitheses in which clarity and simplicity are dismissed in favor of obscurity or nonsense. That which has become intellec-tualized, mastered, explicated is relegated to the junk heap, and the speaker's desire is directed toward that which is beyond the intellect, beyond direct articulation or paraphrase. It is as if the desired world were an obscure poem or song not yet understood, and the familiar world were the stale poem re-duced to cliché by the very fact of its accessibility.[4]

Leggett seems to see Stevens's penchant for nonsense and obscurity as the expres-sion of a desire to transcend the normal possibilities of language rather than a failure to exploit its capacity to represent.

The significance of Stevens's inclination to resort to nonsense in his poems is evi-dent to critics who perceive the formal elements as expressive. Alison Rieke, for in-stance, rejects the idea that communication fails in Stevens: "The position that the poet's recourse to nonsense is symptomatic of a failed and flawed effort to describe the indescribable does not fully account for that which is comic and pleasurable in Stevens' engagement with language."[5] Eleanor Cook, who explores precisely the comic and pleasurable aspects of Stevens's language (without ever overlooking their seriousness), also defends the idea that what appears to be nonsense in his verse is actually a verbal gesture of no small significance. Cook's arguments are the more in-teresting, as she places Stevens in the context of literary tradition at a juncture between charm and riddle verse: "Personally and historically, he began to write at a time of transition from charm poetry to riddling poetry, from incantatory late-Victorian poetry, to modern, riddling poetry."[6] According to Cook, Stevens never quite decided between riddle and charm and practiced them both with equal success.

The distinction between charm and riddle verse belongs to Northrop Frye, and Eleanor Cook uses it to point out discursive differences: "Riddles tend to be visual and conceptual, charms tend to be aural and hypnotic."[7] This is an important distinction, as it also suggests two different sets of assumptions about the nature and functioning of language. Riddling is reminiscent of the representational function of language, al-though representation in this case is complicated by the hermetic or enigmatic features of the utterance. Charm, on the other hand, obliges one to perceive totally different qualities of language: its formal design in sound pattern as well as the power resulting from it.

Besides their formal characteristics, charms and incantations are distinguished by their purpose, which goes beyond communication. Charms are supposed to produce practical results, to heal, to make rain, or to rid us of evil spirits. Such a purpose implies a reversal of the relation between language and reality as we normally conceive of it. For instead of representing reality, and therefore being subordinated to it, charms create, and therefore master and control, a reality. This kind of reversal appealed to Stevens on different levels.

Jacqueline Brogan finds that Stevens shares in the medieval belief that language has an essential role in creation: "The medieval conviction that God's thoughts about creation and creation are connected by the Logos (and that our thoughts about the world and the world are connected by our words) is not essentially different from Stevens' suggestion that words not only 'create the world' but approach the 'living ideal.'"[8] In her book *Stanza My Stone,* Leonora Woodman has suggested a more than casual relationship between Stevens and hermeticism, a tradition that also gives a special power to language. Analyzing "Large Man Reading," Woodman states: "Here, too, a similar possibility is entertained, guided equally by the assumption that poetic text prefigures the poetic 'life'—that, indeed, the text is the element from which 'life' springs."[9] Woodman also foregrounds the role of sound in the language of alchemy, hermeticism, and magic.

Sound pattern is in fact the element that operates the reversal of what we consider to be the normal relation between reality and language. It is therefore necessary to approach Stevens's sound-dominated poems bearing in mind that our usual assumptions about language and sense may have to yield to a different conception of what language can and cannot do. What Stevens's poems demand, in my view, is a change of the very assumptions on which meaning itself is understood. For the assumption that language's only function is to reflect "reality" is proved to have weak grounds in the poems that fail not only to represent reality, as it is commonly understood, but also to validate its sense. But not validating sense—the way we usually perceive it—is far from producing nonsense. Assuming forms similar to those of charms and incantations, many of his poems conjure up a reality instead of representing one. The dominance of sound in Stevens's poems operates thus a reversal of what we see as the normal relation between reality and language.

In what follows, I shall look at several poems in which the reversal of the relation reality/language is quite evident and in which the sound dominance achieves the intensity of verbal magic. In the course of my argument, I shall look with something like microscopic attentiveness at the operation of sound in Stevens's verse, and I will simply say at the outset that the method of reading exemplified in my analysis—what might be called a method of "unreading" followed by a *re*reading or reconstitution in terms of underlying sound patterns—is, I think, nothing other than the primary mode of comprehension demanded by the poems themselves. The unreading is the result of the failure to which a certain kind of discourse is brought by Stevens himself, and it is necessary, because it addresses the habits of a reader whom we have to imagine as the one the speakers of the poems address. Such a reader is defined by the very discursive strategies present in the poems, and s/he is therefore reconstructable as a function of discourse conventions. The *re*reading is required by the whole process of understanding, in which the renunciation of certain conventions and the adoption of others is the sole warrant of sense. My argument concerning the "metaphysics of sound" is, in effect, about the outcome of such a process of reading, about the manner in which sound works in Stevens to dissolve certain normative notions or schemes of reality while gesturing, ultimately, toward something that lies beyond them.

Many of Stevens's poems start with an apparently earnest attempt to construct a representation, for they are not explicitly lyrical but rather narrative or even argumentative. The narrative or argumentative setup creates expectations for an intelligible reference, for an accurate account of action, or for coherent argumentation. But most of the time the compliance to such expectations is quite illusory. Some of the poems evoke traditions and conventions that are mocked rather than honored, discredited rather than recognized. Once the convention within which words have a certain value has been compromised, words seem to become empty of meaning and may strike one as pure sound. "Some Friends from Pascagoula," for instance, brings up such conventions in the form of traditional symbols placed in a parodic context:

Tell me more of the eagle, Cotton,
And you, black Sly,
Tell me how he descended
Out of the morning sky.
[CP 126]

Like many other poems by Stevens, "Some Friends from Pascagoula" seems to belong to a situational context that is left obscure. The prosodic structure of the stanza is reminiscent of a ballad with its regular rhythm, easy rhyme, and four lines' length. The opening exhortation also reminds one of folkloric narratives: "Tell me" implies the presence of the "singer of tales" and the historical or legendary preexistence of the story's material. The *Iliad* itself starts with a similar formula: "Chant, Goddess." *The Odyssey* comes even closer with "Tell me, Muse."

By virtue of this familiar formula, we are placed in a legendary or mythical realm, but its precise context would be difficult to identify, for this stanza evokes mixed mythologies. The eagle is a traditional heraldic symbol in some European countries, where it represents military or imperial glory, but it is also an element in American Indian mythology, where its rich symbolic value relates to the visionary and the divine. All these associations of symbols from the past first come to mind because of the ancient or medieval flavor of the opening formula, but on second thought, the eagle may stand out as a symbol of contemporary America too, as it gazes at us from mailboxes or the cover of *The American Heritage Dictionary*.

The ambiguity of the image gives rise to a special parodic effect. A more precise context would favor one image and exclude the others, but the possibility of getting all of them, alternately or at once, gives way to comic incongruities. The poem's beginning encourages the assumption that the eagle's image has a symbolic, although uncertain, value, for the speaker takes this image for granted and plans the poem as its extension: "Tell me *more* of the eagle." But this attempt at expanding or enriching the image compromises it as well as its symbolic value. Taken out of its proper context, the verbal image loses its power to signify: whatever the eagle stands for does not seem to be substantial. The significance of the symbol is unstable and dispersed rather than concentrated. The symbol itself has a certain autonomy that may easily be interpreted as mockery either of the reference or of the symbolic function. And the impression that this is a parody is only intensified in the lines that follow:

Describe with deepened voice
And noble imagery
His slowly-falling round
Down to the fishy sea.

Here was a sovereign sight,
Fit for a kinky clan.
Tell me again of the point
At which the flight began,
    [CP 126]

The parodic intent becomes clear here, when the description points ironically to the supposed singer's manner, while ambiguity continues to dominate the poem. Knowledge of geography might disambiguate some lines, but it would create further ambiguities. An awareness of Pascagoula's position on the map, for instance, would make "the sea" a more precise and clear reference, and "fishy" could be read in its literal sense. Geography would also indicate an African-American population in the region and designate "Cotton" and "black Sly" as members of the "kinky clan." Geography is deliberately deemphasized, however, by being hinted at in the title and never mentioned again in the poem. Readers of Stevens are used to titles apparently disconnected from the poems' content. Moreover, "fishy" and "kinky" are placed so close to each other that the suggestion of dubiousness common to both their figurative senses makes the latter more probable than the literal. If nevertheless we accept that the poem is about some African-Americans, we would have to deal with the oddity of the symbolic suggestions of the "eagle" that reminds us first of other races. There would also be the cruel irony of calling African-Americans a "clan"—a word so perfectly echoing Klan—which would be hard to attribute to Stevens.[10]

The sum of such contradictions supports the idea that the poem is essentially parodic. But the target of the parody is less clearly defined than the parodic tone. The beginning would indicate that a story, in which the eagle is a symbol, is being parodied, but the second stanza concentrates more on the manner and the style of the singer. And the ambiguities point to a mockery of the language he uses rather than of his story. Meanwhile, the story itself becomes elusive and immaterial, for while one may suppose that it will be told later in the poem, "Tell me again" suggests that it has already been told, that it is either too well known or too unimportant to deserve our attention. Because the story is thus marginalized, the telling, the manner, and the style are of more consequence, stressing language at the expense of the narrative. The story's immateriality, as well as the direction of the parody toward the language itself, gives language a status equal to (if not higher than) events.

Beyond the obvious mockery, a more important change occurs at this stage. If it pointed to only one symbolic value—eagle as symbol of glory, for instance—the phrase could be considered univocal and semantically clear; but as its meaning is pluralized and thus destabilized, the reader's attention is directed to the materiality of the words. As their sense shifts in an unstable context, as neither the straight story nor its parody comes to a satisfactory ending, the words become present, opaque entities. At first, this transformation may occur as a result of the mocking tone that approaches nonsense. Yet " 'Nonsense' is not quite the word for it," as William Pritchard observes, referring to Stevens's work, "but it is a preferable alternative to treating the poem as if it were a statement about or an attitude toward the real world we presumably share."[11] Pritchard here suggests that there is an alternative to sense other than nonsense. The materiality of the words gives them the potential to become meaningful in a different way. Such words seem to function as objects, whose specific properties make it possible for them to be invested with significance, in the way a magical object would. It is quite possible to read the poem as conjuring or incantation.

Because the power of the symbol seems to have been lost in derision, the reader is forced to return to the beginning, to start, perhaps, with the "real" eagle. This new and repeated reading may lead away from the mockery perceived the first time, because, freed from its current meaning, that is, from its depreciated symbolic value, as well as from the ambiguity the context created for it before, the eagle—now recognizable only as a word with symbolic potential—can become a receptacle of new meaning. The traditional usages have been exhausted, and this exhaustion may have liberated the words, for they seem to become clearer:

Say how his heavy wings,
Spread on the sun-bronzed air,
Turned tip and tip away,
Down to the sand, the glare

Of the pine trees edging the sand,
Dropping in sovereign rings
Out of his fiery lair.
Speak of the dazzling wings.
    [CP 127]

Although this second part of the poem begins with virtually the same formula, "Say how" and relies on clichéd imagery, the speaker seems to intend to clarify. The slight hesitation of the rhythm gives the impression that this is a fresh start, as if he were having some difficulty fitting his thought into words. The rhythm is accomplished but with some effort. There is even an enjambment—a discordance between rhythm and syntax unusual for the folkloric form the speaker of this poem has adopted. If the first part looked like an imitation carried to the extreme of parody, the second one looks like an original making, a genuine creation.

In this second part of the poem, however, in spite of the expansion of its physical description, the eagle does not become a clearer, more visible image. The reason may be the fact that, within the unity of these two stanzas, the element of expressive effort—giving the impression that a representation is intended—also manifests itself as a return upon the same words. The semantic expansion of the first two lines, "Say how his heavy wings, / Spread on the sun-bronzed air" is restrained in the next line by a repetition, ostensibly meant to clarify the movement: "Turned *tip* and *tip* away." The stanza closes after this, the closure being reinforced by the rhyme of its final line.

At this point, the weakening semantic precision is in climactic conflict with the growing regularity of the sound. Although the rhyme of "glare" closes the stanza, the syntax creates a continuity with the next one, but continuity is not only syntactical here. "Of the pine trees edging the sand" echoes "the sand" from the previous stanza, thus forming another sound pattern, which overrides the previous one. The repetition also changes the semantic stress on the word. At first, "the sand" seems marginal and replaceable: the eagle could be falling on the land, on the grass, or on the sea for that matter. But when it is repeated, "the sand" becomes central, as if it were a special place where the eagle is supposed to land. No precise meaning can be assigned to it, for this suggested centrality offers not only one possibility but many. Placed in the center, the word exercises power, attracts interpretations, yet is ready not to radiate but rather to absorb meaning.

The repetitions of words and sounds, which seemed to mark the difficulty of the semantic expansion, grow into a pattern, which gives an air of aural self-containment and unity to the two stanzas. The last three lines emphasize this self-containment—the rhythm has become regular again; the rhyme is an almost total sound identity; and some words from the first part of the poem, now repeated, create the effect of an echo. The poem ends with its beginning formula, closing upon itself, as if tamed, mastered, and self-contained. The sound pattern of convention, which dominated the first part, was only temporarily lost, and it is now recovered with renewed energy.

What, then, has happened to the meaning of the poem? The semantic expansion of its second part seems to have been confined again by the dominance of the sound. The final impression, however, is that one can "see" the eagle that lacks a precise symbolic value but possesses the undeniable capacity to become a symbol. Its clarity as an image is mainly an illusion created by the self-contained quality of the language, for if we look more closely at this description of the "real" eagle, we notice that the image dissolves with the speaker's effort to make it clearer. As it details the eagle's physical features, the description gets caught in rhetoric: the image of the eagle in light gives rise to an analogy with light, and before long, there is no way to separate the eagle from light. Thus the eagle is literally dissolved in sunlight, and one would not be able to tell whether the "dazzling wings" belong to a real, physical eagle, or to an image made of light and its reflections, or to no image at all. The symbol has been compromised and emptied of meaning, in the first part of the poem, and now the word is free to absorb new significance, for its symbolic potential is regenerated when the power of the word's presence manifests itself as sound. This is no longer the eagle of worn-out heraldry, or the image from the mailboxes, but a new one that is ready to take on the significance of our ideals and aspirations.

In the verbal pattern that has just grown, with the eagle's symbolic potential regenerated, the new description may appear as a real "noble imagery" mainly because it sounds like one. The very play of memory, which permits the language to mock and discredit the symbol in the first part, makes it possible for the word to recover its force in the second. Words live their lives in human memory and are always reminiscent of their previous uses. This remembrance creates the mockery in the first place, for it evokes distant and uncertain contexts and generates incongruities. But the same mechanism of memory helps the word acquire meaningful power in the second part, where, in a recovered sound pattern, sounds echo each other and give a self-contained integrity to the text.

As in a magic formula or charm, the poem's meaning resides in its aural self-containment that can exert power. Reference has failed twice: the reference to the symbol was discredited by mockery, and the reference to the "real" eagle was lost in rhetorical indulgence. There is thus no way to recover the eagle left behind somewhere in a symbolic or sensory reality, but from the words' sound, from their newly found formula, a power is conjured and stands ready to generate reality. "Some Friends from Pascagoula" thus achieves a gradual detachment of the words from their accepted meaning.

Such detachment has two main consequences: on the one hand it attracts attention to the words' material presence, and on the other it enlightens us to the illusory nature of "reference" by demonstrating that meaning has actually been attached to words in the process of their use. The process in which words become capable of generating reality starts with a clear detachment from the meaning habitually assigned to them. Meaning appears to be the product of the history of the words' usage, which, in this case, is literary/folkloric convention. Their independence from the habitual usage, their readiness to take on reality, to actually generate it, makes Stevens's words similar to those of charms or incantations, for the eagle of his poem is not spoken about or referred to but rather conjured.

An even more evident verbal conjuring goes on in "Ploughing on Sunday," a poem in which reference to action invites the reader to expect a sequence of events from the outset. Such expectations are encouraged even as they are subverted by the poem's grammar. The two declarative sentences that open the poem may seem, in the first instance, quite straightforward:

The white cock's tail
Tosses in the wind.
The turkey-cock's tail
Glitters in the sun.
　　[CP 20]

This might well be the description of fowl on a farm, but there is here a grammatical detail that, while luring the reader into the narrative, lends it a kind of mystery, related especially to the context in which the little story is to be read. For instead of the customary indefinite articles, the main agent present on the scene (actually there may be two cocks, but the repetitive structure suggests two descriptions of the same one) is introduced with definite ones, and such introduction creates again the illusion of a context otherwise left obscure. The utterance appears incomplete and fragmentary because it breaks the conventions of a beginning, but its deficiency can alternatively be perceived as an attractive mystery. It is as if we had stumbled into a story whose telling had begun some time before. If the speaker referred to a farm and to its fowl, we wouldn't know it as intimately as he seems to. As readers, we seem to become an uninvited audience, estranged by the fact that nobody bothers to fill us in but at the same time attracted by the power of a verbal utterance that is seemingly constituted on solid grounds. And because the definite articles suggest that the cock is already known, one may think of some traditional symbolic meanings of the word by ascribing to it the value of a sexual pun or that of a biblical allusion or by placing it in some medieval literary context.

The second stanza, however, turns to a description of weather and may give another symbolic value to the cock, which can be interpreted as a magical sign of a storm:

Water in the fields.
The wind pours down.
The feathers flare
And bluster in the wind.
　　[CP 20]

In just a few sentences, the context in which the poem's utterance is to be interpreted changes several times, multiplying the possibilities of interpretation. But when we have too many possibilities of interpretation, in effect we have none at all. For this reason the meaning of the poem becomes elusive, and communication seems to fail.

This sense of a failure of communication can only grow stronger with the exhortation that follows: "Remus, blow your horn!" Who is Remus? we may ask, and where did he come from? But like the cock in the opening of the poem, "Remus"—the name thrown in without introduction—may invite symbolic interpretations. Leonard and Wharton, for instance, interpret this stanza in the following way:

> These deceptively simple lines open onto a complex of allusion. The plough-man, like Nietzsche's white bull, ploughs the earth and bellows his exuber-ance. Celebrating work on the Sabbath, the ploughman is in company with Christ's radically freeing "It is lawful to do well on the sabbath days" (Matthew 12:12). Fittingly, the poem's "Remus" (literally "an oar," ploughlike and pro-pelling) may be both the freed slave invented by Joel Chandler Harris to plough the soil of the rural South with homely fables and another Remus (like Christ, of virgin birth), co-founder of the "eternal" city of Rome.[12]

Planting the poem on firm philosophical ground is, however, only one possible interpretation, based on the conviction that Stevens was a philosophical poet. Yet at the time he wrote this poem, Stevens would never have been suspected of philosophi-cal intentions. Frank Kermode, for instance, considered this poem a proof of Stevens's wild experimentation with rhythms in free verse.[13] And indeed the structure of the stanza suggests nonsense rather than symbolic sense. It ends quite arbitrarily with the same sentence that started it, and its repetitiveness makes it oddly symmetrical. The whole poem arranges itself in the way a dance or a musical piece is arranged, and one may consider this stanza and the two lines that open the next to be the center on which the poem pivots in its symmetry.

The poem loses sense because the form repeats itself, and the repetition threatens to become infinite:

Tum-ti-tum,
Ti-tum-tum-tum!
The turkey-cock's tail
Spreads to the sun.

The white cock's tail
Streams to the moon.
Water in the fields.
The wind pours down.
  [*CP* 20]

The "Tum-ti-tums" may go on forever, because there is no reason to stop, and once the speaker seems to have abandoned the rules of reason, the "end" does not look like any definite possibility. The symmetrical arrangement of the words has created a domi-nance of sound that, together with the repeated misdirection, the suggestion of infinite repetition, and the apparently outrageous references, creates the impression of a loss of sense. "Tum-ti-tum / Ti-tum-tum-tum" seems to confirm that loss, reducing discourse to the imitation of pure rhythm. Even more than in "Some Friends from Pascagoula," the words become so detached from their habitual meaning that the "Tum-ti-tum" sounds do not appear to be very different from the other "meaningful" words present in the poem.

There should be, however, another possible way to make sense out of the poem's apparent incoherence. As shown above, the impression of nonsense is produced mainly by the fact that our expectations for the poem are formed in an unstable context. The poem is hard to read for what it literally says, for its meaning greatly depends on the context of its utterance, a context at which we can only guess. To borrow Wittgenstein's terminology, as the meaning of the words is their "use" in a certain language "game," the trouble here is that we, as readers, are not completely aware of the game we are playing. Meaning depends on a certain frame, on a set of rules according to which sense can constitute itself. We call "sense" that which respects the rules and stays within the game, whereas we consider "non-sense" everything that is left out. But if the rules are suddenly changed, that which looked meaningless within one game may become meaningful in the newly created configuration. There is a strong possibility that the features of the poem that make it seem nonsensical in one "game" might make sense in another and that our difficulty should be caused by the shifting of rules in the middle of the initial game.

Because their precise context is missing, one tends to give the words an extra dimension, to project their significance beyond what they actually say. Attention is, at the same time, drawn to the words' arrangement in a quasi-ritual movement. This movement forms a distinct sound pattern that grows with the symmetrical repetitions of words or phrases. Some of the repetitions seem to be motivated by the desire to make the utterance more precise, as in "I am *ploughing* on Sunday, / *Ploughing* North America," but they soon integrate a pattern, and the semantic precision becomes an indifferent matter. At the "Tum-ti-tum" point, sense seems to have been completely abandoned, but we have to observe that the line, in its context, bears some significance, for it indicates the basic trochaic rhythm—with the final syllable dropped, as is usual—of lines such as "Tosses in the wind," "Water in the fields," or "Remus, blow your horn!" "Ti-tum-tum-tum," on the other hand, gives us the strong anomalous pattern of complete lines such as "The white cock's tail" or "The wind pours down." The nonsense lines actually stand at the center of the poem and rhythmically contain it altogether. It is as if the speaker were trying to teach us to listen to the poem.

After it culminates in pure rhythmic sound, the poem closes with a repetition of elements from its own beginning. The impression that the words have some extra dimension, some significance that grows out of them rather than being left behind somewhere in "reality" is only increased by this sound pattern. For it is not an entirely conventional pattern, something that the poet would have known and decided to follow, but a nascent one, some form that grows. The direction toward a sound pattern seems first to overwhelm the sense, but soon it grows so intense that the poem becomes incantatory. Because of the extra dimension acquired from their contextual indeterminacy, the words seem not to refer to anything but rather to have a material reality of their own. And the feeling of order to which their sound pattern gives rise makes their own "reality" powerfully present.

The grammar that gives the words an extra dimension, the power of the sound pattern, and the impression of sense with which one is left in spite of being unable to decode the meaning of the utterance indicate a change in the discursive mode. The resulting discourse may be called "poetic" but on different grounds from the conventional, for Stevens departs from the tradition of poetry in many ways. Traditional prosody is here enhanced by additional patterning to achieve an even more powerful effect that is comparable to the effect of an incantation or a magic spell. For the pattern acts upon us, impresses us beyond control, and language becomes significant by virtue of this action. We can no longer be interested in what the words represent, for we must perceive their action, and their "meaning" becomes closer to that of magic:

> Magic is not built up in the narrative style; it does not serve to communicate ideas from one person to another; it does not purport to contain a consecutive, consistent meaning. It is an instrument serving special purposes, intended for the exercise of man's specific power over things, and *its meaning,* giving this word a wider sense, can be understood only in correlation to this aim. It will not be therefore a meaning of logically or topically concatenated ideas, but of expressions fitting into one another and into the whole, according to what could be called a magical order of thinking, or perhaps more correctly, a magical order of expressing, of launching words towards their aim.[14]

Incantation, magic, conjuring—different language games altogether, far beyond common sense and certainly beyond nonsense—give essentially another value to language. According to our commonsense rules, we conceive of language in the following way: things are real, and we perceive them and give them names that refer to them or evoke them. Significance does not go anywhere beyond things, for even the abstractions are derived from things. For this reason, perhaps, we give great attention to things and regard understanding as a sort of unpacking of the thing. But magic discourse is different in that the relation between language and reality changes: the thing is not unveiled but created by the magic word. Malinowski's description of magic discourse may be instrumental in defining Stevens's poetic mode here, for his poems, like verbal magic, privilege sound over sense in a special way. The privilege given to sound changes the role of language from that of a means of representation to that of a generator of reality. The action of conjuring may be the best example and at the same time a metaphor of a discursive mode characterized by a dominance of sound.

Malinowski's description of magic discourse also reveals the differences between magic and commonsense speech, on the one hand, and between magic and nonsense on the other. Unlike commonsense language, magic language does not aim at a usual communication, but it exercises power, and unlike nonsense, it does not break rules programmatically, but it follows its own. Nonsense is a play against sense, a reversal of values,[15] whereas magic operates in a different system altogether. In magic or conjuring, words do not follow things, as we believe they do in our ordinary speech; on the contrary, things gain reality because of the words. The conjuring word is so much more than the referring word: it has the thing at its command rather than serving as its sign. Compared to the magic word, the referring one looks like a debasement. And if such debased words can be reduced to the state of hollow sound, sound without meaning, in magic words such emptiness would be inconceivable. The meaning of magic words is their fulfillment in reality, a fulfillment that is made possible by the power of their sound, which lies at the root of meaning rather than playing its opposite.

Evidently Stevens's poem cannot literally be a magic spell or have the meaning of one, for such meaning would not be possible outside its proper cultural context. In his description of magic, Malinowski stresses the fact that the natives' beliefs about and perception of language play an important role in the "meaning" of the magic utterance. The magic formula would not have the same effect on an audience that does not share such beliefs. For this reason we cannot identify Stevens's poem as a magical spell, although it is technically close to one. The poem relies on our own sense of language, on our rules of inferring representations to change our motivation in reading.

If by some extraordinary chance, the natives whose magic Malinowski describes knew English and came across Stevens's poem, they would certainly take it for a spell, because its form, which we may have identified as "story," is actually closer to that of a magic formula. But because we are not so conversant with magic, or just because we do not expect it here, our involvement in reading goes beyond the recognition of a form. Consciously or unconsciously, we begin to reverse the relation between reality and language. From the secondary, subservient role, the latter takes the lead, and the reality of the things is the one that follows, a mere consequence of the words' power. For while the story stalls, and our expectations remain unsatisfied, our attention must turn to the sound, as we remain compelled to listen, not because we want to find out what happened, for the line of the story is lost, but perhaps because we are under a special kind of spell. And I take this to be the "meaning" of the poem: this event, this change of purpose that, no matter what we expect to begin with, takes place in our reading attitude. The whole process of reading is thus part of the poem's "meaning."

A language of generative power similar to that of verbal magic seems to be the purpose of the poet's endeavor, and Stevens can sometimes declare such purpose explicitly. In "Certain Phenomena of Sound," he "considers speech" and its power to generate rather than reflect reality. Significantly, as the language becomes the origin of things, it manifests itself as sound rather than as sense:

The Roamer is a voice taller than the redwoods,

Engaged in the most prolific narrative,
A sound producing the things that are spoken.

> [*CP* 287, emphasis added]

In part 3 of the same poem, the human beings themselves are endowed with reality by the language that literally speaks them:

Then I, Semiramide, dark-syllabled,
Contrasting our two names, considered speech.
You were created of your name, the word
Is that of which you were the personage.
There is no life except in the word of it.

> [*CP* 287, emphasis added]

The power of language to generate rather than reflect reality emerges thus in the very process of reading Stevens's sound-dominated, magiclike poems. As quasi-verbal magic, a poem may take the form of a gesture of domination. An example of such an assertive gesture, of an uninhibited exercise of power through language is the famous "Anecdote of the Jar."

I placed a jar in Tennessee,
And round it was, upon a hill.
It made the slovenly wilderness
Surround that hill.

The wilderness rose up to it,
And sprawled around, no longer wild.
The jar was round upon the ground
And tall and of a port in air.

It took dominion everywhere.
The jar was grey and bare.
It did not give of bird or bush,
Like nothing else in Tennessee.

> [*CP* 76]

It is difficult to look at the "Anecdote of the Jar," "over which an implausible amount of ink has been spilled"[16] with a fresh critical interest. But perhaps the inquisitive, and sometimes exaggerated, attention that critics have devoted to this poem is just a proof of its compelling magic. The "Anecdote" is intriguing, as I see it, because it achieves an almost ideal balance between the play against the reader's expectations and the patterning of sound, which makes the poem similar to a charm or magic spell.

Most of the critics consider the jar and the Tennessee landscape in which it is placed as two opposite poles. Either the jar represents imagination and Tennessee is the reality, which it modifies, or the jar represents reason (intellect), which spoils the beauty of the nature symbolized by Tennessee, or the jar is order as opposed to Tennessee, which is the wild, or chaos, and so forth. Yet as some other critics observe, the semantics of the poem does not seem to justify this opposition, for if the wilderness is *slovenly,* the jar, in its turn, is *grey and bare,* qualities that would not exactly recommend it as an aesthetic object.[17] Moreover, the jar does not seem to be in disharmony with the landscape; it just modifies it, nature showing itself willing to comply with the jar's mysterious power.

We may wonder, then, why so many critics, and probably many more readers, remain so keen on this opposition. One reason may be that the two elements may be considered at least potential opposites, even if they integrate so perfectly in the poem. Besides, the jar's oddity in the context is bound to attract attention. For its literary context rejects it as rapidly as the wilderness accepts it, and the reader may find that the easiest way to fit it in is to resort to a symbolic interpretation, which practically changes the meaning of the word. Therefore, critics invoke a quality of the jar that makes it a potential symbol: it is man-made, an artifact, representative of man's creative power or intelligence. As such, it can be set against the forces that oppose man's endeavors, the forces of a nature that resists human activity. Parenthetically, we may notice that critics do not (with the exception, perhaps, of Roy Harvey Pearce, who thinks it is a Mason jar)[18] invoke the jar's capacity to contain pickles, preserves, or cookies, and its utter futility after it had been emptied thereof. Such unpoetic connections would disqualify the jar as symbol, although they might support a parodic interpretation of the poem. The possibility is worth considering that the jar may actually be a very successful spoof of Keats's Grecian urn—another object of the jar kind— which probably fulfilled the same functions in its own time but, given the state of technology, was certainly discarded less often than contemporary jars are. But there may be a more serious reason for any critic to perceive an opposition, the tension of a confrontation, for such tension pervades the whole poem, although it is not explicit in its semantics.

The "Anecdote of the Jar" best exemplifies Eleanor Cook's pronouncement that Stevens could never quite commit himself to either riddle or charm poetry but most often combined both.[19] Frank Lentricchia trusts the title of the poem when he places it in the genre of the anecdote, but he also remarks that Stevens's are "cryptically crafted, riddle-like anecdotes."[20] In all its riddling (therefore conceptual) quality, the poem never fails to impress our ear. Lentricchia calls the poem an "aural imperialist."[21] William Bevis is even disposed to hear in the poem the arrangement of a musical piece.[22] But the resemblance to music (of the classical kind) is less intense, I think, than the hint of magic mongering. The relation of this poem to magic has been suggested by Leonora Woodman, who discovered a possible source for Stevens's inspiration in a passage from Jung describing magical practices.[23] Although Woodman's explanation demystifies the poem, which thus contextualized begins to make literal sense, the possibility of perceiving it as a charm remains one of the most attractive ways of reading the "Anecdote of the Jar."

As the title says, it is a little story, an "anecdote" that revolves around an event. Like all Stevens's anecdotes, Lentricchia insists,[24] this poem strongly suggests a situational context that it does not reveal. Nevertheless the actual description of the event looks straightforward enough: the wilderness changes its shape in order to accommodate the jar, and the jar, in its turn, transforms itself into some kind of ugly, but dignified object. This clearly depicted event, however, does not make much sense because of the lack of a real cause. One may accept the rather sudden transformation of nature, the unexplained dignity of the jar, but one may not easily give up the question of why the speaker places this jar in Tennessee after all. The motivation of a human action is the primary interest in a narrative or anecdote, so that, by not declaring it, this poem frustrates one's basic expectations. The placing of the jar is a totally arbitrary gesture, as is also the choice of Tennessee over a thousand other places. Yes, we know that Stevens traveled to Tennessee, that he may have seen a jar when he did so, but there is no specific quality of "Tennessee" mentioned in the poem to make it a realistic locale. Lentricchia's speculation that Tennessee may have been chosen because of the echo of an Indian place name, Tanasi, is by his own admission unfounded, for the name remains arbitrary (why not Manhattan?) even as its intriguing presence in the poem invites historical connections. Once again, Stevens faces his reader with a lack of appropriate context, which renders the reference partially obscure and for that reason endows the words with an extra dimension. The mystery of the speaker's motivation is a vacuum of sense that perpetually lures one to guess about it. Consequently, the event described—the transformation of nature in the presence of the jar—although fairly clear in its limited context remains mysterious as it returns us to the unmotivated gesture that started it.

The whole poem is like a circle described around the jar, and it may literally be so, since the action is one of "surrounding," and the repetition of "round" and several of its variants creates a sound dominance that neither critics nor casual readers can fail to notice:

I placed a jar in Tennessee,
And *round* it was, upon a hill.
It made the slovenly wilderness
Surround that hill.

> The wilderness rose up to it,
> And sprawled *around,* no longer wild.
> The jar was *round* upon the *ground*
> And tall and of a port in air.
>
>   [*CP* 76, emphasis added]

The poem thus constructs itself around the jar, literally surrounding it; and it makes sense only in reference to the jar—the object whose presence there is precisely the element that does not seem to make sense. Like the poems mentioned before, the "Anecdote" threatens a loss of its sense, which is kept in a precarious balance only by its curious "surrounding" movement, a movement that is largely the effect of sound.

The poem has a powerful rhythm, although it is far from being a conventional one, and its elegant symmetry strikes one from the beginning. As Samuel French Morse observes, "the neat quatrains and subtly manipulated consonance create an effect of symmetry without actually adhering to any fixed pattern."[25]

This effect of symmetry may result from the textual repetition of the words, for "round," with its variants and its rhyme in "ground," is not the only repeated word. While we try to make sense out of the poem, these repetitions may appear to be a hindrance. It seems that the speaker is not sure that we get his meaning and unnecessarily emphasizes some words. For instance, "upon a hill" in the second line is recalled for us in the fourth, "Surround *that hill,*" as if, afraid we have forgotten, the speaker wanted to remind us of it. The "wilderness" from line 3 reappears in line 5 and is "no longer wild" in line 6. And finally, the poem ends, symmetrically coming back to the initial "Tennessee," and induces us, again, to wonder at the motivation of this choice: why Tennessee? "That hill" could have been anywhere. But in spite of all its tantalizing questions, the poem seems perfect in its symmetry, and given the option, we may not want to change a word of it, simply because it "sounds" all right.

The dominance of the sound, the symmetry, and the repetitions make the poem sound like a magic spell, whose power one may accept without questioning its meaning. And perhaps the most important element of this similarity to magic is the gesture that the opening line describes and at the same time performs: "I placed a jar in Tennessee." Taking the liberty to say it is as arbitrary a gesture as the action that the line describes, a gesture of exerting power just like the lines that sometimes open magic spells and do nothing but "simply describe what the magician is doing."[26] This gesture of exerting power may seem exaggerated, given that, as a magic object, the jar may look ridiculous, if not grotesque. This comic potential, however, as well as the potential for nonsense, is never achieved. Samuel French Morse intuitively feels the extra dimension that the sense of the poem can acquire: "The deliberately 'commonplace guise,' like the comic magnification of a trivial gesture, is a disguise, for in professing or seeming to profess that it is a kind of joke, the poem becomes something more."[27]

Paradoxically, the jar achieves its "magical" purpose precisely because it is an unlikely magical object. All we know about magic is related to stories, fairy tales, that belong to some indeterminate, remote past. We cannot expect that an object from our kitchen might serve magical purposes. And the magic here is not in the object but rather "in the word of it." For this poem, like the others before it, makes sense by appealing to our normal way of inferring meaning in language, by exploiting our expectations. If the speaker had selected a more likely object and made his speech more closely similar to a spell, the effect would have been lost on the audience. The poem may have been *recognized* as the imitation of a spell but would not have exerted any power on us, modern readers liberated from superstition. But the odd jar, which even after the poem is over "would not declare itself" (*CP* 19) as the "song" from another poem by Stevens, performs the role of a magic object to perfection. For every time we read the poem, we are under its spell, and whatever symbolic dimensions we attribute to it, we remain tantalized by its elusive meaning. Ascribing symbolic dimensions may be a sort of defense we put up when faced with such mysteries.

In another "magical" aspect, the poem is an incentive to an action of mastering nature; it opposes the human to the nonhuman just like magic, which "is essentially the assertion of man's intrinsic power over nature."[28] And it is perhaps the tension of this confrontation that we feel as an opposition in the poem when, going by our usual routes of interpretation, we attribute symbolic value to the jar and to the landscape that it comes to dominate. But the actual opposition lies, rather, between the voice that speaks, between the human will that imposes itself to the world, and the reality, or the nature it addresses with the sole purpose of appropriating it.

And although this effect may seem unexpected in a poem, its power lies in its literal sense, the sense that threatens to be lost with the dominance of sound, rather than in the possible symbolic interpretation. For a precisely decoded symbolic value would create the possibility that interpretation could be univocal and thus restrain the energy that words possess. But as the numerous critical appraisals of the poem prove, interpretation is an endless possibility here. The symbolic value would make words transparent, whereas the literal sense allows words to remain opaque and to *mean* through their function rather than through reference.

Meaning is brought to the jar rather than discovered to be there, and this potential tips the balance of power between the "real" and the humanly significant object in favor of the latter. The arbitrariness of the choice plays an important part in this balance of power. For to exert a power equal to that of magic, to perform the appropriation of nature by the human will, and no less to put us readers under its spell, the jar must be no more than a jar, a trivial object whose choice itself can only be an arbitrary gesture, meaningful solely as an exercise of power. Frank Lentricchia suggests that the power exercised in or rather by the poem is part of Stevens's "politics of lyricism" determined by the "necessity of forsaking action and the genre of action—story telling—in favor of aesthetics, praise's ultimate awstruck medium."[29] But aestheticism, the subtle refinement of language, translates for Stevens into another kind of action that, although only verbal, exerts the authority of action proper.

Lentricchia also remarks that the sound of the poem is precisely the element that makes it unsuitable for either formalist or structuralist reading, and without noticing the poem's similarity to verbal magic, he points to its quality as a cultural artifact, which functions both as an expression of the culture and as a formative agent of it. The jar comes to express, in complicated and indirect ways, the spirit of America, and Lentricchia quotes Michael Herr, who alludes to it in a commentary on events taking place during the Vietnam war: "Once it was all locked in place, Khe Sanh became like the planted jar in Wallace Stevens's poem. It took dominion everywhere."[30] In an exemplary way, Lentricchia's connection comes to prove not only the "magic" of the poem but also the capacity of its language to gather meaning and to dominate reality. For the aestheticism that Lentricchia notes in Stevens is not an isolating retreat from reality but an action in its own right, a verbal gesture of unmistakable authority.

The "magic" structure appears in Wallace Stevens's poetry quite frequently, but the poems completely structured in this way are rare. Most often, the verbal magic is only a stage toward achieving a language free of the obligation to maintain its referential function, its conformity to empirical reality. Through the technique of a quasiverbal magic, the poet demonstrates that language does not have to be representational and liberates the speaker from the task of constructing either stories or arguments, so that he is free to exert his linguistic imagination. After going through the exercise of sound, language proves its dominant role in relation to reality and is able to extend reality's domain beyond the physical. The landscape, unrepresented and undescribed, becomes a landscape of the mind. "Metaphors of a Magnifico" is a good example of such transformation, for its initial quasi-philosophical reasoning is soon caught in a pattern of sound that dominates and even displaces its sense, and its refrain comes as a self-critical remark:

> Twenty men crossing a bridge,
> Into a village,
> Are twenty men crossing twenty bridges,
> Into twenty villages,
> Or one man
> Crossing a single bridge into a village.
>
> This is old song
> That will not declare itself. . . .
> 　　[CP 19]

As the poem develops, tautology comes in as an escape from the ambition, frustrated as if by impossibility, to construct an argument. Margaret Peterson demystifies the poem by showing that its line of argumentation was inspired by William James. In her view, it is a parody of philosophical argument in which the ending nonsense—the fact that the song "will not declare itself"—is a way of showing the weakness of this type of reasoning.[31] The sound pattern of the poem cannot be dismissed as pure parody, however, and I must agree with James Guetti that the poem, " 'will not declare itself' not merely because as a problem it is too difficult but because . . . it has repeated in the imagination so long that it cannot 'declare': because it is 'song,' and song declares nothing. And so, though it is 'certain as meaning,' it is 'certain' in a very different way from 'meaning.' "[32]

The language of this poem literally closes upon itself and diverts its generative power from the task of arguing to that of achieving a pattern, and tautology appears as the only way to make sense. And only after language has been thus liberated from its representational/argumentative function, an image arises:

The boots of the men clump
On the boards of the bridge.
The first white wall of the village
Rises through fruit-trees.
    [*CP* 19]

This is a perfectly clear image, the clearer for all the tautological sound pattern that preceded it, but what is its sense? For it is an image that registers some kind of reality, which grows in the imaginative space of the mind without apparent purpose. It is not part of anything, for neither argument nor story can use it, and the reader may share the speaker's confusion: "Of what was I thinking?" But the power of this apparently senseless image is shown by the fact that it persists even after the speaker has noticed that "the meaning escapes": "The first white wall of the village . . . / The fruit-trees" look like a glimpse into the metaphysical, a fragment of a reality beyond the reach of reason.

Such glimpses are made possible by Stevens's verbal magic, a special use of sound effect to enrich language and make it more powerful than reality. Verbal magic is not merely a technique but a different discursive mode based on radically different assumptions about language and about the relation between language and reality. And the similarity between Stevens's verse and magic is not purely technical either, for it consists, beyond the devices that can be noticed on the surface, in a change of assumptions about the function of language. It is evident that verbal magic is not Stevens's final purpose but a stage toward the discovery of a discourse with a certain specificity, determined by certain epistemological and ontological assumptions. Stevens's explorations into language reach toward a poetic domain that, although based in language, is not exclusively confined to it but expands into the larger area of human existence and cognition.

4

The Aural Foundations of the Real

THE REVERSAL OF what common sense perceives as a normal relation between language and reality is present in most of Stevens's poems. Yet as I tried to show at the end of chapter 3, privileging language over reality is only the first step toward changes that have to do not only with the surface of language but also with the underlying assumptions of its use. These assumptions lie at the basis of a certain linguistic practice and are therefore part of a larger cultural network that keeps them closely linked to conceptions of reality, truth, knowledge, and the self. One assumption cannot be altered without altering the whole practice. Not only does Stevens's sound technique—similar to a verbal magic—endow language with unusual power, but awarding language primacy over reality, it questions the very notion of reality. In fact, such questioning is one other constant feature of Stevens's poems that materializes not only in statement but also in a characteristic way of manipulating sounds.

The commonsense notion of the "real"—closely related to the notion of "objective reality" derived from the scientific trends of the last century—becomes doubtful when confronted with a language that can also represent its opposite, the fictional, in terms that are not essentially different. Actually, the very opposition between real and fictional is a matter of a basic generic distinction between ordinary and literary discourse. As such, the distinction privileges the nonliterary for being more faithful to "reality" seen as independent of human understanding. And it presupposes, of course, that reality is primary in relation to language. But such privileging of "reality" over language and of representations of reality over fictional representations is a matter of language usage, of conventions that themselves sustain the distinction. Stevens's poetic language works toward discrediting the claims of linguistic realism and the very notion of "reality" implied in such claims through its rhetoric, syntax, and especially through its pattern of sound.

Most often, to speak about the concept of reality in Wallace Stevens means to invoke the dichotomy of reality and the imagination that echoes throughout his essays. Following the poet's lead, critics like J. Hillis Miller, Joseph Riddel, Roy Harvey Pearce, Helen Regueiro, Paul Bové, Frank Lentricchia, to mention only a few, have approached the concept of the "real" in Wallace Stevens by opposing it to either imagination or fiction.[1] In fact, it has become an almost ritual gesture to recall such a dichotomy in any discussion of Stevens's poetry. But the frequency of the subject's treatment does not necessarily indicate that all the questions related to it have been answered. In the beginning of their book *The Fluent Mundo,* Leonard and Wharton warn against the danger of regarding the imagination/reality topic as already exhausted: "The route to the poetry via imagination/reality is well-worn, to say the least. But as current critical theory (and Stevens' poetics) insists, the more clichéd an idea becomes, the more it needs to be reconsidered."[2]

Leonard and Wharton argue against a critical orientation prevailing in the 1970s[3] that found Stevens's concept of reality to be similar to that of phenomenologists like Husserl and Heidegger and that eventually related Stevens to deconstruction. Against such a trend, Leonard and Wharton demonstrate that Stevens is in fact closer to Nietzsche[4] in his views regarding the nature of reality. As I shall demonstrate in this and the final chapter of this book, the concept of reality that emerges when Stevens's sound effects are considered is indeed only partly similar to ideas launched by phenomenology and is to my mind closer to, if not identical with, the notion of reality promoted by American pragmatist philosophers.

The main reason (and proof) for the associations between Stevens's ideas about reality and the ideas promoted by Husserl or Heidegger is a certain manner his poems have (this point will become quite clear in the poems I will examine in this chapter) of seeming to advance perception by canceling previous representations of the real. Although this strategy invites analogies with Husserlian "reduction,"[5] I must agree with Leonard and Wharton that the process of canceling standard representations in Stevens "clears the way for new interpretations, not for a Husserlian apprehension of essence; and Stevens's use of the 'object' displaces Husserl's reductive program, as he remedies the monotony of phenomenal change."[6] Tracing Stevens's ideas about imagination and reality to I. A. Richards, J. B. Leggett confirms that Stevens's reductions (sometimes called decreations, according to the term that Stevens borrowed from Simone Weil) result in other fictions rather than in the discovery of an essential reality. Leggett comments on a letter of Wallace Stevens: "The 'thing' here would seem to be the supreme fiction, which can be seen more clearly after the existing fictions are removed. To put it another way, it could be argued that the implication of Stevens's comment here is that the result of decreation produces something that must yet be abstract in the traditional sense of the word, that is, an idea or concept rather than the 'very thing alive and undistorted.'"[7]

Although most critics have done it, to figure out Stevens's concept of "reality" in his poems may lead to contradictory results. Hillis Miller's article on Stevens in *Poets of Reality* starts by placing Stevens's notion of reality in a Nietzschean context pervaded by the awareness that reality is culturally constructed. At the end of the article, however, Stevens has decidedly become a phenomenologist. The difference is explained not simply by the chronology of the poems Hillis Miller examines but by the fact that, wherever one stops in Stevens, one can find arguments supporting either position. J. B. Leggett's perusal of the studies of Alan Perlis and Helen Regueiro leads him to a similar conclusion:

> These two studies, taken together, suggest the dilemma faced by the reader in search of a theory underlying the verse, the recognition that the most careful scrutiny of the poems—Perlis and Regueiro are accomplished and sophisticated readers—yields results that may be contradicted at every turn. We are given at the same moment two poets who bear only the slightest resemblance. Perlis gives us the exponent of the supremacy of the imagination willfully at play in a world of resemblance and metaphor, fatally but happily sundered from the natural world. Regueiro uncovers a Stevens who rejects the metaphorical world of resemblance and who surrenders the imagination itself so that he may experience the chaotic natural world the imagination denies him. These, of course, are roughly the poles between which commentary on Stevens has been located.[8]

Often we must resort to Stevens's more decisive statements in prose to settle the disputes, but we cannot hope for a final answer there either. Studying his essays, Margaret Peterson was able to demonstrate that Stevens's ideas about reality and the imagination (sometimes fiction) are derived from a number of sources ranging from Coleridge to I. A. Richards, from Bergson to Croce, from William James to George Santayana.[9] As Peterson shows, Stevens's theoretical statements are hard to disengage from their (sometimes contradictory) sources and are far from being clearly articulated. According to her, Stevens's theoretical indecision prompts him to explore the issue again and again: "The problem of establishing a valid relation between mind and the external reality is rehearsed in poem after poem, and the possible ways of resolving it become pervasive themes. This vacillation before seeming alternatives of an intractable problem becomes, in fact, an intellectual mannerism as characteristic as the mannerisms of his style."[10]

Stevens's position on the question of reality and the imagination is indeed hard to disentangle from his evasive formulations, and this difficulty may explain the fascination the question exerts on his critics, who perpetually return to it. Articulation of the issue may be not just Stevens's problem but a problem of the age of modernism, an age that gestured toward not only a different mode of perception but also a change in terminology. The distinction between imagination and reality, in one form or another, belongs to a conceptual framework by now outdated, especially in the context of poststructuralism, which, as Gerald Bruns put it, "makes talk about imagination and reality sound prehistoric, like talk about God."[11]

Armed with another kind of conceptual apparatus, Thomas Grey is able to solve Stevens's problem without difficulty. Referring to Stevens's essay "Imagination as Value," Grey comments: "Stevens first repudiates [the imagination's] philosophically idealist interpretation, and then uses it to refer to what we would call the social construction of reality—the fact that most of our ordinary concepts, including our frameworks for representing time and space, are imaginative and culturally specific constructs that well could have been otherwise."[12] If imagination equals the reality socially constructed, it is no wonder that imagination so often merges with and becomes indistinguishable from reality. In the poststructural conceptual frame, it is difficult to say where solid reality ends and socially constructed reality begins. But Stevens was not reading Jacques Derrida or Clifford Geertz: he was reading Richards and Croce, James and Santayana. Indeed Stevens would have benefited from formulations like "culturally specific constructs" to explain what he meant by imagination when he declared that "it helps us live our lives,"[13] for instance. A concept of reality similar to the one implied by Grey emerges from Stevens's poems if we look at the operation of sound.

My purpose here is neither to revive prehistory by talking about imagination and reality, nor to redefine reality as conceptualized by Stevens, but rather to show how the "real" constitutes itself in the process of reading his poems. For this, I shall have to invoke a similar distinction—between reality and fiction—simply because it is part of the poet's conceptual baggage and it is also assumed by his readers. And only by situating himself against such a distinction could Stevens evolve what he once called a "new knowledge of reality."

Many critics have demonstrated that he labors to dissolve the distinctions between either imagination and reality or fiction and reality, and this concern should by now be quite obvious, but my interest is rather in the manner in which he effects such a dissolution, for the new concept of the real emerges, I suggest, from a play upon the reader's expectations.[14] Taking into account such expectations is essential, for seen as part of a dialogue with the reader, Stevens's gesture acquires significance beyond the epistemological breakdown that either a formalist or a deconstructive reading might, in different ways, suggest. In what follows, I shall observe this dialogue very closely in two poems that illustrate Stevens's constructions of reality in exemplary ways.

As Margaret Peterson informs us, having attended Harvard at the time William James was teaching there and exerting a major influence on the young poets/students, Wallace Stevens shares the pragmatist's skepticism about the notion of "reality" that common sense and traditional philosophy entertain, and although his own ideas about it may differ from James's, he would agree that "Both the sensational and the relational parts of reality are dumb: they say absolutely nothing about themselves. We it is who have to speak for them."[15] In a nutshell, one can say that Stevens undertakes to do just that: speak *for* reality rather than *about* it. In "A Collect of Philosophy," he even defines poetry as "an art of perception" and argues that "the problems of perception as they are developed in philosophy resemble similar problems in poetry."[16] Many of his poems justify that definition proceeding, in language, with the caution of an eye watching or of a hand feeling—a manner that also invites analogies with phenomenology.

"Gallant Château," for instance, seems to develop as an attempt to render pure images, images that only "reality" could endow with significance. Probably for this reason Mark Halliday finds it to be a "cryptic" hymn to solitude.[17]

> Is it bad to have come here
> And to have found the bed empty?
>
> One might have found tragic hair,
> Bitter eyes, hands hostile and cold.
>
> There might have been a light on a book
> Lighting a pitiless verse or two.
>
> There might have been the immense solitude
> Of the wind upon the curtains.
>
> Pitiless verse? A few words tuned
> And tuned and tuned and tuned.
>
> It is good. The bed is empty,
> The curtains are stiff and prim and still.
>
> [CP 161]

Like many of Stevens's titles, "Gallant Château" would fit a painting better than a poem, and beyond Stevens's engagement with theories of modern art,[18] one can easily suspect some influence of imagism in this pictorial choice. It would be rather hasty, however, to decide that this is an imagist poem. As James Longenbach points out, "Stevens appears to have Imagist tendencies . . . not because Imagism was so powerful a movement but because the 'diminished' aesthetic it embodies was a common response to the pressure of the achievement of the high Romantics."[19] Imagism is, in fact, betrayed at the outset, because, although it is grammatically simple—a noun, which is normally supposed to evoke an image without any abstract complications—the title can be endlessly suggestive. It may evoke, for instance, the atmosphere of a romantic novel, and because it is in French and explicitly "gallant" (never mind the English spelling), we are free to imagine a particularly exciting romance. When the image that is central to the poem—that of an empty bed in a deserted room—appears, it may provoke an "emotional complex" not directly but through a long series of already conventionalized responses related to other images. The ostensive gesture of the language reduced to names is thus canceled by the very nature of those names, which contain much more than their simple reference. Having been used in language before, they clearly bear the traces of that usage.

Equally subversive of imagist force is the initial question of the poem: "Is it bad . . . ?" An image of reality by itself cannot satisfy as an answer to such a question, because, as Kenneth Burke,[20] following Bergson, observes, reality by itself is neither positive nor negative; it becomes so only when integrated in a complex of human relationships, of which language is only the most salient manifestation. Therefore, although the question itself is formulated in the simplest of terms, its answer sends us to the words' complex history in philosophy, theology, and myth.

The scarcity of context characteristic of Stevens's poems increases the complexity lingering in this apparently simple question, which the speaker poses to himself as if at the end of a journey. For like many other speakers in Stevens, the one in this poem does not warn his audience about the occasion of the poem, so that his question has a shifting frame. The possibility of many answers makes it difficult for the reader to select one, and the speaker's concentration on the data of the senses remains futile. The closer he tries to get to the sensory image, the further away his words seem to take him. For the question, which the answer echoes rather than resolves, solicits meaning, something that the simple image should *say,* and without a human presence, without a history of human affairs, the image remains indeed "dumb."

And perhaps because such history is missing, language falls back on itself and offers the fiction. After the question is formulated, and before the actual answer comes, we find one of those little fantasies that Stevens's syntax unleashes in his poems: "One might have found." Such phrases abound in Stevens, as his poems thrive upon possibilities, upon what is not, what might have been, would have been, and so on. In *On Extended Wings,* Helen Vendler[21] shows the importance of syntax in Stevens's poems, observing that the extensive use of modal verbs, phrases like "as if," and questions makes them sound evasive and undetermined. This syntax makes her imagine a frame of mind dominated by indecision or by a reluctance to make definite statements. The interpretation of such verbal gestures may vary according to the context of the individual poems, remarks Vendler, but their constant presence in Stevens may also be proof of his particular way of thinking.

From the standpoint of the reader, this uncertainty, which becomes dominant because of the syntactical peculiarity of the poems, may very well look like the natural consequence of the speaker's difficulty in representing reality. Laden with "as if's," "might have been's," and other phrases of the same nature, the linguistic medium appears to be slippery and difficult to control. Jacqueline Brogan discovers a similarity between Stevens's use of "as if" and Vaihinger's philosophy. Her commentary on Vaihinger points out the possibilities opened to language by the phrase: "The reason that the phrase 'as if' carries so much weight for Vaihinger is that it manages to combine two contradictory statements in such a way that both statements are formally maintained."[22]

Maintaining two statements at once, language threatens to lose sense and throws shadows of uncertainty on the reality it purports to represent. "Gallant Château" is mostly spent to say what "might have been" found in the room, whose image should have been, in itself, the answer to the initial question. Language that seemed to be offered for its capacity to express "what is," the reality, or truth, is deployed here to picture "what is not," the fiction. The syntactical turns of the language seem to have blurred the distinctions originally assumed between perception and reflection, or between reality and fiction. And although we might feel deceived in our desire to get a "true" answer to the question, we may also have to admit that language does not really present such discriminations.

Yet the hesitant phrase "what might have been" does not end communication or disqualify the speaker; on the contrary the speaker gets a license to continue ad infinitum, since fictions can virtually multiply for ever. And the switch to fiction is marked not only by the grammar but also by the quality of the images that the speaker brings up. In the "tragic hair, / Bitter eyes, hands hostile and cold," or in "the immense solitude / Of the wind upon the curtains," one might easily recognize the conventions of a certain type of fiction—romance. The conventionality of the images points to them as fictions, so that the truth or the realistic adequacy of the image is no longer an issue.

The uncertainty that dominates the syntactical aspect of the poem may thus well be part of the speaker's surrender to a language that does not permit him to separate reality from fiction. The erasure of the distinction between the two domains seems even to result from the action of the language against his will. It is as if language had a power of its own and chose to make it evident by counteracting the speaker's intentions. But one may wonder whether he is as helpless as he seems, or whether he himself has designed the failure, for he has started with a question that refers to an ambiguously Platonic "reality" that, circumscribed by empiricist notions, may appear as fiction. The moral value of the image, which the question addresses and the poem seeks to compose, could be found only in the fictions that he builds starting from it. Language proves, whether by its own design or by the speaker's, to be as good or as bad for both reality and imagination, and a phrase like "as if" or "what might have been" can constitute a bridge between these two orders, which we usually perceive as disconnected.

Once this continuity has been established, the relation of language to fiction becomes the same as its relation to reality, and language continues to seem to evade the speaker, for as it ran away from reality into fiction, it now escapes from one kind of fiction into another. The speaker seems to get entangled not in one fiction that can, in many ways, resemble reality but into the infinite regression of a fictionalizing process. After he had evoked a scene from a book, he evokes the image of a book—the fictional image of a container of fiction. Besides, it is a book of verse, which cannot even claim the stance of realism as a narrative would. At the same time, the images become less and less personal, as if the human presence evoked were more and more abstract. We can guess that the human feelings are still there, because the "pitiless" verse could not be so unless so perceived, and the "immense solitude / Of the wind upon the curtains" can only be the projection of a person's state of mind. But these feelings hang in an impersonal void, further and further away from the initial "reality."

Beyond the "pitiless verse" there seems to be no logical possibility for further regression. For this reason, perhaps, the verse of the poem turns back upon it (upon itself?) as if to emphasize its most strikingly artful feature: "A few words tuned." The reality of the tune has a purely aesthetic foundation, and at this point the poem itself becomes one with its reference. The repetition in the second line of this stanza transforms it, literally, into a little song: "Pitiless verse? A few words tuned / And tuned and tuned and tuned." It appears that Stevens's language here causes a movement toward an extreme fictionality, transforming reality itself into just a lower degree of fiction. In the speaker's struggle to express reality, language itself exhibits its fictional substance, and although one would like to be able to distinguish between the sensory images and the rhetorical ones, the operation becomes impossible, because language does not make such distinctions.

Advancing toward reality in the poem is a process quite similar to the one William James describes: "Our whole notion of a standing reality grows up in the form of an ideal limit to the series of successive termini to which our thoughts have led us and still are leading us. Each terminus proves provisional by leaving us unsatisfied."[23] The poem itself looks indeed like an act of perception, a sensory advancement toward a reality that forever evades it. And this evasion looks like a failure, and the poem's turning into song like an escape. As in many other poems by Stevens, one may suspect here an apparent degeneration into nonsense—language reduced to its sound.

But the poem does not end, as one might have expected, on the repetitive verse. There is another couplet that may surprise with its decisive tone, with its utter simplicity and clear reference: "It is good. The bed is empty, / The curtains are stiff and prim and still." The room appears now vivid and real, and the speaker even has the latitude to focus on insignificant detail, detail that cannot be converted into symbol, and thus make him forfeit realism. And all moral and metaphysical dilemmas seem to have been either solved or dismissed. This order of things is good simply because it *is*. While in the rest of the poem there seemed to be a struggle between the attempt to express reality and the fictional tug of the language, in the last couplet the tension seems to be dissolved. Language appears to have become plastic and seems to fit reality without a crease.

This certainty contrasts sharply with the indefiniteness and evasiveness of the rest. But there is also another kind of contrast here. The last couplet seems self-contained, rounded up, conclusive, whereas the rest of the poem seems loose, unraveled. And maybe it is this conclusiveness, this well-structured aspect that makes the couplet such a successfully "realistic" description. For as William James suggests again, "what we grasp is always some substitute for [reality] which previous human thinking has peptonized and cooked for our consumption. If so vulgar an expression were allowed us, we might say that wherever we find it, it has been already *faked*."[24]

We thus perceive as "real" those things that look self-contained and definite, as the various ways in which philosophy, history, art, or mathematical formulas represent reality may easily prove. The algebraic formula is probably only an extreme expression of this self-containment, and not surprisingly, there is nothing that we would consider truer and more real. Most philosophical systems identify the knowledge of reality with a certain limitation. In *Philosophy and the Mirror of Nature,* Richard Rorty argues that "the desire for a theory of knowledge is a desire for constraint—a desire to find 'foundations' to which one might cling, frameworks beyond which one must not stray, objects which impose themselves, representations which cannot be gainsaid."[25]

One may wonder why such self-containment comes so easily in the last couplet, whereas the rest of the poem seemed vainly to grope for it. In fact, the realistic, even imagist, quality of the last couplet is nothing but the result of the previous development of the poem. For a foundation, a limit, is what the poem aims at from the very beginning, fighting off the threat of infinity that fiction poses to it. The speaker seems incapable of finding that middle path of common sense, which would make his story acceptable as real, and instead he multiplies the fictions. This very play with infinity leads to a means of ending his description, however, for naturally he falls into the easiest way to perpetuate speech: repetition. And repetition is not only a way of going on forever but is also one way to create a limit.

The first repetition that occurs in the poem looks like an echo. For some reason, perhaps because he is involved in a poem, the speaker comes back to "pitiless verse," and it would seem that the attempt to define this in detail ends in repetition: "Pitiless verse? A few words tuned / And tuned and tuned and tuned." The repetition seems here the only logical solution for ending the poem, although it is precisely not a logical ending. But when the fiction has been thus contained, language can become "proper" and "literal," although not in the way we would normally assume, that is, not because of its adequacy as a commonsensical representation of reality. We get the definite illusion of "reality" simply because repetition has created a limit and, with it, a foundation that satisfies our desire for knowledge. The last couplet itself is a repetition, since even as it answers the initial question, it repeats its structure. If we put them together, the question and answer may remind us of catechism—another linguistic expression of final knowledge actually achieved through repetition.

The final image comes after the fiction of the poem has become self-contained due to the repetitions, and because it is itself a repetition, it strikes us as self-contained too. The interpretation of the words' meaning can no longer be free, hence the illusion that the words can refer precisely and that the room is "real." Only when it is repeated can the image get the force of reality, for it becomes self-contained by virtue of containing its previous occurrence. And it is not as if we discover it with the freshness of a first perception; rather we reach it after a laborious process of cleansing a chaotic mass of sense data, memories, and fictions. Reality, as we come to know it here, is rather the end or result of conception and not the beginning of perception.

The process of composing this "pure" image—a process that is the poem itself—is very similar to what Santayana describes, in *The Life of Reason,* as a process of acquiring knowledge, which, contrary to expectation, seems to exclude the intellect:

> To catch the passing phenomenon in all its novelty and idiosyncrasy is a work of artifice and curiosity. Such an exercise does violence to intellectual instinct and involves an aesthetic power of sinking into the stream of sensation, having thrown overboard all rational ballast and escaped at once the inertia and the momentum of practical life. Normally every datum of the sense is at once devoured by a hungry intellect and digested for the sake of its vital juices. The result is that what ordinarily remains in memory is no representative of particular moments or shocks—but rather a logical possession, a sense of acquaintance with a certain field of reality, in a word, a consciousness of *knowledge.*[26]

Santayana's emphasis seems to be here on the "aesthetic" quality of the cognitive process. He speaks not even of knowledge proper but of a "consciousness of knowledge," and this seems to me to support the distinction I have been trying to make between "reality" as it is usually defined and what is actually perceived as reality. The poem has been an experiment in approaching reality, and its action upon us demonstrates that we cannot accept the real in its "raw" form. We are ready to declare the poem a failure as long as it attempts to advance into the domain of pure sensation, but we perceive as successfully "real" an image that appears only after the fiction has been carried to its extreme. Santayana's "consciousness of knowledge" is probably the best term to describe the way the last couplet of Stevens's poem affects its readers.

Due to repetition, this image converts the failure of language to render sensory experience into a certainty of knowledge beyond fiction, "at the end of the mind" like the "palm" of another poem by Stevens, and thus its success is directly connected to the sound of the poem. For although the failure to represent the real may be construed as a degeneration of language into sound without meaning, in that sound, there is a "consciousness of knowledge" impressed on the reader by the pattern. Resulting out of this pattern, the image appears to be contained, founded, and to have a form that imposes it as "real." The paradoxical power of repetition to create closure while preserving a movement that threatens to go on infinitely accounts for the fact that, when language fails to compose visible, pictorial images, it may find another kind of clarity in the sound patterns unavoidably generated by repetition.

The failure of the language to remain as purely referential as Pound's imagist doctrine required should not surprise us (and it probably did not surprise Stevens, whom one might suspect of having designed the failure), simply because our perception of reality is always a quasi-conventionalized process. Some forms or conventions are considered more realistic than others, according to the extent to which they are capable of providing foundations. In agreement with Rorty, Hayden White points out that narrative form is prized for precisely that reason: "This value attached to narrativity in the representation of real events arises out of a desire to have real events display the coherence, integrity, fullness, and closure of an image of life that is and can only be imaginary."[27]

Interestingly enough, Stevens's poem demonstrates the importance of foundations by revealing them in an aspect of language usually considered meaningless: its sound. His gesture demonstrates not only that the formal foundation is more important in the perception of reality than any empirical proof but also that there are alternatives to the most trustworthy forms of representation familiar to us. By proving that the "conscious-ness of knowledge" resides in form rather than in sensory perception, "Gallant Château" compromises the directness of imagism, but imagism is not the only target of the poet's subversion. The poem that I would like to consider next, "The Hand as a Being," experiments with and subverts, from the inside as it were, the narrative form itself.

Stevens's poems always imply questions about knowledge, and the knowledge they seek seems to be of a direct, unmediated nature. And it is perhaps the singularity of that purpose that eventually leads to a revelation of the inevitability of mediation. A direct access to reality, which is in many ways more similar to touching than to seeing, or the illusion of it, is most of the time the apparent purpose of a poem's action, and sometimes it can become its subject. "The Hand as a Being" dramatizes this explo-ration of the immediate. Thomas Hines[28] enlists the poem as proof of phenomenologi-cal reduction in Stevens. The poem does indeed offer numerous instances of stripping off fictions, but it also convincingly demonstrates that the end of Stevens's "reductions" is not an essential reality but another fiction. The reason why Hines is blind to the evidence is the fact that, eager to draw the philosophical parallels, he overlooks the biblical and Miltonic allusions in which the poem ends. As will become evident in my analysis, these allusions, duly noted by Eleanor Cook,[29] make "reality" appear definitely to have foundations in culturally constituted forms and particularly in the sound pattern of the poem.

The poem's title, which at first does not seem to have much to do with the rest, is suggestive of the sense of touch, of knowledge obtained by direct perception. This exploration of the immediate starts, as it should, at the point farthest from it, in a work of fiction:

In the first canto of the final canticle,
Too conscious of too many things at once,
Our man beheld the naked, nameless dame,

Seized her and wondered: why beneath the tree
She held her hand before him in the air,
For him to see, wove round her glittering hair.

    [CP 271]

Unlike the speaker of "Gallant Château," who is faced with a static scene, the present one is a narrator who has to deal with a sequence of events. He is faced, however, with the same paradox in his task: he must render the immediate through a series of mediations. Reference itself is a mediation already implied in language, but here mediation is brought to a superlative degree, since several fictions are imposed upon one another. The fictional status of the poem as "poem" is recognized from the very beginning, for it starts "in the first canto of the final canticle," and from such a songlike creation one cannot expect directness, not even intelligibility. Moreover, we seem to catch here a moment when the speaker approaches the end of the fiction: this is the final canticle, and the story is about to accomplish its fictional existence. For if during a story's development we may be entranced to the point where we may believe it to be real, at the end, when we part with it, we are more than ever aware of its fictional nature.

In admitting that he refers to a fiction, the speaker reinforces the unreality of his hero, who himself seems to be aware of his fictional status. Fictionality seems thus to be acknowledged by all the persons involved with the poem: reader, speaker, hero. And there is a sense of identification between the hero and the speaker, for the speaker, who is supposed to be only the teller of this story, which has reached its final canticle, seems to participate in it more than is required from an observer. The snatching quality of his verse may easily lead us to believe that he is himself "too conscious of too many things at once." But caught in the process of reading, so are we, the readers. Like the hero, we are offered "too many things at once" and become conscious of them without being able to order them.

The absence of such order creates a vacuum into which we are forcefully absorbed, and we may feel that we should already have read or listened to all the other canticles to be able to accomplish our fate as readers in the final one. At the end of a story, we also expect knowledge, though not exactly of the kind we aspire to in real life; within the limits of the fiction, we seek a resolution, a clarification, some kind of an end that may give us the illusion that we *know*. This point too can identify us with the hero and with the speaker, since although the knowledge they aspire to is the "real" one, *they* are fictional, and we cannot make much difference between what they seek and what we seek.

The result of these successive identifications is that speaker, hero, and reader meet in the same realm. And although we very well know that we are at the end of a fiction, as far from the real as possible, in spite of it all, everything looks like a beginning, like the first contact with "reality": our hero, speaker, or self is conscious of "too many things at once" as we usually are in a new environment; he (we?) is confronted with the unknown in the person of a "naked, nameless dame" without identity but alluring and familiar. Like ourselves, the hero trusts his senses and takes the perception of the object of knowledge for knowledge itself, and like most of us, he is fated to be disappointed by the elusiveness of that object. It would seem that, because the identification between reader and hero has become so close, we could also just stretch our hand and touch, and with him, we may wonder why we simply cannot do it.

For whether we realize it or not, the illusion that everything is real has been growing out of the fiction. And as the fictionalizing process begins to follow a regressive movement, one fiction nesting into another, the illusion of reality becomes more and more dependent on it. The presupposed narrative becomes a vital necessity. It is as if in order to be real at all, we must be in a canto of a canticle and be composed by a hand, which itself is a creation of some artist or poet:

> Too conscious of too many things at once,
> In the first canto of the final canticle,
> Her hand composed him and composed the tree.
>
> The wind had seized the tree and ha, and ha,
> It held the shivering, the shaken limbs,
> Then bathed its body in the leaping lake.
>   [CP 271]

The paradox of the situation is that the more fictional everything becomes, the more real it appears to be to us, to the hero, and even to the speaker. The limits between reality and fiction are blurred. It is only after the woman draws the contour of the tree with her hands that this tree seems to acquire existence, and the wind can begin to blow on it. But for all this blurring of limits, the woman's creative act interposes a distance:

> Her hand composed him like a hand appeared,
> Of an impersonal gesture, a stranger's hand.
> He was too conscious of too many things
>
> In the first canto of the final canticle.
>   [CP 271]

I have argued above that the limiting, containing function of representation makes reality look "real" to us, and that the distinction between real and fictional does not hold. As if to support that idea, the hero of this poem advances toward a knowledge of his own reality by surrendering to rather than opposing the fiction that has been around him from the very beginning. This surrender itself accelerates the blurring of the limits between fiction and reality, but as if prompted by some regenerative force, fiction recreates its limits, the aesthetic distance that, according to Santayana, is so important in order to gain a "consciousness of knowledge." The limit is textually reinforced by the repetition of the poem's refrain at this point, where it might be almost forgotten and where one might be tempted to form expectations for a narrative sequence.

Narrative itself is a way of representing reality, which is often considered its warrant, especially in historical accounts. As Hayden White observes, "It is historians themselves who have transformed narrativity from a manner of speaking into a paradigm of the form that reality itself displays to a 'realistic' consciousness."[30] But although dominant, narrative is not the only form that can appeal to the realistic consciousness, and Stevens explores precisely the alternative paradigm of sound pattern. Although for a while the poem looks like a story, any possible expectation for a linear development is frustrated. For we are back where we started, and the illusion of development may have been nothing but the infinite regress from the "real" toward further and further removed degrees of the fictional. If we try to summarize the details mentioned in the first five stanzas, we shall see that their place in the structure of the story—which the poem had promised to be—is uncertain, perhaps because the story is not really structured in the way we expect.

The man in the story is conscious of too many things at once, and the speaker seems to be so as well, who continues telling it regardless of coherence. His repetitions and returns bring us to the same state of mind, and we get the distinct feeling that everything happens at the same time. This simultaneity of the actions is reinforced, again, by the very verbal device that damages the linearity of the story: the repetition. The first two lines "In the first canto of the final canticle / Too conscious of too many things at once" are repeated in this order or in reverse all through the poem, producing a musical effect, or perhaps I should say an effect similar to that of music, for not simply do we perceive the verse as rhythm and melody, but we get the same impression—that time itself is being manipulated, structured, and contained—that we have when listening to music. The normal assumption about verbal repetition is that it is meant to emphasize. But such a function becomes paradoxical, because the more repetition emphasizes the fictional, the more we have the distinct feeling that something is certain and defined, that there is a meaningful space that we would like to call real.

The poem thus faces us with the paradoxes of our own sense of reality, since on the one hand we think it starts in the immediate sensation, whereas on the other, we do not recognize the result of that sensation as "reality" until it has been aestheticized, fictionalized, founded in forms. Repetition, when used to create pattern, is essentially an aesthetic feature of speech, because it creates the illusion that the text is self-contained. We keep returning to "the first canto of the final canticle" as to a sort of center, around which the reality of the poem organizes itself. And although the exigencies of realism have it that the resemblance with the "reality perceived by our senses" should be maintained closely in order for speech to be considered true, reality cannot be recognized as such, unless it is structured in a forcibly fictional whole. And once again, repetition performs the role of limiting and containing the fiction to the point of making it seem real.

The effort to maintain the tie with the "reality" of the senses is obvious in the poem, and it accounts for the speaker's return to the same formulations over and over again. The end of the poem looks like a new attempt to recapture the authenticity of pure sensation, and it symmetrically reproduces the beginning. At the beginning the man, fictional as he may have been "in the first canto of the final canticle," tried to seize the woman, whose appearance was sudden and whose reality remained uncertain—for all we know, he might have dreamed her up. In the end, it is this woman, whose creative gestures have fictionalized everything, or rather have moved everything to a further degree of fiction, who seizes the man. There are no doubts about the fact that everything is fiction. As Eleanor Cook[31] points out, the choice of the verb "seize" gives a Miltonic resonance to what was a biblical scene. The biblical allusion is thus doubled by a literary one heightening the fictional; however, there is something about the gesture, perhaps the fact that it reduces sensation to touch, which is more direct than seeing or hearing, that makes the final embrace seem "real," and together with the hero, we might feel that now we finally "know":

> Her hand took his and drew him near to her.
> Her hair fell on him and the mi-bird flew
>
> To the ruddier bushes at the garden's end.
> Of her, of her alone, at last he knew
> And lay beside her underneath the tree.
>
> [CP 271]

The final lines, although quite similar, do not exactly repeat the refrain of the poem, but the sensation of familiarity persists: we know this, because we have heard it before, because it has always been there, because it is such a familiar myth. And we may realize perhaps only now that this is indeed the "first canto of the final canticle," where we have been from the very beginning. It is actually only the fourth chapter of Genesis, but for any lay reader of the Bible, the story of the Fall more or less ends there. And when, in its final stage, the poem borrows the actual language of a myth, it seems to have achieved that similarity, the resemblance that we, as supporters of realism, want to maintain between fiction and reality. It may even have achieved much more, for the story of the story and the actual story flow together here, and the mere resemblance is carried to the point of continuity with what we identify as "real." And although it has perpetually been trapped in fiction, the poem seems now to have found real roots in a reality that defies the very notion of fiction. For this reality is not the end of a discovery process, which should only be described by language, but the result of a creative act; and this creative act cannot be manifested, cannot be fulfilled without the language that speaks it, as in: "God *said,* Let there be light, and there *was* light."

It is not an accident that in "The Hand as a Being" the initial tension between "reality" and "fiction," between the speaker's evident desire to stay close to sensory images and the slippery language that makes him regress into fiction, is resolved by an all but expected encounter with an actual myth. The blurring of the distinctions between reality and fiction is characteristic of myth, for as Hayden White points out, "What we wish to call mythic narrative is under no obligation to keep the two orders of events, real and imaginary, distinct from one another."[32] Under this aspect, having nothing to do with romantic or even modernist notions of myth, most of Stevens's poems starting with tensions between the desire to be realistic and the fictional nature of language achieve, if not a literal transformation into myth, a concept of reality close to the one underlying mythology. For myths deal with "creation" on a larger, cosmic scale, and not only does their "reality" depend on that creation—which is divine—but it also relies on the imaginative space of the language that sustains it. Myths found knowledge in limits and provide limitations for reality, and at a more clearly verbal level, so does Stevens's verse.

In fact, the similarity of Stevens's poems to myth has to do with the challenge he presents to an epistemology based on a particular notion of the real. When Gerald Bruns proposes to read Stevens "without epistemology," he has precisely this kind of challenge in mind, which addresses the way the problem is posed rather than proposing a solution. According to Bruns, "the main problem for Stevens is not how the mind links up with reality but what to do about other people."[33] The notion of the real as founded by the limitations created in language therefore brings Stevens as close to the pragmatic notion of truth resulting from negotiation promoted by William James as to the verbally negotiated "real" of myth.

The idea that, for the human spirit, reality depends on the forms in which it is presented, on the shapes that it takes in the imagination as it were, belongs to a dissenting orientation in philosophy, but it does not, by any means, postdate Stevens. James and Santayana debate it in different ways, and they may constitute direct sources for the poet. What is more interesting than the idea itself is, however, the fact that Stevens does not launch it as a thesis but rather makes it work. He engages readers in a discovery of their own assumptions about and attitudes toward language and reality. Stevens's poems offer indeed images of the real, but these "images" seem to constitute themselves in language beyond the distinction real/fictional in the realm of a musical or quasi-mythical experience. Before being able to perceive such images, we have to relinquish a certain crude identification of the way the eye can see and the way the mind can take in the world. Paradoxically, the evidence of clarity, of convincing images, is to be found rather through a listening activity in the perception of sound patterns. And if the foundations of reality appear to be in language and in its forms, the engagement of the reader situates poetry in a much larger cultural sphere. In Stevens's own words, this sphere, which he calls nobility, "seems, in the last analysis, to have something to do with our self-preservation; and that, no doubt, is why the expression of it, the sound of its words, helps us to live our lives."[34]

5

The Image of Sound

IN THE PREVIOUS chapter I examined a couple of poems that reveal the paradoxes of linguistic representation by emphasizing the discrepancies between sensory images and the images created in or by means of language. The "real" of the common sense, which is supposed to be perceivable and expressible, vanishes into a created realm circumscribed by its self-imposed limits. The way out of the crisis is nothing other than a realization that the real is actually constructed—"imagined," Stevens would say—and such a reality is validated by the form of its expression. The sound pattern, as I have demonstrated, generates another kind of "image" that transcends the opposition between real and fictional.

The failure of the poems' speakers to achieve an identity between the sensory reality and verbal expression hints, beyond a linguistic dilemma, at an epistemological crisis. The parallels between Stevens and Heidegger (mentioned in the previous chapter) suggest that the poet may be directly and openly opposed to epistemology. Heidegger himself formulated his philosophy by arguing that both idealist (Kant) and materialist (Descartes) traditions are mistaken to found their theories of knowledge on the subject/object dichotomy. The implied autonomy of the subject is, in Heidegger's opinion, an illusion, since subject and object are both conditioned by history. Epistemology is thus, for Heidegger, the wrong way to approach the question of knowledge, and it must be replaced by an inquiry into the nature of being, that is, by ontology.

It would be hard to attribute to Stevens such insight; however, as shown in the previous chapter, his poems invite comparisons with Heidegger's (and Husserl's) philosophy as they seem to seek pure perceptions and fail at the task. In such poems we encounter the same kind of distrust in our cognitive powers that is to be found in phenomenology. Thomas Hines gives perhaps the best description of a typical Stevens poem of this category: "The subject of the poetry becomes the process of perception through which the objects of the exterior world are grasped. Stevens develops what several poets have called a 'poetry of process,' in which the processes of the mind provide both the subject matter and the structure of the poetry."[1]

In Hines's view, by focusing on the mind itself in the process of perception, the poet endorses Heidegger's shift from epistemology to ontology. Paul Bové[2] finds further proof of Stevens's inclination to think like a phenomenologist (and like a deconstructionist-to-be) in the fact that the acts of perception performed by the poems end in the discovery of "nothing" at the center. From Bové's perspective, they ultimately reveal that all reality is fiction and that all fictions can do is build upon other fictions. This revelation again puts epistemology in crisis by depriving the cognitive activity of an object.

There can be no doubt that Stevens's verse indicates his aversion to epistemology (understood in the useful formulation of Gerald Bruns as "the way the mind links up with reality").[3] Yet this aversion must be seen in the more complex context in which Stevens's ideas about matters of knowledge developed. This context might reveal that Stevens's grounds for rejecting epistemology were aesthetic rather than philosophical. Margaret Peterson suggests that Stevens's distaste for science originates in his desire to prove the importance of art: "The opposition [between science and art] is fundamental to Stevens' thinking. In a 'culture based on science' the imagination is given exclusive salutary power. Its functions are associated with 'escape,' 'illusion,' 'deliberate fictions'—in short, with a conscious retreat to an imaginary world invincible to science."[4]

Peterson also shows how difficult it is to determine who had the most powerful influence on Stevens's thought in matters of knowledge: "Since the problem of knowledge is an ubiquitous concern among modern philosophers, it is scarcely possible to single out those writers who may have been significant influences. It is possible, however, to establish the general context of Stevens's interest through those philosophers with whom he was acquainted, those to whom he refers on several occasions and whose ideas on aesthetic theory, and the problems of knowledge generally, are related to his own. For this purpose, the most useful figures are I. A. Richards, Benedetto Croce, Henri Bergson, William James, and George Santayana."[5] In fact, it is this difficulty of establishing his affiliations that makes Stevens's own position on the matter hard to define.

Peterson traces Stevens's progress from German idealism to American pragmatism by examining the poet's vocabulary and formulations that closely echo his sources. Her findings indicate that James's "radical empiricism" can account for Stevens's "perception" poems even better than phenomenology, and her description of James's and Santayana's epistemologies shows that, to understand what Stevens was doing, one does not need deconstruction: "We must 'trust our senses,' but as James readily admitted, the sensible world would not suffice, and for Santayana the only remaining epistemological step was the step into nonexistence or a fictional world."[6] Stevens's search for an answer to questions about knowledge represents, in Peterson's view, the "philosophical heritage of modern aesthetic." Poets like Stevens inherited an idealistic frame of mind from Coleridge, but they were also powerfully attracted to pragmatist ideas. Following his aesthetic purposes, Stevens did not clearly differentiate between aesthetic idealism and pragmatism and used them both to reject realism, for instance. This lack of discrimination might explain why, in his work, questions about the nature of poetry cannot easily be separated from epistemological questions.

The importance of the historical context in which Stevens conceived his ideas about art and knowledge is well emphasized by Ronald E. Martin in his book *American Literature and the Destruction of Knowledge*. Martin sees Stevens as only one of a number of modern poets and writers who, by subverting the prevailing notions of knowledge, implicitly militated against the oppressive order of their society. According to him, the attack on epistemology took the form of a destruction of normative linguistic structures. By showing the role of stylistic innovations in the destruction of socially and culturally acceptable knowledge, Martin emphasizes again the opposition between epistemology and aesthetics. The aesthetic, in the case of modernism, denied the established ideas about knowledge. And as Martin does not fail to notice, the significance of this nihilistic gesture extends beyond the aesthetic into the realm of politics:

> The destructionist writers impugned, by implication at least, social and political as well as literary and philosophical regimes. They pioneered an absolute skepticism about the language of ideology and of social control, and that attitude has been invaluable to subsequent social movements arguing against race- and gender-based oppression. They undermined customs of genre, text, and linguistic representation in ways that foreshadowed subsequent Deconstructionist thought. If such knowledge destruction be nihilism—the denial of an objective basis for truth—this episode in our cultural history provides a case study in the constructive uses of nihilism.[7]

In agreement with Peterson, Martin acknowledges the influence of philosophers like Bergson, James, and Santayana on the modernists and especially on Stevens. He also agrees with Bové on the similarities between Stevens's representation of knowledge and deconstruction. Yet he must also observe that the poet did not actually achieve a deconstructive stage and that his thought was characteristic of his time:

> However accurate [Bové's criticism] is as a characterization of all Stevens, we can certainly see in his work at various times the world represented as unstably changing, part human projection; the human mind represented as category-ridden, self-confined, and partial; cognition as tenuous, relative; and representation itself as hypothetical and arbitrary. The anxieties of the age of epistemology possessed his imagination, and he envisioned poetry at its profoundest as defining and bridging the gap between humankind and the bare possibility of our knowing the reality around us.[8]

My argument about how Stevens's use of sound reflects his distaste for epistemology accords with criticisms proposing that Stevens's preoccupation with knowledge must be seen as an aesthetic concern, a concern that, I would add, is also linguistic.

For most of the changes Stevens brings to the notion of knowledge (as I think Ronald Martin would agree) reside in the ways he manipulates language. It is Stevens's change in the use of language that leads to alterations in the way we think about knowledge.

Here I will explore the epistemological implications of Stevens's sound techniques, which are especially apparent in a group of poems having sound itself as their theme. This extraordinarily complex theme—complex because it is played against the poems' performance—in Wallace Stevens's poetry has normally been approached through the idea of one or another dominant opposition: between, for instance, sound as brute noise and as music,[9] between "natural" and "artificial" sound,[10] between the sound of speech and the silence of writing,[11] or between objective and subjective reality as these are fused or dissolved by sound in Stevens's verse.[12] Nor is it difficult to see why the notion of such reigning oppositions has dominated discussion of sound in Stevens: they are all essential to a logic of poetic representation that Stevens wants to call into question in a certain radical way, such that epistemological breakdown or dissolution becomes, within the context of a modernism haunted by questions of "reality," the great subject of his poetry.

Yet the ultimate truth about Stevens's verse, I suggest, lies in the way it operates to dissolve or discredit all such traditional oppositions between sound and sense, meaning and meaninglessness, and thus to lay bare the alternative domain of reality that otherwise remains perpetually veiled by all logics of representation or systems of signification as such. It is with this alternative domain that the "sound image," as I shall be calling it, is associated in Stevens's poetry, a domain that comes into view only when we have seen the level at which sound operates at once to dissolve a certain epistemological order traditionally associated with poetic representation while summoning into existence another—the unrepresented, the (otherwise) unrepresentable—in its place.

A poem that permits us to glimpse this process at work in an exemplary light is "Autumn Refrain," in which sound works to dissolve a certain representation of reality associated with the romantic sonnet, a particular idea of nature as simultaneously constituted by external world and subjective mood, by subverting conventions honored by both the sonnet as a traditional form and by romanticism as a distinct movement in English poetry.[13] For Stevens's poem, as it appeared in the *Collected Poems*, containing fourteen lines and written in slightly varied iambic pentameter, so closely observes the formal conventions of a romantic sonnet concerning nightingales and evening sadness that it might, at first glance, appear to be almost an outright parody:

> The skreak and skritter of evening gone
> And grackles gone and sorrows of the sun,
> The sorrows of sun, too, gone . . . the moon and
>   moon,

The yellow moon of words about the nightingale
In measureless measures, not a bird for me
But the name of a bird and the name of a nameless air
I have never—shall never hear. And yet beneath
The stillness of everything gone, and being still,
Being and sitting still, something resides,
Some skreaking and skrittering residuum,
And grates these evasions of the nightingale
Though I have never—shall never hear that bird.
And the stillness is in the key, all of it is,
The stillness is all in the key of that desolate sound.
    [CP 160]

But as Eleanor Cook observes, "Stevens begins his refrain well past obvious sorrows, and satires too. His first line is one of the noisiest lines he ever wrote, and all the noisier because we are expected to cut the sound effects abruptly with the last word."[14] There is indeed more than parody here, for the conventions are not only reversed in the theme or strategically disobeyed in the meter; they are also "discussed" in a manner that betrays an analytic purpose. Although this would-be sonnet is most of the time dominated by its plaintive tone, while intelligibility is rendered vague by repetitions, there is an attempt to distinguish pairs of opposites, a clearly analytical step. The opposition between real and imagined, natural and artificial, is sketched in the contrast between the "skreak and skritter of evening" and the song of the nightingale. The latter seems to be privileged by virtue of the fact that it belongs to literary tradition, whereas the former is trivialized as a source of quotidian annoyance. It is at the end of the day, when these irritating sounds begin to disappear together with the agitation and distraction that stands in the way of mental concentration. Paradoxically, the speaker's attention is directed toward the perception of a sound he has never encountered except in poetry. And the paradox is double, since the sound he wants to "hear" is only the fiction or "image" of a sound, which could only mentally be "seen."

The speaker's mental concentration is only a stage of a meditation made possible by silence. In its own turn, it is disturbed and distracted not by literal "noise" but by the interposition of memory and fictionality. Because the song of the nightingale is a fiction descending from romantic poetry and is present only as a memory, its fictionality stands in the way of its perception—"I have never—shall never hear that bird"— in the same fashion as the residuum of the "real" sounds does. Reduced to a residuum, surviving only as a memory of their immediacy, the real sounds become virtual fictions themselves, even as the song of the nightingale begins almost to take on reality in the silence that the speaker so intently listens to. The real sound, passing into silence, has been semifictionalized, while the fictional one, which has become an object of inward perception in spite of its fictionality, acquires the same uncertain status.

We do not know whether "that desolate sound" at the end of the poem is the song of the nightingale or the "skreak and skritter" of the grackles. In fact, Cook argues that the "grackles" themselves belong to an ironic, parodic tradition and therefore are as fictional as the nightingales.[15] The opposition between fictional and real, artificial and natural, is thus dissolved, frustrating rather than satisfying the expectation of an analytical distinction that its occurrence, in the first place, created. We are left, in short, not only with a failure of the language to deal with reality but with a failure of the whole process of apprehending reality, of distinguishing between real and fictional.

As we should expect in this context, sound and silence represent another pair of opposites. But instead of maintaining this opposition, the poem moves toward an awareness that silence is only the other face of sound. In the speaker's present meditative mood, stillness comes to mediate between reality and fiction, to facilitate perception, be it of the intellectual or of the sensory kind, so that in the end stillness itself is the only perceivable "reality." The intense concentration on the act of perception makes its object disappear and offers itself as the only possible end of cognitive activity. Sound, on the other hand, is perceived as noise, as a disturbance of the concentration necessary to a mental act, being in many ways the physical counterpart of the mental turmoil that is preventing the speaker from making distinctions among his present perceptions. Yet even when we consider it in this way, the opposition is dissolved, because the stillness cannot be achieved but "in the key of that desolate sound."

The poem as a whole, meanwhile, has its own "sound," which forms the recognizable pattern of a sonnet. This pattern undercuts the speaker's apparent inability to compose a sonnet with the limited inspiration provided by the homely grackle. For the speaker's efforts are definitely directed toward the composition of a romantic sonnet. Although "Autumn Refrain" was initially published as a fifteen-line poem, and the Holly Stevens edition presents it in that form, it can be inferred that the fourteen-line version was Stevens's final choice. The line "The stillness that comes to me out of this, beneath" may have been left out for its sheer clumsiness, but its omission may also indicate that Stevens wanted the poem to be a sonnet. Determining Stevens's intention is beside the point in the present argument, however, which is concerned with the poem's effect, with the intentions that can be inferred from its final form. The poem's rhythm, even as it hints at parodic intent, creates and maintains the expectation of a sonnet thus working to sustain the very form its discursive aspect undermines.

At an even more fundamental level is the sound pattern produced by repetition, of which there are several important types in the poem. Some of the words are repeated in quick succession or at short intervals, as in "the moon and moon, / The yellow moon" or "not a bird for me / But the name of a bird." In the second half of the poem the word "still" and the related "stillness" zigzag among the other words as if they wanted to dominate this part of the discourse or maybe to suggest that they have a dominant place in the speaker's mind.

There are also words that are repeated partially in derivatives like "name of a nameless air," "measureless measures," "still" and "stillness," "resides" and "residuum." They give the impression of attracting one another's presence, as echoes do. And this is not a pure phonic coincidence, because it has meaningful implications. The sameness of the sound creates identity between words that otherwise find themselves in very diverse logical relations. "Name of a nameless air" and "measureless measures," for instance, contain contradictory terms, and their sound similarity not only obscures the contradiction but mystifies the reference as well. In "still" and "stillness" the shift of grammatical category accentuates the difference inherent in any repetition, whereas "reside" and "residuum" send us to distant etymologies that validate the sound coincidence.

Such repetitions in everyday conversation would give one the feeling that the speaker was hesitating, that he could not find words for what he had to say, or conversely, that he had nothing to say and was thus mechanically deriving every word from a previous one without following the sense. The fact that we have to do with a sonnet does not prevent us from forming expectations that we would have from a conversational situation, since the classical sonnet, as well as its romantic form, contains a "theme" and an "argument," a lyrical communication indeed but a communication nonetheless. It does not often allow for repetition, and even when it does, the repetition is felt as an emphasis, whereas Stevens's repetitions have nothing to do with emphatic intent. Here repetition robs the message of its pointedness and discredits the speaker's authority; at the same time, it mystifies the content of communication.

But another type of repetition in the poem produces a different effect. Groups of words are repeated incrementally:

> But *the name of* a bird and *the name of a name*less air
> *I have never—shall never hear.* And yet beneath
> The stillness of everything gone, and *being still,*
> *Being and sitting still,* something resides,
> Some skreaking and skrittering residuum,
> And grates these evasions of the nightingale
> Though *I have never—shall never hear that bird.*
> *And the stillness is in the key, all of it is,*
> *The stillness is all in the key of that desolate sound.*
>
> [*CP* 160, emphasis added]

While the echolike repetitions may be attributed to the speaker's hesitancy, the incremental ones make us recognize a pattern and a certain incantatory quality encountered elsewhere in Stevens's poetry. The sound pattern acquires power here, not only because it becomes more obvious, but also because it occurs at a point in the poem when the speaker seems utterly to have lost control over language. The multiplication of negatives and the repetitiveness of his utterance seem to suggest a failure for which the poem has been preparing us from the start.

For everything now begins to suggest that this is the voice of a modern poet all too acutely aware of a reality that contradicts his romantic aspirations. Therefore from the very first line we may suspect that this poem will not achieve a logical or rhetorical closure, that its message will not be rounded up. And the end will indeed confirm this expectation if we take it for its "message" value, but now the very poetic form, which through repetition of sound has given the poem status as a self-contained aural unit, compels us to forget the expected failure. For the last line, which literally includes most of the repeated words, is heard as a conclusion in an alternative mode, with the circling effect of the repeated phrases making the form cohere on its own, as in an oral poem, where "patterns of repetition can provide structure and coherence . . . —a necessary aspect in a medium as ephemeral as the spoken or sung word."[16]

Through its repetitions, the poem thus acquires an aural/oral intelligibility clearly distinct from the intelligibility of an utterance that attempts to represent a world external to itself. According to Gilles Deleuze,[17] within the conceptual frame of representation, repetition can be defined only in a negative way: "One (language) speaks because one (the word) is not real. . . . One repeats because one cannot hear. As Kierkegaard put it, this is a kind of deaf repetition, or rather a repetition for the deaf, deaf words, deaf nature, deaf unconscious. The forces that ensure the repetition, that is, the multiplicity of things corresponding to one concept that remains always the same, can, in a representation, be determined only negatively."[18]

Such repetition is mechanical and excludes the difference, as it presupposes an identity of the repeated elements with the concept. Deleuze calls this kind of repetition "naked" and distinguishes it from the kind of "clothed" repetition that includes the difference. Such is the repetition one can find in nature and one can define positively as evolution. For in nature, every element that repeats does so under a guise that includes its previous one but also differentiates itself from it. Under this aspect, "repetition constitutes the power of language, and far from being explained in a negative manner by a default of nominal concepts, it implies an Idea of poetry that is always excessive. . . . It is thus as function of its most positive and ideal powers that language organizes its whole system as a clothed repetition."[19]

What has emerged in the above reading of the poem can be seen as a transformation of the linguistic representation into the kind of excessive poetry that Deleuze describes. The mechanical, naked repetitions have become clothed, obliging our attention to shift from representation to "excessive poetry" and to search for meaning there. And in this context it would not be inappropriate, I think, to call meaning a "sound image" by way of differentiating it from the "deaf" image/meaning of representation.

Due to the sound's complexity, we as readers may achieve the condition toward which the speaker himself aspires: the stillness in which one can hear. For as long as we are interested in the unavoidably fictional representation, we shall experience the sense of failure in the same way the speaker does. But as soon as the effort to follow the images becomes too hard to sustain, we are prepared to yield to the sound, to perceive its incantatory power. As R. P. Blackmur points out, the sound of Stevens's poems never assumes a total privilege that would eliminate intelligibility: "Somewhere between the realms of ornamental sound and representative statement, the words pause and balance, dissolve and resolve. . . . The ambiguity of this sort of writing consists in the double importance of both sound and sense where neither has direct connection with the other but where neither can stand alone."[20]

Thus Stevens cannot be accused of excessive concern with the form at the expense of meaning. After debating Stevens's preoccupation with Croce's idea of "pure poetry," George S. Lensing observes: "Stevens' defense of his work in terms of its variously contrived effects ('sensations,' 'images and sounds,' 'gaudiness,' 'Feeling of the words') underscores the importance of a special craft to him, the sound of a poem, how it was arranged on the page, and how it engaged the reader in all its attributes. Such concerns do not invalidate his many remarks on the meanings of the poems; in absolute terms Stevens was never a maker of 'pure poetry.'"[21]

The "contrived effect" of sound does not only allow meaning to develop but actually produces it. For it is sound that brings us to the stage where the distinctions between fiction and reality, sound and silence, and perception and conception are transcended, and by virtue of the word's power, there is one single "reality."—that quasi-mythical realm in which things exist because they are spoken of. And we may even be able to "hear that bird," the nightingale that poems speak of, unhindered by the noise of any grackles, because neither grackles nor nightingales can *be* before a poem speaks of them. The sound (effect) silences the "noise" of the fiction the poem otherwise constructs and allows us to perceive a reality beyond the physical world. What we finally come to know are neither the birds nor their song, nor even the feeling that made the poet think of them, but our own feeling stirred by the poem's sound.

Repetition is always at work in poems that have sound itself as their subject. My next example is "Domination of Black," about which Stevens wrote: "I am sorry that a poem of this sort has to contain any ideas at all, because its sole purpose is to fill the mind with the images and sounds that it contains. A mind that examines such a poem for its prose contents gets absolutely nothing from it."[22] But the habit of reading for the "prose contents" is hard to ignore, and perhaps the poem's effect would not be possible without it. Although the sound pattern may strike the reader from the start, attention is first drawn to the status of sound as a metaphor of an enigma presented in visual terms. The poem opens with a setting reminiscent of the situations in which stories are told: "At night, by the fire . . . " This sounds like a promise to tell a story, and for the whole of the first stanza, we could get the illusion that the narration is on the way. We could even tell the genre of this story: a bit from the dark side, one of those stories about giants or dragons that eat human flesh and produce a kind of turmoil when they come upon the scene:

> At night, by the fire,
> The colors of the bushes
> And of the fallen leaves,
> Repeating themselves,
> Turned in the room,
> Like the leaves themselves
> Turning in the wind.
> Yes: but the color of the heavy hemlocks
> Came striding.
> And I remembered the cry of the peacocks.
>   [CP 8]

It would seem that this is the description of an optical feast, a real, moving rainbow: the colors of the leaves and those of the fire, which will be matched in the second stanza by the colors of the peacock's tail. But curiously enough, although Stevens wants us "to get heavens full of colors," with the exception of the "black" in the title, no other color is named. The speaker defines them by mentioning the objects to which they belong, and thus the visual appeal of the colors is doubly mediated. If we are to imagine the colors, we have to use our mind's eye not merely to replace the name by the picture but to compose the picture and fill in the colors as well. This is a visual space of the mind: if we "see" a lot of colors, it is because we are used to identify the objects mentioned in the poem by association with a multitude of colors. So that in trying to compose the picture, we are already engaged in "an act of the mind." The description of the room, this scene itself, solicits an intellectual activity similar to seeing.

The feeling that we are engaged in an act of cognition is also created by the presence of the analogies that grow in complexity as the poem advances. At first, there is the analogy between the colors of the fire—the element present to the speaker's senses—and the colors of the leaves in the fall. It is not clear whether the leaves are just hidden from the view, outside, or whether they reside only in the speaker's memory. In any case they are not present to him. It appears that the speaker would engage us in a simple intellectual operation—to look at something and remember a similar image—but he does not stop at observing this simple resemblance that can have only

a limited significance. The memory of the cry of the peacocks brings to mind the peacock's tail, which makes the speaker observe another resemblance:

> The colors of their tails
> Were like the leaves themselves
> Turning in the wind,
> In the twilight wind.
> They swept over the room,
> Just as they flew from the boughs of the
>   hemlocks
> Down to the ground.
>   [CP 8–9]

This resemblance is more remote, as it is not based on the strict coincidence of
colors but is only suggested by their variety and movement. The fact that this resemblance is not so obvious makes us look again for some significance to it. In any communication, there is a presupposition of relevance:[23] there must be a reason why these
things are seen under the same aspect, a sense to this resemblance, or the speaker
would not bring it up. This certainty of meaning makes us expect a revelation, but the
poem, instead of progressing toward an answer, seems to get caught in a pattern of
repetitions:

> I heard them cry—the peacocks.
> Was it a cry against the twilight
> Or against the leaves themselves
> Turning in the wind,
> Turning as the flames
> Turned in the fire,
> Turning as the tails of the peacocks
> Turned in the loud fire,
> Loud as the hemlocks
> Full of the cry of the peacocks?
> Or was it a cry against the hemlocks?
>   [CP 9]

The only sense of these repetitions seems to be that everything is reminiscent of
everything else. The colors and shapes in "Domination of Black" represent and are
represented, become in turn vehicles and tenors not of a metaphor but of a chain of
metaphors. Instead of one single correspondence, which would give us the key to the
cipher, we get a chain of correspondences. Each of them has the potential to represent
the others, but none of them gets this privilege, and consequently they "mean" nothing. Besides, as Jacqueline Brogan[24] observed, the "as's" that mark the analogies may
also suggest simultaneity. This may be the perfect example of what Deleuze calls

clothed repetition, as there is no "concept" here that the words could reproduce and with which they could remain identical. Representation is subverted by its own multiplication, and repetition is the clothing of a phenomenon/word in the guise of a new one. The metaphoric chain itself comes close to being metamorphic, because while representing each other, the colors of the fire, of the leaves, and of the peacock's tail transform into each other and participate in the same movement.

The auditive analogy, already present in the first stanza, does not give a sense to this chaining but raises more questions. The story that we have been led to expect loses its contours, while the description of the setting expands into aural imagery. As the colors before, the visual and the aural are transforming into each other in synesthetical combinations: the hemlocks are loud and full of the cry of the peacocks. Thus the sound does not get the chance to become the opposite of the visual effect, since from the point of view of communication they remain equally opaque and resistant to intelligence. The last stanza pushes the analogies even further by adding some cosmic elements to the series:

Out of the window,
I saw how the planets gathered
Like the leaves themselves
Turning in the wind.
I saw how the night came,
Came striding like the color of the heavy
    hemlocks
I felt afraid.
And I remembered the cry of the peacocks.
    [CP 9]

The resemblance between the colors in movement and the planets is even more remote than the one between the leaves and the peacock's tail: movement is probably the only common feature of the two images. This remoteness makes the comparison sound like a riddle and creates the expectations for one: that it has an answer, and we are supposed to find it. For this reason, although there is no question being asked here, we feel that we are called upon to answer one. Some critics find it convenient to equate the answer to this question with death: "Death is the 'Domination of Black' (*CP* 8), felt in the cry of the peacocks which haunts the mind of the lonely, isolated poet. . . . There are few modern poems which better evoke the experience of cosmic fright. The turning world, caught in the motion of leaves (and through an ominous anaphora), enshrouds the poet in fear, and the refrain of the crying peacocks echoes through 'the color of heavy hemlocks' to catch a melancholic struggle of the self with its fate."[25]

The suggestion of death is very strong indeed, but death seems to take a place in the chain of metaphors already existing in the poem. For as in the case of the other metaphors, we cannot tell whether "death" is tenor or vehicle, whether the poem was written to represent death as enigma, or whether death is just one more enigma that remains undeciphered like "the color of the heavy hemlocks" or "the cry of the peacocks." The poem ends more or less where it began, with the memory of the mysterious cry that, rather than being interpreted with the help of the images, renders them mysterious too.

Harold Bloom has also noticed the contradictions in the poem's meaning: "To get started, [Stevens's] lyric has to say the exact opposite of what it meant."[26] Although this remark may imply that the poem's meaning can finally be clarified, Bloom's additional remarks point further to its vagueness: "To explain how and why that observation is accurate is to arrive at a theory of poetic interpretation. This theory depends upon the verifiable pronouncement that the language of British and American poetry, from at least Wordsworth to the present, is overdetermined in its patternings and so necessarily is underdetermined in its meanings."[27] As in the poems analyzed before, the vagueness of the meaning in "Domination of Black," as well as the possibility of multiple interpretations, attracts attention to the poem's sound patterns.

Repetition or near repetition forms the basis of a powerful sound effect that changes the register in which meaning must be considered. Due to the irregular pattern of these repetitions, our action of following the communication of the poem is considerably slower and less significant than usual. The descriptive progress of the first stanza is interrupted by the entrance of what seems to be the main character of the drama that promises to develop on the scene: "the color of the heavy hemlocks." The second stanza, although moving to the description of a new element—the tails of the peacocks—merely picks up where the description was interrupted by repeating almost identically: "[Were] like the leaves themselves / Turning in the wind." And as if imagination had been exhausted, the next verse repeats incrementally: "In the twilight wind."

Because the description is done in the same words, the advance toward a new term in the chain of analogies is canceled or reduced to the bare minimum. By virtue of this sameness in description, the "tails of the peacocks" become not analogous but identical with the leaves and the fire. This identity blocks any progress on the cognitive plane—some progress that the poem has made us expect—since the analogy that could have said something, could have had a "sense," is now canceled. For there is nothing to distinguish these peacock tails from the leaves and the fire, nothing that their resemblance with the first two images could reveal. This contradicts one's expectations, for the purpose of comparing one object to another is to discover its otherwise hidden qualities. In a quite unnerving way for the analyst, the question that starts with "Was it a cry against the twilight" is completed only at the end of the stanza, and it actually forms a tautology. Its direct reference to the cry of the peacocks is wearing off, as the speaker tries to define it better:

I heard them cry—the peacocks.
Was it a cry against the twilight
Or against the leaves themselves
Turning in the wind,
Turning as the flames
Turned in the fire,
Turning as the tails of the peacocks
Turned in the loud fire,
Loud as the hemlocks
Full of the cry of the peacocks?
Or was it a cry against the hemlocks?
  [CP 9]

The cry does not make sense without the repetitions and the correspondences that accompanied it in the first place, and the contradiction that the end of the question contains—the cry in the end is against the hemlocks, with which it had almost been identified—does not really matter, as long as we, as readers, can hold onto the same context that validates the existence of the cry for us. After having been caught in the pattern of these repetitions, our alertness to the logic of the question is slackened, and we do not even notice the contradiction. We begin to take the repeated "turning" of flames, leaves, or tails for granted and to accept it without question.

The leaves turn, and this "turning" begins to look unquestionably "real," perhaps because the repetition of this word is in itself a turning, a coming back made significant by the very gesture of repetition. For repetition makes us presuppose an original, in whose "reality" we are ready to believe even if we ignore it. Surrounded, closed in by the "turning" of the leaves and by its own repetition, the cry becomes a "nothing" out of which a benevolent God might create the world, a beginning of a word, or the word that was in the beginning. And like all beginnings, it is frightening, not because the cry of some peacocks is the best metaphor for fear, or can best "represent" it, but because, placed among the repetitions of "turning," it produces a void, an enigma that threatens to absorb us. Against the void, the nothing of the beginning, we can only repeat; repeat the gesture of a divine agency, which we suppose to have been there and created everything out of nothing. A cry is a word without meaning, a nonword uttered before or beyond language. And only by being repeated can this cry become something, a "real" cry, "a cry against the hemlocks."

The process of cognition enacted by the poem I examined above seems to end in an enigma that blocks its progress and seems to be caught in a circle, as its final images are similar, if not identical, to those of its beginning. The poem dramatizes a language failure: faced with the nothing of beginnings one cannot represent. But this failure is even more dramatic than the unsuccessful attempt to make language correspond to reality. For what seems to fail here is the very effort to understand, to "know" reality or nature. The confrontation of the image of sound with the actual sound pattern of the poem thus generates questions about cognitive processes, about the very nature and status of knowledge.

That knowledge should be identified with poetry is a sort of a paradox in modern times. In a section of *A Grammar of Motives* dedicated to the imagination, Kenneth Burke notes that modern thought is deeply permeated by "scientism." Although modernist theories of poetry try to define it by opposition with science, they have their root in a "scientific" view of life. Burke's example happens to be Stevens's essay "The Figure of the Youth as Virile Poet," where the latter defines imagination in terms that can easily be identified as "scientific": "The important thing for our present purposes," comments Burke, "is to note that the key term 'imagination' here figures in a theory of poetry that is basically scientist. For poetry is here approached in terms of its search for 'truth' as a 'view' of reality, as a kind of 'knowledge.' "[28]

Burke's observations may be accurate as far as the respective essay goes, since one can indeed see in Stevens's theoretical writings a tendency to place poetry in competition with science and philosophy. Some of his poems also refer to poetry as "a kind of knowledge." In "Man and Bottle," for instance, poetry appears as the satisfaction of reason and as the only product of the human mind strangely involved in violent action. But Stevens's poems do not lack that quality of "act" that Burke finds essential for genuine poetry, and their action, as described above, seems to reveal what T. J. Reiss[29] has called "the uncertainty of analysis," the doubts about the possibility and validity of representation. They bring to an almost ritual failure representations of reality based on the scientism of Stevens's century, albeit covered by romantic overtones, and hint at the possibility of another horizon of knowledge.

Gerald Bruns talks about the possibility of reading Stevens "without epistemology," if we define epistemology loosely as "a concern for how the mind links up with reality."[30] Indeed, according to such definition, epistemology becomes cumbersome for reading Stevens. But what I want to suggest here is that an even looser definition—epistemology as a way of conceiving of knowledge—would permit the acceptance of the idea that there are alternatives to epistemology. The domain of myth, for instance, is a good example of an alternative. If there is a way of conceiving of knowledge for Stevens, it belongs to a cultural space that could be deemed poetic rather than "scientific." It is a domain claiming the independence of its own discourse from the dominant one even as it proposes a different way of knowing. For this reason in my argument, I actually started from the changes in the discursive mode that, from the reader's point of view, come first and produce the change in the way we conceive of knowledge. For what we perceive as failing in Stevens's poems is not only the visual (sensory) image in the restricted sense whose sharpness declines as representation advances but also the whole conception that assimilates cognitive activity to seeing. There is a whole "visual" code that collapses because it is pushed beyond itself, and it is ever so subtly replaced by an excessive poetry, a kind of "aural" language made fuller and more significant by the clothing of its repetitions. Beyond the deafness of representation, the sound of language sustains its poetic sense and validates its reality in audibility.

Stevens does not deny the existence of reality or the utility of empirical knowledge but proposes alternatives and prompts us to a pragmatic kind of questioning: what notion of reality is more useful, and what kind of knowledge is more likely to benefit us? When we read poetry we shift our attention from a reality independent of human thought to a cultural reality, a reality constructed in the very process of communication. The alternative notion of knowledge promoted by Stevens therefore implies creativity, a creativity manifested in a language that undoubtedly claims itself as poetic. Performing toward the attainment of this special kind of knowledge, poetry can be said to acquire the value of a ritual in words. Knowledge is engendered in repetition, and the purpose of the cognitive activity is directed no longer toward the "standing reality" but rather toward a reality itself constructed within the limits of a culture.

6

Meaning and Repetition

THE STUDY OF Stevens's discursive shifts, operated mostly through a patterning of sound, has brought us to an insight into what his philosophy might have been if he had ever articulated it as such. As Thomas Grey points out, Stevens shied away from constructing a philosophical system, but he was nonetheless haunted by philosophical questions: "He *was* a philosopher in one sense, and knew it, just as in another sense he knew that he was not."[1] His inclination to philosophize has to be seen as part of his general endeavor to define his position as a modern poet. For this reason his stylistic innovations and especially his use of sound are intimately connected with his views on questions normally deemed philosophical.

The fact that Stevens offers an alternative to epistemology through his crafty handling of repetitions and of sound patterns places him among those modern writers who attacked the established view of language and the world. The logic according to which his thinking appears to be similar to phenomenology (especially Heidegger) would lead us to see his attention to language and his distaste for positivism as steps leading to the replacement of epistemology with an ontology. Heidegger's objection to epistemology was based on his observation that the thinking subject's existence is as time bound as the object's. The subject cannot, therefore, contemplate the object from a transcendental standpoint, as Husserl had suggested. Yet Heidegger does not succumb to agnosticism either but proposes that the philosopher should contemplate the nature of being, a property common to both subject and object. By rendering the opposition between subject and object insignificant, Heidegger marked the dissolution of a whole tradition in Western philosophical thinking.

Stevens's version of this dissolution has been taken to be his gesture of effacing the distinction between reality and fiction (imagination). Since the notion of reality is very frequently debated by Stevens, most critics who raise the question of ontology in his work return to an analysis of the process of decreation by which the poet demolishes the current notion of the real and arrives at something similar to the phenomenal world of Husserl. Leonard and Wharton provide a useful summary of such views in chapter 3, "The ABC of Being."[2] But even Leonard and Wharton, who are very careful in making distinctions between Stevens and Heidegger, assume that for Stevens reality and being are interchangeable notions. This is not the case. Because the parallels between Stevens and Heidegger are so attractive, one often forgets that the dissolution of the opposition reality/fiction does not lead Stevens, as it does Heidegger, to a contemplation of being. Being for Stevens is not a quality of things but a quality of the mind, so much so that it has led some to explain his poetry through analogies with transcendental meditation.[3]

Another point of intersection of Stevens's ideas and Heidegger's, which might blind us to the differences between the philosopher and the poet, is their view of language. Heidegger thinks that being is revealed in language especially of the poetic kind, and so does Stevens. The effort, repeated in poem after poem, to dissolve the dichotomy reality/fiction indicates that Stevens is aware of reality as a cultural construct bound by forms that are mainly those of language. Stevens never meditates upon how such forms came about, however, as does Heidegger in the "Origin of the Work of Art." The poet is, nevertheless, intent on finding out how the self comes about, how the individual consciousness arises in and from language. As Gerald Bruns pointed out, the reformulation of the question of knowledge beyond epistemology implies that the subject-object dichotomy is replaced by self and other and it becomes "a problem of dialogue, of speech that presupposes and even engages the discourse of other people."[4]

For Heidegger, human agency is not clearly distinct from things. Leonard and Wharton do not fail to notice that, by privileging language over reality, Heidegger makes the individual seem passive, a mere product of language. Language is invested with transcendental powers by Heidegger: it is like an autonomous force that controls the speakers rather than being controlled by them (I shall return to this point in chapter 9). The sheer brilliance of Stevens's manipulation of language would be enough to suggest the contrary. The following analyses will demonstrate that not only does Stevens allow the speakers to take control of language but he is also aware that language is the place where the self (ultimately, for him, being) is negotiated, where the individual both integrates his culture and appropriates it. Repetition plays a crucial role in this process of appropriation, which is also an ontological process.

Most of the significant sound patterns in Stevens's poetry result from textual repetition. Stevens is, in many ways, a repetitive poet: some of his poems have the aspect of a theme with variations, and quite often he repeats his subjects and metaphoric structures to such an extent that one may consider some of the poems rewritings of older ones. This fact is not unusual, since, as Marius Bewley observes, "there is a sense in which a poet rewrites his collected work every time he writes a genuinely new poem."[5]

His critics have not as readily accepted Stevens's textual repetitions as they have his rewritings. Like his too intense sound effects, the repetitions have often been characterized as nonsense. (See chapter 3.) For while the rewriting is understood as the repetition of a theme, which may improve its treatment, the verbal repetition is perceived, at best, as "musical," as a meaningless embellishment. But as my previous readings suggest, verbal repetition can intervene in the process of understanding and may radically change the perception of meaning in language. Along with our perceptions of meaning, the basic assumptions about notions closely related to language use—reality, knowledge, and being—are also altered.

Here I propose to reveal how the self comes into being in Stevens by taking a closer look at the phenomenon of verbal repetition itself. I shall focus first on two poems—"The Death of a Soldier" and "Contrary Theses (I)"—which treat the same theme and are both dominated by textual repetition. These poems contain a transformation of simple word repetition into a verbal ritual, the result of which is a founding of being in the poetic act. The same transformation appears in a more refined version in "Tea at the Palaz of Hoon," where the ontological theme of the poem doubles the effect of its performance.

"The Death of a Soldier" deals thematically with an epistemological challenge, for the poem purports to be about death, a reality that resists the human effort to know more than any other. As Heidegger remarks, death, "which cannot ever *be such as* any experience which pretends to get Dasein in its grasp would claim, eludes in principle any possibility of getting experienced at all."[6] Death can be experienced only in others or as a "not-yet" datum of existence. Language has its own way of dealing with the challenge, since it offers a number of ways of speaking—phrases or commonplaces— about what cannot essentially be either experienced or represented. In fact, the poem itself resorts to such a commonplace from the outset:

Life contracts and death is expected,
As in a season of autumn.
The soldier falls.

He does not become a three-days personage,
Imposing his separation,
Calling for pomp.

Death is absolute and without memorial,
As in a season of autumn,
When the wind stops,

When the wind stops and, over the heavens,
The clouds go, nevertheless,
In their direction.
    [CP 97]

The poem's central metaphor, "as in a season of autumn," works as a reminder of an archetypal analogy between the end of human life and the death of nature in the "season of autumn." It constitutes, in the first place, the speaker's way of giving in to the common or collective perspective, since the trope of the seasons of life is, to use a phrase of Robert Frost's, one of the "metaphors we live by."[7] It is not only very old but also central to mythical thought—the race's way of understanding the mystery of life and death. Most of the ancient myths of the world are based upon patterns of recurrence analogous to the succession of the seasons. As Mircea Eliade[8] shows, the "myth of eternal return," which is almost universal, can take a variety of forms, but one of its main models, especially relevant to Western culture, is the pattern of nature's regeneration. Thus the analogy between human life and the life of nature in the seasons is, in a way, an act of acceptance of the natural way of life that leads to death, but on the other hand, it offers the means to resist its inevitability by also suggesting regeneration. When he uses the traditional metaphor, the speaker subscribes to the collective view of death as a natural occurrence but discovers, at the same time, the collective way of canceling misfortune.

The statement of the poem can thus be reduced to the reiteration of an old adage, which may even be missed. For instance, James Longenbach—an otherwise attentive reader—dismisses the metaphor as weak precisely because he thinks it was meant to be original. In addition, he also devalues repetition: "Even the one rather weak metaphor offered for the death ('As in a season of autumn') is protracted into meaninglessness when it is repeated in the third tercet, not to enlarge the single death by locating it in a natural cycle, but to reveal that this seasonal decline is indifferent to human sorrow."[9] There are reasons for Longenbach's misreading here. He does not notice the old adage because Stevens does not reproduce it but rather echoes it. The significance of the adage could remain limited if it were not for the almost imperceptible imperfections of this repetition of a commonplace.

As is customary for Stevens, the poem's speaker wrestles with his own language, this time in order to compose an original representation of death beyond the old adage, although the traditional image is difficult to avoid, since it bears the authority of that tradition. The speaker's initiative resides in minor grammatical alterations that should eventually change the meaning of the metaphor. Such changes are subtle, and for a while, they seem to do nothing but reinforce the traditional representation of death. For instance, in "as in a season of autumn" the use of the indefinite article does not entirely rob the analogy of its generality but frames it in a narrative way, giving more power to its validity for a particular case. In such a context "the soldier" appears to be at once generic and individualized. Working simultaneously with and against the traditional analogy, the speaker makes the example—the death of a soldier—at once an illustration of the general truth and of a personal tragedy. The soldier, *this* soldier, is not treated to the customary ritual meant to alleviate oblivion; he is forgotten in the indifferent manner in which nature itself forgets its losses or destructions.

In a way, the analogy between human life and the life of the vegetation becomes more literal in Stevens's hands, and actually its meaning stretches beyond the limits of its normal usage. For pushed to its limits, the analogy is no longer only about acceptance of death and consolation but reveals something of death's mystery that does not make itself available in the language's normal intelligibility. This movement toward an exploration and enhancement of the analogy would seem to lead to its elucidation, when the speaker arrives at a formulation in more precise semantic terms: "Death is absolute and without memorial." But this is precisely not what the analogy means, or is commonly used for, since the acceptance of death as part of the natural cycle works against its being "absolute and without memorial." In the cycle, one death repeats another as one life repeats another, and repetition is its own memorial. There is a tension here between the established usage of the analogy and its latent and unexplored possibilities. For Stevens's speaker may be right to suggest that nature is cruel and forgets and that indifference is the condition of its very regeneration.

But the frightful possibilities of the analogy remain unfulfilled, because, as if in spite of the speaker's will, "as in a season of autumn" returns in repetition and restricts his deviations. Being repeated, the analogy becomes a refrain that performs precisely the function of refraining, restraining, the attempt to reach beyond the meaning established by usage. The repetition of this line clearly performs the function of maintaining the poem's own value as repetition, as reiteration of an old adage. But another repetition counteracts these restraints. When the speaker seemingly submits to the authority of the tradition and expands on the repeated analogy, he also repeats his own addition in apparent hesitation: "As in a season of autumn, / When the wind stops, / When the wind stops and, over the heavens . . . " This repetition may look like a hesitation on the speaker's part, but it is only through its power that the image of the clouds, which "go, nevertheless, / In their direction," becomes possible. The clarity of that image is essential to the poem's sense, for only through its intelligence can the traditional analogy be given a new meaning, and only through such new meaning could the speaker detach himself from his tradition and acquire his own authority. Thus besides reaching toward the metaphysical, the poem teaches a lesson about language: meaning is established in repeated, collective usage, and only a repetition (full or clothed, as Deleuze[10] would have it) can make individual usage meaningful.

In "The Death of a Soldier," the repetition of a sentence thus performs a double role. On the one hand, it embodies in language the trope of recurrence and regeneration that dominates the whole poem, for the cyclical perspective, which comes into the poem via the metaphor of the seasons, is in perfect accord with a repetitive style. On the other, it offers the speaker the means to gain an authority comparable to that of the tradition and to identify himself both as part of that tradition and as an individual. Through such an act of repetition the speaker asserts his right, not to disobey or defy the language, but to appropriate it, to make it his own so that his own being may claim his existence. As Deleuze[11] points out, such meaningful repetition constitutes a liberation of being. For although it looks superficial, a purely verbal event, it derives its force from the more profound repetitions constitutive of the culture.

And the curious fact remains that, although the poem is beautifully accomplished in this way, the poet felt the need to rewrite it as "Contrary Theses I." According to James Longenbach,[12] "The Death of a Soldier" is the product of Stevens's effort to come to terms with the reality of the war, and the banal (to him) imagery of the poem can be redeemed only by reviving the context of the letters that served as its inspiration. The letters belonged to a French soldier—Lemercier—and Stevens wrote a whole cycle of poems inspired by them. Although Longenbach has Harold Bloom on his side when he finds "The Death of a Soldier" unsatisfactory, his reading misses precisely the cultural context in which all of Stevens's poetry was produced. Yet Longenbach may be right to notice the difficulty that Stevens has in tackling the topic. In *The Great War and Modern Memory,* Paul Fussell has shown how difficult it was for writers to find a language adequate for the unspeakable reality of the First World War.[13] In fact, it was not until the Second World War that the horror of the modern battlefield found its proper linguistic equivalent. This may also be what happened to Stevens: "Contrary Theses (I)" repeats "The Death of a Soldier" a couple of decades and one war later in a language that the poet has more thoroughly made his own.

The similarities between the two poems are so obvious that no one could fail to notice them: both are dominated by the atmosphere of "a season of autumn" and by the presence of the soldier who dies. They also share the elegiac tone, which is pervaded by a mild resignation. The gesture of repeating the same subject and the same tone seems so superfluous that, as far as I know, critics ignore this second variant altogether. But there are substantial differences in the discursive genre adopted in this second variant. For whereas "The Death of a Soldier" progresses from the general statement about death toward a particular illustration, which is, again, lost in generality, "Contrary Theses (I)" proceeds narratively—from the particular—and its insistence on particulars seems at first to forbid generalization:

> Now grapes are plush upon the vines.
> A soldier walks before my door.
>
> The hives are heavy with the combs.
> Before, before, before my door.
>
> And seraphs cluster on the domes,
> And saints are brilliant in fresh cloaks.
>
> Before, before, before my door.
> The shadows lessen on the walls.
>
> The bareness of the house returns.
> An acid sunlight fills the halls.

Before, before. Blood smears the oaks.
A soldier stalks before my door.
> [*CP* 266]

This new version of the soldier's death creates a different expectation, for the main interest is no longer in the argument about death but in the narrative development concerning the soldier. The description of the season, which unfolds itself according to the rules of scene setting, paves the way for the growth of a story. The very first couplet introduces us to a moment ("now," qualified by the description of the grapes, which indicates that it is autumn) and a place, ("before my door"), and it thus composes a scene. But according to a pattern more or less typical for Stevens, the poem is spent in this description, and the promised action is barely initiated. And although the setting of the scene seems to indicate that a drama is being prepared, and the soldier is the only available protagonist, he appears to be as neutral as if he were just part of the description. This neutrality may be determined by the description itself, since it refers to aspects of nature that are usual or typical for the coming of the season.

The very familiarity of these images deprives them of any capacity to represent the particular and gives them the value of a generalization. But it is not the kind of generalization that might be obtained in abstract argument, since the images remain concrete. The fact that they are typical and repeatable, however, makes them look general. For to acquire the value of something general, a phenomenon does not necessarily have to be reduced to essentials; it is enough that it is repeated. This spontaneous way of generalizing without abstracting and without eliminating the details is the way oral cultures make generalizations. As Eric Havelock points out, in a society that ignores writing, generalization is achieved mainly "in the verses which were repeated and remodeled, and what was at one time or occasion specific turns into what is typical."[14] The seasons offer a natural endorsement to this spontaneous type of generalization, since, by virtue of their repetition, they already have the value of a generality. The very subject of the poem seems thus to have offered a way to undermine the narration by its latent generality.

The sketching of a narrative situation is also undercut, from its very beginning, by the fact that the temporal dimension (the season) is stressed at the expense of the spatial one. The descriptive elements may seem to refer to the place: the grapes, the hives, the house, the oaks, may be what the landscape has to offer to the viewer, but their lack of specificity transfers the reference to the season. Thus the season becomes the scene of action, and having lost the specificity of place, it acquires also a general, typical quality. And all these elements may explain why the protagonist appears as almost passive; although surprised in action, he seems to melt into the scene. The sentence of the second line, "A soldier walks before my door," is caught in this context of semigeneralized statement, which makes the event described look like one of the usual things that happen in the season: it is the fall, the grapes turn ripe, the hives are full, and . . . soldiers come to a door to die.

The beginning of the poem thus establishes a tension between a narrative development, which is by its nature time bound, and a tendency to generalize that the trope of the seasons' repetition seems to be providing for language. Besides the insufficient particularization, several other things do not fit with the narrative frame. One of them is that the description of the landscape does not seem to have the proper consistency for a scene setting. First it looks like a short description of nature, in which the entrance of the soldier seems to be the central event. But the gesture of composing the scene is repeated in each new couplet, so that the marginal role of the description is changed to a central one. Like the "stalking" itself, the end of the poem looks more like an interruption, a stumbling in the way, and we may easily consider it an unfinished meditation on death.

The quality of this meditation reveals another difference between this poem and "The Death of a Soldier." While the earlier poem named death and was marked by the overt intention to describe it, represent it, find its meaning, the latter one just lets itself be haunted by it, by impressing us with images that we traditionally connect with death: the harvest or "reaping," the representation of celestial creatures, and the adumbration of the end connoted by the image of the shadows that "lessen on the walls." One can easily state that such images are repetitions of traditional representations of death or afterlife, but even more than in the previous poem, they are couched in a grammar that radically alienates them from the original, a grammar that creates a difference and makes it possible for the speaker to claim them as his own creation, thus warranting his individual authority.

But this originality is not the main source of his authority: authority grows out of the pattern of repetitions. As I have pointed out above, the narrative development of the poem is stopped by the disproportionate length of its descriptive stage, on the one hand, and, on the other, by the repetitive structure of the lines. Every couplet repeats the scene setting, the preparation of the event, and the event itself is thus pushed somewhere outside the poem. Besides, there are many textual repetitions. The incremental repetition "Before, before, before my door" has the self-contained quality of a refrain, but in the last couplet, this refrain is only partially repeated, and the interruption shocks with the force of an event. The action, whose description is the expected development in a narrative, is thus displaced by the action of the language itself. Detached, even alienated, from their reference because of repetition, the words themselves become sound events, because they attain significance only when perceived as events.

But such "meaning" is naturally different from our everyday notion of linguistic meaning. Its structure can best be described by an analogy to the way meaning is produced in music. For the melodic quality of the words' repetition gives way here to a subtler sound effect, which looks like the phenomenon of recurrence, as Leonard

Meyer describes it in a theory of music. Recurrence is to be distinguished from reiteration, says Meyer, which is another form of musical repetition. While reiteration implies a comparison with previous similar patterns and creates a tension by stressing the deviations from those, "the recurrence itself represents not tension but the relaxation phase of the total motion. It creates closure and the feeling of completeness."[15]

The incomplete repetition "Before, before" may be regarded as such a recurrence, in the last couplet of the poem. It does not create tensions, as it is an identical repetition, and its very "meaninglessness" gives it the power to act as a musical sound pattern. The phrase itself is syntactically incomplete and therefore even more similar to a musical turn, in which not the reference but the form, the pattern, and the recurrence constitute the meaning. For in music too, the very incompleteness of the sound term makes the return more effective in creating closure: "The law of return appears to operate most effectively where the given sound term is left incomplete. Since the sound term is a Gestalt which sets up forces towards a particular kind of closure, the only way in which it can be closed is by repeating it with a new and more final ending."[16]

If the narrative development, as I have pointed out, is incomplete, or rather unachieved, because the description of its scene does not follow the usual rules, is not specific and particular enough, the poem resolves, closes, and gives satisfaction to the reader in its "musical" form. The repeated line provides the stable, fixed point around which the poem can revolve but not because of what it represents. "Before my door" is not translatable into a picture of a "real" door in front of which some event is going to take place; its repetition obscures the reference. But the phrase *is* the scene in another sense: that of a purely linguistic background, a verbal arrest at the threshold between language and song. Like the commonplace metaphors it reminds us of, "gate of Heaven" or "Death's door," the line is also a passage to another state of language, which may also be another state of being.

The poem thus acquires the quality of a ritualistic gesture, in which repetition itself draws on the power of superior creativity. Repetition transforms language into a succession of events, since once the words are repeated they lose transparency and become present—they happen. And the events of language gain significance from repetition, as any event does in ritual or celebration (see notes 8 and 11 on Eliade and Deleuze). It thus becomes possible for the sense of the poem to develop without any apparent reliance on external meaning, because both the event and its repetition are contained within the same utterance. This independent development takes place more forcefully in "Contrary Theses (I)" than in "The Death of a Soldier." On reading the two poems, the first impression may be that "The Death of a Soldier" is the original one; it was written first and treats its theme without indirection. "Contrary Theses (I)" is not only repeating the same theme but goes away from it, as if rehearsing an impossible performance. But the first poem makes sense mainly as a stylization, actually a repetition, of an old adage, and relies, for significance, on our tolerance for such repetition. The event that this poem repeats is outside it, in our own experience, and the repetition makes sense because our experience provides the event. The individuality of the voice is only partly achieved toward the end.

The second poem, on the other hand, pushes toward the achievement of that individuality, toward a liberation of being through the appropriation of language. Its sense develops mostly from its internal repetitions; it does not acquire significance as a ritual but builds its significance in a quasi-ritualistic manner. Its ties with an external context, as well as its appeals to our preexistent memories, are circumscribed, such that memory is completely and exclusively engaged with the poem itself. This apparently mechanical repetition derives its force, however, from the other repetition, the imperfect repetition of traditional images. As Deleuze points out, "a material repetition occurs as a result of a more profound repetition, which develops in depth and produces it as its outcome, as an outer envelope, a detachable shell which would lose all meaning and capacity of self-perpetuation if not propelled by its cause, the other repetition."[17]

"The Death of a Soldier" already modifies our notion of meaning in language, for its meaning resides not in what it says about death but rather in the act of saying, actually repeating, something we already know. The poem fulfills its meaning because it assumes our knowledge, because it obliges us to recognize the ancient formulation and its force. With "Contrary Theses (I)" the assumption is even stronger. There is no ancient formulation that we could directly recognize here, but the verbal pattern of the poem behaves as if there were. Traditional images of death, reordered by the poetic imagination, inspire familiarity, but it is the pattern itself that endorses the poem's utterance as common knowledge. In order to make sense of the poem, we must accept it as ritual, as the consecration of a (linguistic) event. Instead of bringing our knowledge to it, we must accept its verbal universe as our own. The speaker achieves here the greater authority of a collectively endorsed discourse simply by borrowing its pattern, in which his own being has been given significance.

In such a process of verbal ritualizing, which is quite frequent in Stevens's poems, language acquires a certain independence, which sometimes may raise doubts about its own source, its speaker. For if language is a series of events, reality appears as the result of a creative activity in language. And if reality is our own creation, who then are we, and who or what validates our own reality? This question lurks in the speaker's hesitations, which are perceivable in every poem. For the speaker seems to get lost in language before language becomes his own and gives him an identity. The world created from words first engulfs and then recreates its creator. "Tea at the Palaz of Hoon" is a poem in which self-making in a world created in the act of speech is most poignantly evident:

Not less because in purple I descended
The western day through what you called
The loneliest air, not less was I myself.

What was the ointment sprinkled on my beard?
What were the hymns that buzzed beside my ears?
What was the sea whose tide swept through me there?

Out of my mind the golden ointment rained,
And my ears made the blowing hymns they heard.
I was myself the compass of that sea:

I was the world in which I walked, and what I saw
Or heard or felt came not but from myself;
And there I found myself more truly and more strange.
        [CP 65]

Most of Stevens's titles shock with their apparent inadequacy to describe the content of the poem, but in the end they prove to be part of its language universe. "Tea at the Palaz of Hoon" is no exception; it can strike anyone with its arbitrariness, and it has inspired more interpretations than the poem itself. The question most often asked concerns the identity of Hoon, and Stevens's famous answer that he might be "the son of the old man Hoon" is no less intriguing. To me, the strangeness of Hoon's name is more important than his real or symbolic identity, precisely because its oddity generates the "who is . . . ?" question, around which the whole poem develops. The "palaz" is suggestive of the opulence of an exotic place, and it seems again rather odd that it should be owned by a man named Hoon and that tea should be served there. But the "tea" may be a useful indication of the time of day, midafternoon, and may explain the impression of sunset that the first stanza leaves without actually speaking of it. There is no straight connection, and the mixture of pretense and snobbery in the title clashes with the solemn, almost religious tone of the poem's utterance. The very possibility of a connection between the eccentric title and the contents of the poem threatens to upset the order of words/things that we perceive as natural.

The "I" who speaks the poem is the main riddle here, and although many critics call him Hoon, there is no indication whatsoever that the peculiar name has anything to do with this voice that, when the poem opens, is yet unidentified. In spite of the resolute tone in which he says "I," the speaker of the poem seems to need identification. The grammar and rhetoric of the first stanza combine to give at once the impression of arrogant self-assurance and extreme insecurity. The rhetoric consists in what I would call overreaching metaphors, metaphors that would be hard to translate into anything literal and that seem to claim for themselves a world of their own. Any attempt at interpretation immediately reveals this quality: to "descend in purple" may mean to descend in some purple light, or in the purple robes of a king, or simply with a certain religious majesty, but no one of these possibilities is excluded, so no one is singularized. To descend "the western day" may imply that time can be regarded as space, but the spatial epithet "western" actually indicates the time of the day that, in turn, is a place to descend in. The air, which we normally regard as space, is "lonely," as if a creature forsaken by the other, who descends. Not only the differences between time and space but also those between the self, the person, and the impersonality of time and space have been erased. The metaphors are there not to elucidate a world we live in and know but to construct another, a different one, in which the need to verify one's sensations becomes an urgent need to find oneself.

The grammar in which these metaphors are set does not clarify them but rather increases the obscurity of their newly created world. "Not less" may suggest a restriction, a negative definition that contrasts with the spatio-temporal metaphors. But the same restrictive "not less" is afterward repeated to transform the tautology of "was I myself" into a self-definition. The self defines by resistance to the outside pressures, to the otherness that surrounds it, to the strangeness of this fluid universe. The whole utterance seems to be motivated by the simple desire to say "I, myself," to define the self against the rest of these undefined and undifferentiated entities. For the indistinguishable time and space of the poem threaten to absorb the speaker, to make him part of their indefinite and fluid reality.

The need to speak, to assert a voice against this verbal universe, which seems to have been created in another's speech, and where definitions are erased, gives rise to the questions of the second stanza. And the sensations of the body seem to be the best assurance of identity. "What was the ointment sprinkled on my beard? / What were the hymns that buzzed beside my ears?" The first two questions create a contrast between the strange otherness surrounding the self and its own material limit, the body. There is a slight annoyance at this invasion of the body, a sort of protest against this infringement of its limits. The curious thing is that the body finds itself in conflict with not a natural world, as we might have expected after the first stanza, but some elements of a ritual, of a world made sacred by human action. The second stanza seems to pick up not on the general impression of a natural grandeur of the sunset but on some secondary meaning, or rather a peripheral suggestion of pontifical majesty contained in "purple."

Their grammatical similarity makes the first two questions seem quite literal and easy to understand, in spite of their suggestions of mysterious sanctity. But it is, again, the marginal and not the central meaning, the mystery and not the clarity, that is reinforced in the third question. The speaker seems continually to shift his focus and finds the important meanings on the fringes of his utterance. The questions serve self-definition partly because they form a pattern: they have virtually identical beginnings and a similar grammatical structure. This pattern forms a background against which the speaking voice can distinguish itself. And in the third line, the pattern is slightly altered, and the alteration creates a difference. "What was the sea whose tide swept through me there?" launches again an overreaching metaphor that raises the poem's figurative power, for the arch of this metaphor goes over and beyond a handy or beautiful analogy and projects a verbal universe where the beginnings are. The "I" suggested at first by fragments of the body, "my beard," "my ears," appears now total and metaphysically able to host the tide of the sea.

The "I" thus projected into a mythical space is reasserted and confirmed in the next stanza, which is constructed in an "answer" form. The very structure of these answers reinforces the mythical dimension, because, by a switch in word order, the body becomes the source of those elements that produced its sensations before. The repetition of the same words in reverse order also creates a falling, conclusive sound pattern that in a way seals the answer in the same verbal unit with the question and thus validates it:

Out of my mind the golden ointment rained,
And my ears made the blowing hymns they heard.
I was myself the compass of that sea:
    [CP 65]

There is another shift here that places even more emphasis on the "I." In the questions of the previous stanza, there are two possessives, "my beard," and "my ears," and a prepositional object, "me," which occur toward the end of the lines. In the answers the possessives are foregrounded by being placed closer to the beginning of the line, and in the third "answer" line, "I was myself" appears as a very emphatic beginning that confirms the sought-after identity. While in the questions there is an indefinite and rather insignificant "I" looking for its "self," for the meaning of its existence, the answers give the image of a mythicized, aggrandized "I" who is master of all the overwhelming forces that seemed to dwarf him before. This transformation is also noticeable in the verbs that are used in the answers. They are semantic equivalents of the verbs contained in the questions, but their connotations are different. "Rained" replaces "sprinkled," and "blowing" replaces "buzzed." While the verbs of the questions suggest some kind of garden domesticity, those of the answers are related to elemental nature and echo mythical contexts. The incorporation of nature in the "I" is thus a double-edged sword that cuts both ways, for the absorbed nature transforms the body itself into an elemental force.

Stevens's speaker bears a striking resemblance to Mircea Eliade's "archaic man." Like the archaic man, he "sees himself as real only to the extent that he ceases to be himself (for a modern observer) and is satisfied with imitating and repeating the gestures of another. In other words, he sees himself as real, i.e., as 'truly himself,' only, and precisely, in so far as he ceases to be so."[18] But the newly found "I" at the end of the poem is in possession of mythical proportions and powers, when it speaks in self-description as the source of everything that surrounds him, as the self-appointed master of a thoroughly humanized universe. Like the "Anecdote of the Jar," this is a poem of appropriation, of taking possession of the world through language and making it over again as one's own territory. Speaking the world in a poem becomes the necessary human action that can generate "reality," and within that reality, it can define the self as the source of speech itself. Self-definition is thus a return to the beginning, a circle described around itself, a supreme ritual repetition that generates significance.

The pattern of repeating the question within the answer is also reminiscent of catechism. Catechism is a form of religious teaching in which the apprentice is initiated, and therefore given identity, within the community of belief. The answers as well as the questions are standardized and must be learned and repeated. The language of catechism is different from the ordinary in that it functions as an event, serving not communication but communion. The apprentice is asked not to inquire into the mysteries of the divinity but to accept the already formulated answers. This acceptance on his part ensures that he himself is accepted as a member of the community. Something similar happens to the reader of Stevens's poem, to whom the questions are directed but whose right to look for answers is denied. The answers are already there, contained in the poem, which attracts us within its own universe. To read the poem means to commit oneself to its way of making sense, to participate in, or rather partake, of its language. It is a universe that can make sense to us only on the basis of our acceptance of its parameters and a universe in which indeed we can find ourselves "more truly and more strange."

The self that the poem generates belongs thus to the reader as much as to the speaker. For the language that appropriates "reality" and defines the speaker is itself to be reappropriated and redefined in an endless process of repetition. In its "ritual" repetitions language validates its existent significance and our significant existence. Repetition obscures the transparence of language and transforms it into a series of events that in turn become significant only through repetition. It may seem to achieve a self-containment and a power of its own, to function outside or beyond us, but the repeated events of language depend on us, as they happen to us and are formative of our selves. Set in its repetitive mode, poetic language is not only the expression but also the continuation of a thoroughly humanized universe, whose harmony makes significance itself possible.

Mircea Eliade summarizes the ontological conception of archaic man as follows: "an object or an act becomes real only insofar as it imitates or repeats an archetype. Thus, reality is acquired through repetition and participation; everything which lacks an exemplary model is 'meaningless,' i.e., it lacks reality."[19] Transposing this statement in terms of language, we could say that verse becomes meaningful only insofar as it imitates or repeats an archetypal poem, and its reality is acquired solely through repetition. At this point we would meet Stevens's "A Primitive like an Orb":

The central poem is the poem of the whole,
The poem of the composition of the whole,
The composition of blue sea and of green,
Of blue light and of green, as lesser poems,
And the miraculous multiplex of lesser poems,
Not merely into a whole, but a poem of
The whole, the essential compact of the parts,
The roundness that pulls tight the final ring

[CP 442]

Archaic ontology could be useful in clarifying some aspects of Stevens's poetics, but his thinking cannot be called archaic per se. He rather shares Eliade's own awareness that the sacred is man-made and responds to the spiritual needs of man. Poetry too responds to such needs, as it offers centrality and foundations in its formal pattern. Finding that such foundations do not exist in the world of objects—in the world as nineteenth century science saw it—does not mean that we have to give them up. According to Stevens, all we have to do is "to believe in a fiction, which [we] know to be a fiction, there being nothing else."[20] The echoes of William James's views on belief are clear in this adage, and as Lyall Bush[21] argues, they can explain the ironies of Stevens's meditations. (I shall return to William James in the final chapter.) Beyond the irony, however, there is Stevens's desire to give poetry the central role in human spirituality, to make it the sacred space where words give meaning to the self that speaks them.

7

The Metaphysics of Sound

I N THE PREVIOUS CHAPTERS, Wallace Stevens has emerged, somewhat in spite of himself, as a poet philosopher. His affiliations can be placed with either phenomenology or pragmatism. As far as philosophy is concerned, my readings may tilt the balance toward the latter rather than the former. Although I think that arguments like those of Thomas Hines or Paul Bové, which relate Stevens to Husserl and Heidegger, are compelling, my study of the sound effects tends to endorse criticisms like those of Margaret Peterson, Thomas Grey, or Richard Poirier that point out Stevens's ties to William James or George Santayana. But my argument is not ultimately about philosophy. The changes that Stevens effects in notions of reality, knowledge, or self are, in my view, the result of his exploration of language. With this chapter, I wish to continue the debates around philosophical notions but at the same time to return to the question of discourse. In "Sunday Morning," "The Poems of Our Climate," and "Crude Foyer," I will explore the dissolution of another classic philosophical opposition, the one between objectivity and subjectivity. This dissolution, I will argue, marks the shift from a representational discourse to what we might call a poetic one.

According to my readings so far, it would seem that Stevens's main purpose is to direct cognitive attention away from objects. The difficulty of assessing his "philosophical" position derives from the fact that, in the outlook adopted by his poems, the alternative to objectivity is not, as we might expect, subjectivity. Like William James, Stevens opposes at once both idealism and empiricism, and the dual nature of the target may explain the ambiguity of his attack. Idealism and empiricism form an established opposition, and the normal expectation is that if one rejects the former, one would embrace the latter. But the originality of the pragmatic orientation in philosophy, which largely influenced Stevens, is that it rejects both, and it directs its main objections against what they actually have in common.

As Margaret Peterson shows in "*Harmonium* and William James,"[1] what bonds idealism and empiricism together is a lack of interest in human affairs, for while idealism situates certainties in the absolute world of essences, beyond human reach, empiricism concentrates on material aspects, closer to earth but still unrelated to human activity. To this I would add that both idealism and empiricism share the language of representation, which remains essentially the same whether its warrant is transcendental or material. The unsystematic character of James's own lectures signals the need for a different kind of discourse, and we could credit Stevens with the attempt to forge a language that, in being nonrepresentational, remains nonetheless intelligible and can be shared by members of the same community.

Gerald Bruns remarked in "Stevens Without Epistemology" that the poet perpetually tries to escape the voices of others, which inevitably can be heard in one's own voice. The paradox of having to speak a language that essentially belongs to others extends even beyond expression to the very core of being, for one has to learn to *be* from others, on their terms, and the only manner to become oneself is a repetition and an appropriation: "appropriation of the voice of the other by the discourse of the self that in turn is characterized as a monologue or song of world-making."[2] But I think Stevens's purpose reaches, beyond that of finding an individual voice, toward founding a type of discourse that could eminently be characterized as poetic. Poetic discourse emerges as a language based on notions of reality, knowledge, and self that, influenced by some innovative developments in philosophy contemporary to Stevens, are basically opposed to the ones current in that time and culture. One has to notice, from the start, the provisional character of this discourse, for it never achieves the point of stability that could confer on it absolute authority. For Stevens, poetry is always in the making, and the other discourse—of which we may conceive either as the nonpoetic or as the discourse of the other—is always the starting point of his creative acts. Nowhere does the other's voice more clearly assume the form of representational discourse than in "Sunday Morning."

"Sunday Morning" is perhaps the most talked about and admired poem by Stevens. Its interpretations are too many to invoke here, and I shall refer only to those that have some relevance to my argument about the dissolution of the opposition between subject and object. As I have already noted, Wallace Stevens would often start a poem by naming a few objects as if trying to paint a picture or to establish a space for some action. In the same fashion, the opening of "Sunday Morning" discloses a number of objects arranged in a scene:

> Complacencies of the peignoir, and late
> Coffee and oranges in a sunny chair,
> And the green freedom of a cockatoo
> Upon a rug . . .
>   [CP 66]

Whether inspired by Stevens's own bourgeois surroundings, as Frank Lentricchia[3] argues, or representing "the harbinger of death itself," as James Longenbach suggests,[4] the enumeration of objects is a definite stylistic marker leading to the recognition of a certain type of discourse. Early critical appraisals describe the poem as an argument, since for those critics, the setting of the scene invokes the premise of argumentation.[5] And indeed it may constitute such a premise, since argumentation usually starts with the examination of the facts. Later critics, like Joseph Riddel and even Harold Bloom, follow in the same vein, discussing the poem mainly for its content of ideas.[6]

Argument is a discursive genre, actually a type of discourse, with certain characteristics based on a particular ideology. A good description of this kind of discourse and its ideology is offered by Timothy J. Reiss, who identifies it as the "discourse of modernism" and aptly calls it analytico-referential. Reiss's "modernism" refers to the historical period between the Renaissance and the twentieth century and is not to be confused with literary modernism. Following Foucault, he places the beginnings of the analytico-referential discourse in the second half of the seventeenth century, when it developed as a means of dealing linguistically with the new (for that time) reality of scientific discoveries. Basically a language of science (later also adopted by philosophy and literary realism), the analytico-referential discourse is characterized by a certain precision of reference (which we would normally call objectivity), the effacement or occultation of the speaker, and a logical coherence that validates its truth. It is in sum "a discursive practice purporting to be at once transparent to the truths it communicates and an ordered system whose coherence is alone responsible for the 'value' of those truths."[7]

The beginning of "Sunday Morning" bears the markers of the analytico-referential discourse in its crudest form: naming objects. Names are supposed to leave language transparent, and to lead us directly to the reality they stand for. The speaker, "occulted," as Reiss puts it, disclaims all participation in the transfer of objects into words, and his listener becomes a spectator to a dispassionate exhibition of things to which no intention is attached. But as Mikhail Bakhtin has noticed, this orientation of the language toward the object can never be completely successful, because "no living word relates to the object in a *singular* way: between the word and its object, between the word and the speaking subject, there exists an elastic environment of other, alien words about the same object, the same theme, and this is an environment that it is often difficult to penetrate."[8] And indeed, in spite of the insistence on naming objects, the scene set at the beginning of "Sunday Morning" is not free from the impurity of suggestiveness. If the "peignoir," "coffee and oranges," "sunny chair," and "rug" are just objects, their enumeration in a single sentence suggests their agglomeration in a single space that, in its turn, hints at the time of breakfast and the leisure of a middle-class family. Besides, "complacencies" mitigates the strictly objective manner from the very beginning. The lateness of the coffee, the light on the chair, to say nothing about the "green freedom of a cockatoo," are part of the complacent feeling rather than of the images that they qualify. In spite of its impurity, however, the impression of having to do with a simple catalog of objects, of the kind one can find in realistic novels like those of Flaubert or Balzac, is the dominant one and helps us recognize here a discourse whose main purpose is indeed transparence.

Objectivity is also stressed by the use of the third person. The speaker, whose identity we don't know and are not even urged to inquire about, is a hidden voice that does not acknowledge his intervention into the reality described. Description is supposed not to interfere with reality but only to represent it in words in a neutral manner. The neutrality of the language transforms the person present among the objects into another object. The description of the woman, of her thoughts and feelings, is informed by the objective stance of the unidentified speaker, and she becomes one of the "things" spoken about. This portrayal of the woman as an object may not be an exception for Stevens. As Jacqueline Brogan observes, "Stevens' female figures do not only rarely speak, but they rarely move. Consider the difference between his earliest and most famous male and female characters, 'The Comedian as the Letter C' and the complacent woman of 'Sunday Morning.' In a very disturbing way, women in his poetry remain too obviously figures—empty ciphers for masculine rumination and scripting, even de-scription."[9] But the speaker's effort to disguise his presence may have been quite successful, since many critics, starting with Yvor Winters, discuss the poem as if it were the woman's own meditation. It is also true that the critic's own assumptions about language may account for such an interpretation.

It is quite clear that the poem is not the woman's meditation. The feelings and thoughts of the woman are not expressed but analyzed here as part of the development of a larger theme. In a letter addressed to L. W. Payne, Jr., Stevens is careful to stress the general import of the theme: "This is not essentially a woman's meditation on religion and the meaning of life. It is anybody's meditation."[10] As I see it, the poem is a progression from the speaker's analysis of the woman's meditation toward "anybody's meditation," or as Frank Lentricchia put it, "from isolate sensibility to community, from poems as aids to perception to poems as aids to connection, from the singular image and its support in the lonely imagination to the long poem and its support in a community of interpreters."[11]

The analytico-referential discourse is allowed, in the course of the poem, to encounter all the pitfalls to which its own purposes expose it. From the start, the woman is not left to meditate alone. The carefully neutralized speaker intrudes, albeit covertly, by claiming to know her thoughts. But the pursuit of her thoughts as objects is a dangerous venture, because thoughts are subjective and might assert "Her" against his objectivity. The speaker's neutrality can be maintained only within a strict objectivity, which he reasserts in adopting the attitude of a scientist: he observes, he deduces, he infers, and he wants to conclude. Calling the speaker "he" is a mere convenience, as that clearly separates "him" from his object, the woman. Actually his neutrality is not only willed uninvolvement but also apparent genderlessness. Careful not to be distracted by the woman's subjectivity, he turns back to the scene to emphasize its most striking colors while apparently following her dream. It would seem that visual stimulation is most powerful here, and that everything else—the woman with her thoughts and dilemmas—will have to be conceived of in this space:

She dreams a little, and she feels the dark
Encroachment of that old catastrophe,
As a calm darkens among water-lights.
The pungent oranges and bright, green wings
Seem things in some procession of the dead,
Winding across wide water, without sound.
    [CP 67]

But it is at this point that the generic purity of the discourse is more powerfully threatened by the signs of what Bakhtin would distinguish as another layer of language. The dream grows out of and merges with the reality objectively rendered in language. The difficulty of keeping reality and dream apart creates an imbalance for the speaker, whose purpose remains analytical. His classifications lose ground because of linguistic equality, and under such conditions, language cannot grant objectivity or verity to things. When he attempts an explanation of the religious feeling, the speaker is forced to resort to a metaphor, and the objectivity characteristic for analytico-referential discourse falters: "She feels the dark / Encroachment of that old catastrophe / As a calm darkens among water-lights" (CP 67). Metaphor diminishes the authority of the hidden speaker, which has so far been based on a strict objectivity—that is, on the capacity of the words to stand for objects—but it seems that he has no other choice. And the metaphor gains ground even as the speaker returns to the description of the scene. "As a calm darkens among water-lights" leads, because of a sound coincidence characteristic of Stevens, to "water without sound" and thus creates a connection between the woman who meditates and the object of her meditation. As the thinking subject and its object are becoming continuous, objectivity loses its ground. The avoided mythical, "dead" world fuses with the woman's reality and dream.

At this point, the loss of objectivity is accompanied by a weakening discursive assuredness; the so far clear statement becomes repetitive: "Winding across wide water, without sound. / The day is like wide water, without sound" (CP 67). Even at the end of the first stanza, there is a change in the speaker's stance: his objective, analytical attitude seems to be subverted by the language's inner forces. For in its exploratory linearity, this kind of discourse works against its referential purpose. The repetition of "wide water without sound" is differently contextualized and marks a shift from a quasi-allegorical representation to a (much more unstable) metaphorical one. The leap into the metaphoric register is huge, but it may pass unnoticed because the repetition gives the two lines a sort of unity and makes them sound adequate to each other. For the rest of the stanza, metaphor extends into myth. The woman is seen walking Christ-like over the waters toward some inevitable tragedy:

The day is like wide water, without sound,
Stilled for the passing of her dreaming feet

Over the seas, to silent Palestine,
Dominion of the blood and sepulchre.
[CP 67]

The difference between the opening description of casual bourgeois domesticity and this visionary ending of the stanza is staggering, but it does not disturb its smoothness because another sound factor intervenes: the meter of the poem. The prosody of "Sunday Morning" is somehow unique in the Stevens canon through its apparent uniformity, a fact that prompts James Longenbach to call the poem's music "a mighty act of ventriloquism"[12] of the high romantic poets. Longenbach argues that adopting the high romantic sound, Stevens is seeking to give an epic scope to his philosophical preoccupations, at that time related to the reality of the war. This statement may be true, but at the same time the choice of classic meter opposes the poem's analytical tendencies. Sound pattern always works against analysis. The elegant dignity of the blank verse and the smooth transition achieved through repetition also cancel the potential parody of the poem's beginning. Read in retrospect and in view of the stanza's ending, the "Complacencies of the peignoir" and so forth acquire an unusual elevation to the rank of sacred objects. This effect, of course, is not what the speaker of the poem, whose attempts to achieve an accurate, objective representation are quite obvious, had intended.

The discursive mode has definitely changed, for what is important here is no longer the transparency of the discourse but its rhythmicity, the pattern that the sound of the verse creates. Rhythm is, according to Bakhtin, that which gives poetry its apparent monologic quality: "*Rhythm, by creating an unmediated involvement between every aspect of the accentual system of the whole* (via the most immediate rhythmic unities), destroys in embryo those social worlds of speech and of persons that are potentially embedded in the word: in any case, rhythm puts definite limits on them, does not let them unfold or materialize. Rhythm serves to strengthen and concentrate even further the unity and hermetic quality of the surface of poetic style, and of the unitary language that this style posits."[13]

There are two discourses that I have identified so far, one analytico-referential, objective, and transparent and the other "poetic," dominated by rhythm, and rather opaque. They are not only in dialogue with each other but also competing for supremacy, as the authority of the analytico-referential discourse is counteracted by another kind of authority. For the poetic, in its ideal form described by Bakhtin, the best example of which would be the Homeric epics, gains authority from a collective endorsement, whereas the analytico-referential discourse relies, as mentioned above, on its own logical coherence for validation. That coherence, together with the neutrality of the occulted speaker, is repeatedly threatened by the unmistakable markers of the "poetic" as literary tradition conceived of it.

In fact, the analytico-referential discourse reasserts its presence in every stanza only to be subverted, if not totally displaced, by the other discursive mode. The speaker proceeds with his determination to analyze the situation, subjecting it to a quasi-scientific scrutiny. Opposed to this determination is, in the second stanza, a certain subjective and romantic kind of discourse, recognizable as such because the elements of nature are connected to emotional states to the point where they become interchangeable. Critics acknowledge the presence of this discourse by signaling here echoes of Keats or Emerson.[14] It is again a variety of "poetic" discourse, which works against the analytico-referential one. This counteraction is weak, however, for as Lentricchia observes, commenting on this passage: "The passions, grievings and moods have no intention: they are directed to nothing in particular."[15] The analytico-referential stance is simply sustained by grammar. "Passions of rain, or moods in falling snow" seem, in spite of denoting emotions, quite impersonal, since they are enumerated as if to constitute proof in a case. Thus the speaker maintains his analytical intention and is able to conclude again: "These are the measures destined for her soul." The concluding gestures show that the speaker is still in control of his utterance, and the analytico-referential discourse is still the dominant one. Romantic subjectivity does not threaten objectivity; on the contrary it confirms it. In fact, subjectivity and objectivity are dependent on one another, and the romantic excess of emotion defines itself against unemotional science. Stevens distances himself from both, in search of a way to surpass the distinction itself.

After having considered this particular case, the speaker, in pursuit of his analytical goal, proceeds to generalize but not before having examined other cases. Paganism offers itself as an example, because it shows that religious feeling is possible without asceticism or discipline. The second stanza provides a hint in that direction:

> Shall she not find in comforts of the sun,
> In pungent fruit and bright, green wings, or else
> In any balm or beauty of the earth,
> Things to be cherished like the thought of heaven?
>   [CP 67]

The full development of the argument about paganism occurs, however, in the third stanza, after the incursion into romantic poetic discourse has been completed:

> Jove in the clouds had his inhuman birth.
> No mother suckled him, no sweet land gave
> Large-mannered motions to his mythy mind.
> He moved among us, as a muttering king,
> Magnificent, would move among his hinds,
> Until our blood, commingling, virginal,
> With heaven, brought such requital to desire
> The very hinds discerned it, in a star.
>   [CP 67–68]

The example serves the analytical demonstration, but again it contaminates the discourse with its subject matter, which cannot remain neutral. This contamination is somehow recognized by Stevens himself, who in the letter mentioned above states: "The poem is simply an expression of paganism, although, of course, I did not think I was expressing paganism when I wrote it."[16] Talking of paganism, the speaker turns to myth, and myth is (if at all) a different kind of discourse. Or we can say that myth does not share the assumptions on which the discourse of the poem is built, for in myth the notions of subjectivity and objectivity do not exist. There is no "I" and the object but rather "we" and divinity. A voice that speaks collectively as "we" to divinity is the same as the voice that speaks immaterially from divinity, and it needs no objective endorsement.

Because he has freed himself of the representational framework, the speaker should feel free to assert himself, and to give up the neutrality required by objectivity. But the contamination of the discourse by myth becomes apparent in the fact that an assertion of subjectivity does not materialize here, although it would be the expected event. On the contrary, a collective voice emerges and covers both subjectivity and objectivity. This voice, which has the authority of collective knowledge and seems to benefit from a divine endorsement, changes the description of objects into an action upon the objects, which begin to transform, as metaphor becomes metamorphosis. And by the end of the poem, the voiceless discourse, which was analyzing the woman's reluctance to observe the religious ritual, is displaced by this voice. Speech is no longer neutral, but in being voiced, it is no longer transparent. The last eleven lines of the poem resist analytical effort:

> We live in an old chaos of the sun,
> Or old dependency of day and night,
> Or island solitude, unsponsored, free,
> Of that wide water, inescapable.
> Deer walk upon our mountains, and the quail
> Whistle about us their spontaneous cries;
> Sweet berries ripen in the wilderness;
> And, in the isolation of the sky,
> At evening, casual flocks of pigeons make
> Ambiguous undulations as they sink,
> Downward to darkness, on extended wings.
>   [CP 70]

Harold Bloom's interpretation of the stanza points out that here all the rules by which meaning is usually reached are being violated: "There are no causes, only temporal effects, in this concluding topos, where the ripening is all and where the extended wings of the evening birds have ambiguous significances but no actual meanings. Resemblances have receded here, because these tropes turn only from previous tropes. There is just a premonitory, introjective gesture, downward and outward, into the darkness, appropriate to a world where no spirits linger."[17] At best an analysis may reveal a paradox: that although we claim ourselves as the inhabitants of chaos, our world displays the beauty, order, and design of God's creation. The "darkness" toward which the pigeons "sink," however, throws another ambiguous shadow on this beauty.

But when the authority of discourse is not derived from objectivity, understanding no longer presupposes analysis. The opacity of the discourse does not have to make it unconvincing or senseless. Beyond its ambiguities, the stanza sounds conclusive as the voice that speaks it is calm and composed, and there is no reason for us to question that

> We live in an old chaos of the sun,
> Or old dependency of day and night,
> Or island solitude, unsponsored, free,
> Of that wide water, inescapable
>
> [CP 70]

however paradoxical it may seem to be free from something inescapable.

The poise of the collective voice discovered along the poem's development is achieved here, in the final stanza, at the expense of a renunciation. And it is not only objectivity that is renounced, for with it goes subjectivity, the possibility of having something hidden under the pretense of impersonality and from that hiding to impose an individual authority over others. The new authority of the discourse comes from a collective endorsement rather than from neutrality and dispenses poetry rather than truth or rather changes the substance of truth and knowledge into poetry. Such authority validates uncertainty by aestheticizing it, that is, it preserves the mystery and gives it a place in some kind of human order instead of attempting to reveal it.

Stevens's gesture of discrediting objectivity definitely addresses certain expectations, which are not difficult to infer, given that the immediate response to the poem is fairly well documented. Stevens's letters to Harriet Monroe, who first published "Sunday Morning" in *Poetry,* show that he agreed, rather easily, not only to cut, but also to rearrange some of the stanzas. Monroe does not seem to have been interested in the "argument" of the poem but to have had in mind only aesthetic considerations, as can be seen in Stevens's concession that stanza 7 was "not too detached to end with."[18] This attitude may show that even Stevens was less intent on the argument than one might have thought. The rearrangement of the stanzas was possible, I think, because the whole design of the poem is based on the coexistence and dialogue of the analytico-referential discourse with other discursive modalities; however, in its initial form restored in the *Harmonium,* the poem seems to let the analytico-referential discourse lose to its "other."

On the other hand, in spite of the resistance to analysis that the final stanzas display, the first major critical appraisal of the poem by Winters details its argument, which would be impossible to follow in a different stanzaic order. The interpretation is based, of course, upon Winters's own penchant for analysis. The expectation for aesthetic integrity, persistent in Monroe's response to Stevens, is replaced by a determination to analyze, for Winters clearly expects the poem to forward knowledge. And it would seem that Stevens might have had in mind exactly this kind of expectation. In a letter written to Delmore Schwartz, he states that, "poetic order is potentially as significant as philosophic order."[19] Poetry addresses thus an expectation for philosophical reasoning, but it distinctly constitutes another order, satisfying also the desire for aesthetic integrity.

It is this kind of mixed expectation that explains the success of an argumentation that is actually thwarted by both its rhetoric and its rhythm, for when analysis is no longer possible, the aesthetic integrity can become the substitute of transparence and coherence. The prosody of the poem does not follow the shifts and switches, the insecurities and uncertainties of the speaking voice, which the desire for objectivity condemns to inaudibility. On the contrary, it advances with the determined rhythm of the authority identified as "we." This is probably why the changes in the discursive modes—their actual dialogue—are not immediately noticeable, and the poem seems to have all the force of a philosophical argument. The poet confronts us again with the paradoxes of our own sense of what is real and true. For the aesthetic quality of the language validates for us a truth and a reality that we assume to be altogether independent of our actions. Aesthetic expression may seem as transparent as analytical discourse, but its effect is actually produced by a rhetoric and a rhythm endowed with traditional authority, which acquire the value of statement even as they make language quite unclear for analysis. The poetic, as well as other discourses diverging from the analytico-referential, gains the upper hand in "Sunday Morning," betraying the readers' desire for transparent argumentation in a major way.

In *Ariel and the Police,* Lentricchia argues that Stevens was torn between his masculine duty, which he perceived as being useful and productive, and his inclination to write, which he saw as frivolous and feminine. The dialogue between the useful (objective, transparent) discourse and the excessive, poetic one may reflect that duality. On the other hand, the priority that the poetic discourse gains toward the end of the poem suggests a desire to assert poetry against the practicality of analytico-referential expression. But poetry does not triumph here as trivial and "feminine" occupation. On the contrary, it appears to be the virile and seminal discourse that Stevens himself described in "The Figure of the Youth as a Virile Poet."

While seemingly satisfying the contradictory expectations of his readers, Stevens undercuts the domination of analytical discourse and concurrently dissolves the subject/object dichotomy, on which classical philosophy is based. As the previous chapters have also shown, the enterprise of objectivity comes, in the verse of Stevens, to a sort of spectacular failure that may be, and has been, taken for a failure of language. Language seems slippery, and no sooner is an object named than some associations are stirred. The poet seems to lose control and to be driven by the stubbornness of the language itself. I want to emphasize here, again, that Stevens's language does not dominate its speaker, but we may have to do with a deliberate staging of a failure that reveals the possibility of an alternative discourse. "Sunday Morning" offers a good example of the failure to objectify, but it may also demonstrate that the retreat into subjectivity is only the other face of the coin. Actually, the impasse of objectivity is transcended only when the opposition between objective and subjective dissolves.

The poem has thus achieved a transition from an object-based, analytical discourse, characteristic of realism and science, to an even more authoritative one, based on a collective endorsement rather than empirical proof. The latter may be seen as poetic or as the voice that the poet has been looking for, but it should be noted that such discourse cannot claim individual authority or originality, since it relies on a collective authority and on the reader's previous acquaintance with the thematic material. The shift itself, the transition from one kind of discourse to another, is the element that constitutes Stevens's originality. The poetic emerges thus rather as the confrontation of discourses, as a revolution of poetic language in a much more literal sense than Julia Kristeva[20] would give the phrase. The poem opposes more than just two discourses, for it also brings head to head two different conceptions of the world: one realistic or objective and the other mythical, imaginative, where knowledge does not seek empirical verification and, as such, does not destroy the mystery.

The pragmatic doubts about absolute knowledge, as well as the Heideggerian suspicion that language will have its way with the speakers, leads Stevens to discover the power of sound in the practice of poetry. Ironically and parodically situated toward traditional prosodic forms, Stevens's poetry displays new patterns of sound emerging in the very effort to make things more clearly visible. In "The Poems of Our Climate," visibility seems to be at once the purpose and the theme of the poem. The opening lines place it among Stevens's imagistic exercises, and the attempt to render a "pure image" in language is successful, as far as the first sentence goes, "Clear water in a brilliant bowl, / Pink and white carnations" (*CP* 193). The stark clarity of this image may let the reader assume the presence of a painter, carefully arranging his "still life," confident in the power of the image not only to strike our eye but also to convey something to our intellect. Harold Bloom also notices the still life quality of the image and connects it to the intellectualism connoted by the wintery atmosphere of "The Snow Man": "He has arranged his still life so as to make 'the light / In the room more like a snowy air / Reflecting snow.' Hence the choice of a brilliant or shining bowl, reminding us that 'brilliant' means 'full of light,' and hence also the emphasis upon the clarity of the water and upon the pink and white as chosen colors."[21]

The accent is indeed on clarity and transparence, for every element seems to have been selected for precisely these qualities: the brilliant bowl, in which we can see the clear water, and the carnations, whose pale colors are so close in shade as to give the illusion that we can see one through the other. If there is a painter, he is certainly not composing this image for pure sensory pleasure, for it is by far too simple, of a calculated simplicity meant to give some intellectual satisfaction. Glen MacLeod thinks that the poem makes a case against abstract art that is "overly intellectual."[22] One can thus feel from the very start that this is an arrangement, an image already artificialized, and its perception is not so much a sensory starting point as the reduction of a complex intellectual activity to its simplest form: seeing. This image is not where the beginning of cognition is but rather a possible end of it, where the object of knowledge is reduced, abstracted, and simplified so that it might be controlled. But as James Longenbach suggests, the attainment of abstraction is not final in Stevens: "We push ourselves toward the complete simplicity of abstraction and in doing so we push ourselves back to the complicated multiplicity of representation."[23] At a verbal level, the apparent imagistic strategy, together with the simplicity of the vocabulary, contains its own defeat, because, for being too well done, the image serves not to produce an intellectual or emotional reaction but rather to restrain it. The poem may well be an attempt to limit, circumscribe, and contain the activity of the mind in search of knowledge, an activity that can get so prolific and ramified that its purpose might be lost.

Having chosen visibility as a means to discipline the activity of "the never resting mind," a speaker has to deal with the difficulty of rendering the visible in language. The image, "so long composed," is represented in the poem through what are considered the simplest grammatical means: nouns. In enunciating the bare names of the objects that compose the image, the speaker attempts to efface himself and to give the right of presence only to things. Like the speaker of "Sunday Morning," he hides behind an affected objectivity. But this effacement cannot stay for long, because the slightest analogy creates connections that extend beyond the mere presence of the things:

> Clear water in a brilliant bowl,
> Pink and white carnations. The light
> In the room more like a snowy air,
> Reflecting snow. A newly-fallen snow
> At the end of winter when afternoons return.
> Pink and white carnations—one desires
> So much more than that. The day itself
> Is simplified: a bowl of white,
> Cold, a cold porcelain, low and round,
> With nothing more than the carnations there.
>
> [CP 193]

As it progresses, the description loses concentration and digresses into analogies, which seem to pull away from the description of a simple arrangement of objects, distancing them from the speaker. The very reduction of the image to a set of objects, as well as the stress on its clarity, brings light into discussion, and the whole picture is expanded and diffused, when the frigidity of the composition stirs an analogy to "a snowy air." The apparently innocent epithet makes its way to the center of our attention as, perhaps still animated by the desire to keep the image simple, the speaker repeats the word in its nominal version: "snowy air, / Reflecting snow." As a noun, "snow" cannot remain peripheral, and the insistence on its repetition brings it closer and closer to the sentence's semantic center. In "a newly-fallen snow," a certain ambiguity of the grammar—since the sentence is fragmentary—does not allow us to determine whether "snow" is the subject or the object of the sentence, but the word has its own qualifiers, which indicate that it is important. And the rhetorical importance increases accordingly. "Snow" is not only an analogy to describe the "snowy air," but it extends, beyond the idea of coldness, to the idea of winter (the cold season) and from there to the idea of time. So far the mind has concentrated on a frozen space "in an instant of time," but the winter, the afternoons, and the "day" that "is simplified" may break the impression of immobility and dilate the instant beyond itself.

As if aware that he is losing his proximity and faithfulness to the image, the speaker returns to the simple formulation of the opening, but he is constrained, by his own frustration, to reflect on his own and his interlocutor's state of mind: "One desires so much more than that." The line never fails to attract critical attention and is considered a turning point in the poem. Thomas Hines, who sees the poem as an exemplification of Husserlian reduction, is forced to conclude that, by proclaiming the insufficiency of simplicity and abstraction, Stevens parts company with Husserl.[24] The line indeed turns the poem away from abstraction and back to concrete multiplicity. But as usual with Stevens, a sentence dominated by syntactical ambiguity has an unstable reference, for it may be a reflection on the previous digressions—one desires to say more— or the declaration of a desire for even greater simplicity, which would explain why the description returns to the carnations and repeats itself with variations. The impression that the stanza leaves on the reader is not of abstract thought but of a clear, material image.

Much of the effect of clear visibility that the stanza eventually achieves is due to the repetitions and variations, which end up by forming a pattern. But the pattern fulfills here yet another interesting function, as it creates an expectation of regularity, which is not completely satisfied. While most of the words belonging to the description are repeated and point again and again to the image of the bowl with pink and white carnations, "one desires so much more than that," although it determines another return to that image, integrates neither the sound pattern nor the insistent concentration on those objects. Its inadequacy to the sound pattern reinforces its inadequacy to the logic of the utterance, for if the rendering of the image was the purpose, then bringing up one's desires is totally irrelevant. Yet what may appear to be a minor dissent turns the whole poem into something else, the achievement of pure visibility fading in favor of an introspective meditation. As the pattern of sound closes the stanza, sealing it up as it were, the little loose end enables the poem to continue as an inquiry into subjectivity. There is a switch here from objects to subject whose imperceptibility dissolves the opposition between subjectivity and objectivity.

Since its reference extends to some undisclosed metaphysics of the cognitive process itself, which is obscured rather than clarified, it is only to be expected that this loose end should be resumed in the second stanza, in order to be resolved. The "complete simplicity" as well as the desire for more is pushed toward the revelation of "I," self, or subjectivity, which was only suggested by the reference to "one" in the first stanza:

> Say even that this complete simplicity
> Stripped one of all one's torments, concealed
> The evilly compounded, vital I
> And made it fresh in a world of white,
> A world of clear water, brilliant-edged,
> Still one would want more, one would need more,
> More than a world of white and snowy scents.
>   [CP 193–94]

Before becoming patterned itself, the second stanza is a recognition of and a reflection upon the first. Acknowledging the incapacity to reduce cognition to objectivity, to the perception of a confined, simplified, visual space, the second stanza also discloses the motives of the attempt to know: "all one's torments" and "the evilly compounded, vital I" appear now to be the generators of the reductive action of the first stanza. But having failed to concentrate on the simple image, the mind is liberated from the task of reducing the cognitive process and becomes self-reflective. Cognition of and through space changes thus into self-cognition. The attention to the object turns into an attention to the subject, and the transition from the objective to the subjective appears now as the clear result of the change from space to time. But the problem remains the threat of expansion. Once the space has been confined to the image, and the subject turns upon itself, it continues to expand in time. Even after it has become a part of the limited, confined world of the bowl with pink and white carnations, "the evilly compounded, vital I" continues to break the limits, projecting itself into the future, for the element of desire of whatever sort, which marks the presence of a subjectivity, perpetually extends beyond the present moment. This is what the final lines of the stanza seem to suggest; however, reading them, one gets the feeling of a conclusion, of a satisfactory end, something quite similar to the feeling with which we read: "and they lived happily ever after."

If desire cannot be contained, if even after it has been made fresh in "a world of white and snowy scents," the subject still cannot stop its expansion, the possibility of containment appears in the musical arrangement of the language. Contrary to expectation, the sense of having exhausted the time, of having confined desire comes from the very indeterminate "more." Repeated at intervals, "more," the word that indicates expansion, becomes the very means of self-containment. For the operation of containing time, which seems intellectually impossible, is obtained by verbal repetition, by the musical effect it creates. As it becomes almost a song, the poem does to the temporal flow what usually music does: it patterns it, contains it, makes it tame and human. Here, as elsewhere, Stevens finds a foundation of the real in the very symmetry of sound.

The verbal circularity of the second stanza closes, once again, upon the image of transparence. And again, this temporal, musical closure gives rise to a semantic expansion probing deeper into the motivation of this quest for knowledge. Having exhausted the image but not the desire to explore, the mind will turn again upon itself following its own working. And since this working is the poem itself, the last stanza constitutes its best self-criticism:

There would still remain the never-resting mind,
So that one would want to escape, come back
To what had been so long composed.
The imperfect is our paradise.
Note that, in this bitterness, delight,
Since the imperfect is so hot in us,
Lies in flawed words and stubborn sounds.
    [CP 194]

As the poem turns upon itself and self-describes, the speaking (writing) voice merges with the reading voice, and we accept without reserve that what is being said is about "us." The progress of the pronouns is from none at all, when the poem refers only to objects; to the impersonal "one," when desire first insinuates itself in the cognitive process; to the "evilly compounded, vital I," that is more of a concept than a person; and finally to the fully personal "us," which is so adequate in the context that we accept it almost without noticing the change. Thus the study of the objects seems to be impersonal, at best an individual activity, whereas the delight in the "stubborn sounds" of the language is shared. This progress from an objective presentation to a subjective introspection and beyond it to a shared "delight" that replaces absolute truth, transcends again the opposition objective/subjective and establishes the authority of a collectively negotiated truth.

After meandering in subjunctives, the poem returns to the indicative present in its final lines and becomes assertive. But what is asserted is not of the initial image, for after having failed to present objectively, the speaker has contaminated it with subjectivity and can no longer speak of it as of a pure presence. The indicative present asserts now only the language materialized in sound. As it is created and perceived at the same time, at once given and taken, the language of the poem is both subjective and objective and renders this dichotomy insignificant. The poem, an utterance of sound in language, contains synchretically and indiscriminately the subjective and the objective, the general and the particular, the individual and the collective, and any other binary opposition that philosophy might have invented. The poetic discourse evolves again in transition, marking itself as a self-transcendence of language. The poem thus transcends the impasse of rational knowledge through its existence as sound.

Since the poems examined above are mainly oriented against empiricism, I shall now have a look at a poem in which idealism is subjected to the same kind of attack, or rather dissolution, clarifying Stevens's pragmatist inclination. The analytical attitude of the mind in the process of acquiring knowledge, which leads to dissatisfaction in many of Stevens's poems, is plainly thematic in "Crude Foyer." Leonard and Wharton find it to be a satire of "the rational metaphysical bias (that intellect 'can penetrate the deepest abysses of being') underlying the scientific orientation of Western thinking."[25] In spite of its metaphorical title, this poem may seem more clearly descriptive, almost expository, as it opens with an attempt at definition, in a manner strongly reminiscent of a philosophical text:

> Thought is false happiness: the idea
> That merely by thinking one can,
> Or may, penetrate, not may,
> But can, that one is sure to be able—
>   [CP 305]

But the utterance, which started almost like a lecture meant to achieve a demonstration, begins to betray hesitation after the first two lines. The repetitions show that the argument cannot continue in abstract terms, and indeed it is literally interrupted. The speaker seems to be fighting a failure, as he picks up his demonstration in the next stanza, where metaphor appears as the last expressive resort. It seems that the quality of the mind can be defined only in the concrete terms of a landscape:

> That there lies at the end of thought
> A foyer of the spirit in a landscape
> Of the mind, in which we sit
> And wear humanity's bleak crown;
>   [CP 305]

What follows may be considered either a critique of Platonism or a cultural history in a nutshell:

In which we read the critique of paradise
And say it is the work
Of a comedian, this critique;
In which we sit and breathe

An innocence of an absolute,
False happiness, since we know that we use
Only the eye as faculty, that the mind
Is the eye, and that this landscape of the mind

Is a landscape only of the eye; and that
We are ignorant men incapable
Of the least, minor, vital metaphor, content,
At last, there, when it turns out to be here.
    [CP 305]

There is a clear allusion to Dante in "the critique of paradise,"[26] but the manner in which it is continued adds to it an ironic twist. In Dante's sense, "comedy" means the achievement of harmony, and it is divine. I suppose in the context one could, by derivation, call God a "comedian"; but to the modern reader—the reader implied by Stevens's text—the word may fail to maintain its original dantesque flavor and may become almost derisive. The dignity of the divine is not lost, however, as this God/comedian brings to mind another image of God given by Stevens in a short poem called "Negation." The image, although it challenges religious conventions and is pervaded by some skepticism, is more sad than irreverential: "Hi! The creator too is blind, / Struggling towards his harmonious whole" (CP 97). Margaret Peterson attracts attention to the fact that in "Negation," "Stevens appropriates James's philosophical strategies"[27] and attacks the idealist view of the world rather than the traditional God of Christian theology.

In the context of "Crude Foyer," the "work" of the comedian, who by virtue of the dantesque allusion is divine, is thus our world, which we "read" as if it were a book in our "foyer of the spirit." Consequently we see emerging here, in a modified form, under a French name and with Italian overtones, the old image of a "quiet house," in a "calm world," where any reader can become one with the "book of nature," just as he does in "The House Was Quiet and the World Was Calm."[28] And in what looks like very modern language, a universe of pre-Renaissance imagery begins to take shape, and Plato's metaphors follow in one of their most natural contexts. Plato's analogy between the mind and the eye is presented here not simply as a way of describing an intellectual activity but as an enforced rule of our thinking ways or a habit of mind that limits us. As Leonard and Wharton point out, "The terrain, the context of this 'crude foyer' (and humanity's thorny/metaphysical 'bleak crown'), originates in the 'eye' for which, again ambiguously, 'the mind is the eye': the mind/eye gathers the phenomena of perception for its landscapes."[29] A criticism of this attitude becomes apparent at the end of the poem, where the limitations of the "eye" are emphasized. This criticism turns against the whole poem, which although disclosing a limitation of thought is itself based upon that very limitation.

The description of the "foyer of the spirit" is performed in visual terms and depends on the notion of space: it is a place, a landscape in which we "sit." This is an unusual way to speak about thought; our everyday metaphors would have it fly, move quicker than the senses, whereas Stevens makes it a place to sit, like a library, maybe. That would make the description extremely realistic, since thinkers literally "sit." But the verb comes back in the next stanza, and besides the image of the modern scholar, it brings to mind a monarch or God figure sitting on his throne: God sits on his throne in paradise. This suggestion lends the whole image an aura of power and authority: this foyer of the spirit is the seat of a sovereign. And since Plato's ghost haunts the poem anyway, it would probably be natural to remember that his "reason" is king and "rules" the other parts of the "soul."

Summing up all the suggestions of "sitting," we get the idea of a privileged element that "rules" over the others, as the eye rules over the other senses. The activity of the thought has a center, a stable point to which the work of all the senses must converge. Elsewhere, Stevens speaks about the "central man," the "central things," and no less about the "central poem." But the poet's attitude toward this centrality remains ambivalent, for the poem is imbued with the Platonism that, toward the end, it seems to criticize. And at its sharpest point, Stevens's critique of Plato resembles Plato the most. "We are ignorant men," perhaps because we follow Plato, because we think in the way we see, because we construct an interior "foyer" and organize it around the center of the ruling reason. But in doing so, don't we actually look like the prisoners in Plato's cave, who are content to look "there" at the shadows instead of "here" at the real thing? Again, is this a way to agree with the master of the dialogue or just an enactment of his image that may prove him wrong? Without having two voices, the poem too is a dialogue, in the sense of a text that sustains two different or contrary attitudes. That neither side is privileged, and that they should get so easily mixed, makes the poem opaque to analytical scrutiny. The simple opposition of "there" and "here" is in the end of the poem completely dissolved: the "foyer" was described as interior to the human mind and is now called "there" as if it were remote, outward, and foreign, leaving us to ask where "here" is after all.

As Stevens put it, "the poem is the *act* of the mind," a comedy in which "seeing" fails just in order to demonstrate that "thought is false happiness." And the failure pertains precisely to the attempt at seeing, for philosophy is, after all, a way of seeing the world. Stevens opposes to it not another way of seeing but another sense altogether, since for him the world is both built and known as poetry, as words "that are, in poetry, sounds." And the world as poetry, the world as sound, is above dualism and paradoxes, above the "torments of the evilly compounded vital I," a world created in speech, where one exists by virtue of speaking to others. To the Platonic metaphysics of seeing, Stevens opposes a metaphysics of sound.

Toward its end, the poem submits to a subtle kind of pattern that, although repetitive, seems to follow thought to its resolution. And perhaps the only way to solve the riddle of "there" and "here" is to think of the former as remote and absent and of the latter as close and present. It does not matter if the home of the mind is within or outside; what matters is that it be present, to itself and to the other, as sound. With the eyes we create the remoteness; we are in a domain of shapes, forms, that are far away from us because we need the distance to see them. And anything the mind creates in the fashion of the eye might have the same fate, to be forever "there." The need that the object of knowledge should be self-contained remains constant, but when such self-containment is achieved in language through the pattern of sound and therefore is not projected on the reality outside it, the knower and the known, the subject and the object, become continuous or rather present to each other.

The poems I examined above belong, respectively, to the early, middle, and late career of Stevens, and besides providing further illustration of Stevens's effort to find his voice as poet, they chart the evolution of the discourse that results from such an effort. This evolution shows that, toward the end of his career, Stevens may have settled for a certain manner of voice that moves with the thought, and his purpose may always have been to establish poetry as a way of thinking, not just a way of speaking. The earlier attempts, however, show him shifting from one established discourse to another and letting the poetic reside, as Emerson would say, "in the moment of transition from a past to a new state, in the shooting of the gulf, in the darting to an aim."[30] But such differentiations are not essential to the understanding of Stevens's poetic work, since he frequently returned to his earlier poetic experiments, and his constant preoccupation remained to blend, in the language of poetry, the abstract quality of thought and the natural vibration of emotion. The sound-dominated discourse becomes effective in Stevens's poems by creating a special kind of intellectual emotion that chapter 8 will illustrate in more detail.

8

"And if the music sticks"

So far I have shown how Stevens's special use of language affects basic concepts of classical philosophy. Yet his ultimate purpose, I think, is to find a place for poetry in modern life. In a more or less romantic tradition, common sense relates the idea of poetry to emotion, but Stevens's acute awareness of language and its functioning, as well as his fondness for abstraction, may seem to distance him from such a tradition. Modernism itself developed as the antithesis of romanticism, and we would not be surprised to find Stevens among those poets who despise displays of emotion. Yet emotion is not beyond Stevens's scope. Here I shall argue that Stevens's stylistic innovations are directed toward producing emotion; however, as in the case of all his other notions, emotion must be understood in a different way. And the difference consists in the way emotion is produced, for Stevens succeeds in awakening feelings by a subtle manipulation of his reader's expectations.

Stevens's play upon the reader's expectations is consistent throughout his poetry, but it is never more thoroughly at work than in his first long poem, "The Comedian as the Letter C." What makes the poem immediately dependent on the reader's reaction is its obvious parodic quality. Parody, if it is to be read as such, requires that the reader be familiar with an original and thus places the work in a tradition, which in the case of "The Comedian" is romanticism. As Harold Bloom notes, "Its place in literary history is, in one sense, very clear, because it is the satyr-poem or parody that culminates and almost undoes the tradition of the High Romantic quest-poem."[1] Helen Vendler, Joseph Riddel, Paul Bové, and others join Bloom in identifying the romantic tradition of the narrative and philosophical poem not only as the target of Stevens's mockery but also as the model he emulates in "The Comedian."[2]

In a way, such ambivalence is to be expected, for Stevens is a modern poet, and high romanticism, while rejected, continues to exert a powerful influence in modernism. But Stevens does more than take issue with romanticism, for parody here, as elsewhere in his work, is not fully achieved, and its mitigated quality indicates that we may have to do with something more complex than a simple mockery. The parodic mode is accompanied by many other verbal effects, which influence more fundamental expectations regarding not only poetry but also language in general. In fact, romantic discourse would be too easy a target for the formidable verbal performance that is

"The Comedian," and clearly Stevens has more at stake than the negation of a tradition that had already been discredited.

The poem's end, with its gently teaching tone, may give us a clue as to its purposes:

> Score this anecdote
> Invented for its pith, not doctrinal
> In form though in design, as Crispin willed,
> Disguised pronunciamento, summary,
> Autumn's compendium, strident in itself
> But muted, mused, and perfectly revolved
> In those portentous accents, syllables,
> And sounds of music coming to accord
> Upon his lap, like their inherent sphere,
> Seraphic proclamations of the pure
> Delivered with a deluging onwardness.
> Or if the music sticks, if the anecdote
> Is false, if Crispin is a profitless
> Philosopher, beginning with green brag,
> Concluding fadedly, if as a man
> Prone to distemper he abates in taste,
> Fickle and fumbling, variable, obscure,
> Glozing his life with after-shining flicks,
> Illuminating, from a fancy gorged
> By apparition, plain and common things,
> Sequestering the fluster from the year,
> Making gulped potions from obstreperous drops,
> And so distorting, proving what he proves
> Is nothing, what can all this matter since
> The relation comes, benignly, to its end?
>   [CP 45–46]

We are advised here, retroactively as it were, that we have been engaged in listening to an anecdote with a strong didactic purpose. The teller of this anecdote seems to be certain that the philosophical conclusions are, or should be, the most important part of the story for us. He fears, however, that we may not have got the moral of his story, because he has tried to disguise his pronunciamento "In those portentous accents, syllables, / And sounds of music coming to accord." The danger of this disguise designed to entertain us is that the music may "stick" and thus render philosophy empty of meaning. The notion that music may damage philosophy is based on an opposition—which we usually discount, since the two terms are rarely allowed to stand on equal footing—between narrative (and/or philosophy-in-disguise), on the one hand, and music, on the other; or between representation of action (and/or ideas) and sound. According to the narrator, the success (or rather excess) of the latter would jeopardize the former, but his final argument is that this kind of danger does not matter, "since / The relation comes, benignly, to its end." He is finally saying, then, that the whole purpose of the narrative is only to come to an end, whether its lesson is learned or not, and that its relation, its telling, is more important than whatever it has to tell.

The narrator obviously relies on our willingness to listen to the relation, and to go on trying to make sense of it, even if his hero, Crispin, does not manage to make sense of his own philosophy. For as long as we are engaged in listening to "the sounds of music," the story can fulfill its purpose even if it proves nothing. Stevens seems thus to be offering us the failure of Crispin's endeavor as the main point of attraction, so that the absence of meaning should itself become meaningful. How can significance lie in emptiness, and what does this absence of sense have to do with music? The answer to this question is suggested by Kevin Barry's study *Language, Music, and the Sign*.[3] As I have mentioned in my first chapter, the study concerns the disputes around the nature of language and significance in the eighteenth century. Those disputes are relevant to Stevens's poetic practice, as the positivist model of language established in the eighteenth century has dominated Western culture ever since, and it has started to lose ground only recently. The pragmatic philosophy, contemporary and congenial to Stevens, may have been the first serious challenge to that trend. But according to Barry, even at the start, the positivist theories of language developing out of the Enlightenment found opposition in theories of music, which problematized the positivist notion of meaning and intelligibility. Basically, the pictorial model of language was opposed by an aural one: "The specular analogy with painting, on the one hand, and the aural analogy with music, on the other, indicate opposed ideas about language and poetics."[4]

Music presents a problem to rationalists, because it appears to be meaningful, while it is not representational and cannot be translated into images. Music is undoubtedly signifying something, but one cannot tell what its signs stand for. These signs are thus empty and promote uncertainty and doubts about meaning. On the other hand, musical theories of meaning direct attention toward the value of that emptiness and toward the listener's response: "At the moment when eighteenth-century epistemology noticed that the signs of music evade the categories of distinctness and clarity of ideas, it became possible . . . to locate the significance of music in its emptiness, in its absence of meaning, and therefore in the act of listening, in the energy of mind which its emptiness provokes."[5]

The reason why music appears to be meaningful at all is precisely its capacity to elicit a response from the listener, to provoke a special kind of emotion. But the quality of such an emotion may seem different from anything a literary text can convey. Language can stir emotions by evoking emotions or circumstances connected with emotions, as it does in lyrical poetry; or it may let the reader identify with a character's predicament and thus feel his/her emotions, as it usually does in narratives. But music offers neither such occasions, nor circumstances and characters to identify with. The emotional response to music is at once deeper and harder to explain. Leonard Meyer points out that music impresses the listener due to the arrangement of the sounds rather than to the sounds as such. Taken individually, sounds have no meaning and cannot evoke anything.

But when sounds succeed each other and are repeated, they form a pattern and engage the listener in an activity of perception that eventually becomes meaningful. Following a pattern, the listener forms expectations: "In any particular musical work certain melodic patterns because of their palpable and cohesive shapes become established in the mind of the listener as given, axiomatic sound terms. They set the mode of continuation, completion, and closure which are the norms of the particular work. And if part of such pattern is introduced, it will arouse definite expectations as to the manner of continuation and completion."[6] A melodic line may fulfill such expectations and give satisfaction, or it may frustrate them and thereby produce suspense. The final result of this action of the pattern is an emotional participation on the listener's part, which, according to Meyer, constitutes the meaning of music.

The relation between meaning and emotion may reveal another aspect of the strange injunction that the narrator of "The Comedian" addresses to us at the end of the poem. He may be inviting us to enjoy the music of the poem, to find meaning in the emotion it arouses, rather than in the representation of events or ideas. But the question is: how can the poem work musically at all? Stevens has puzzled many of his critics by urging his readers to listen to the sounds of the letter C.[7] Harold Bloom finds the hint, to say the least, unhelpful. But if the proposal to listen to the sounds of the letter C may seem a little aberrant, since from a strictly phonetic point of view they are not related, Stevens's musical design is evident in the poem, maybe too evident, so evident that it may escape the attention of a reader who starts out with strong expectations for a romantic narrative poem.

There are, however, many reasons for the reader's interest to shift. From the start, the poem draws attention to its own language. Virtually every critic notes the "dazzling surface" of this language, which may seem to provoke more interpretations than its presupposed semantic core can endure. Harold Bloom notes a typical reaction: "No one can discuss the Comedian without an opening wonderment at its language, which carries rhetoricity or word consciousness to a pitch where many readers cannot tolerate it and where no reader can be comfortable for long."[8] The reason why "no reader can be comfortable for long" has to do with a habit of reading based on the very assumption, which the narrator brings up at the end of the poem, that what one has to find in the poem is a philosophical statement, a "pronunciamento," disguised as narrative. Interpretation is supposed to result from analysis, and in Bloom's view, the poem must "sustain" it. His own (excellent) interpretation determines the poem's starting point in "Cartesian dualism" and points toward abstract questions about selfhood that are not fully accounted for.

Bloom's attitude is only typical, and his desire to provide the best, the incontestable, interpretation is shared by all his peers. But all interpretations are liable to be questioned, not because the critic or the critical method would be in any way at fault, but because what this poem (to an even greater extent than the others) demands is a different way of reading based on entirely different assumptions about poetry, language, and the world. For as I have shown, what constitutes Stevens's most important achievement lies not in his scattered philosophical remarks but rather in his poetic performance. Actually, a number of criticisms starting with Helen Vendler's and continuing with more recent ones, such as Gerald Bruns's, Jacqueline Brogan's, or Eleanor Cook's focus on the action of language rather than on the thematic content of Stevens's poems, but although the significance of rhetoric and grammar becomes evident in their work, the role of sound remains unexplored.[9]

The criticism focused on form emphasizes in one way or the other the nonrepresentational possibilities of language, the effects Stevens obtains from obscurity. For instance, in her recent study of Stevens, Eleanor Cook compares the final version of "The Comedian," as we know it from the *Harmonium,* to the earlier "Journal of Crispin" and concludes that Stevens seems to avoid rather than promote clarity in the final version. The revision moves from a more coherent narrative to one dominated by wordplay, which itself is headed to self-destruction: "In *The Comedian* . . . rather than playing with tropes so as to prevent easy reading or easy writing, Stevens begins to shut off their possibilities. The later tropes turn savage and bitter, as if Stevens were questioning the possibility of any reading."[10] Thus the wordplay, which in Cook's opinion constitutes the key to reading Stevens, comes here to the same kind of failure that the more conventional means of poetic representation do in the other poems. But the implication that it was Stevens's purpose to defy the reader or proclaim some kind of triumph of obscurity may be a little hasty, since rhetorical play is not the only alternative to what we might consider straightforward representation. As I shall argue here, in "The Comedian" logical, narrative, and rhetorical sense are all complemented and completed by a musical meaning. My manner of reading here may resemble a piece of musical rather than literary criticism. The musical approach is not only possible but also desirable in order to explain how Stevens endows his poetic language with emotion.

The language of "The Comedian" is so brilliant as to seem self-destructive, and Frank Kermode's statement that the poem is "a sustained nightmare of unexpected diction"[11] has become its classical description. This nightmarish language obscures the sense of the story, be it literal or symbolic, and its rhythms conspire with the quality of the diction to create a dominance of sound that ultimately affects its meaning. If the sense of Crispin's adventure remains ambiguous and undeclared and elicits a plurality of interpretations, the poem's sound effect sustains the reader's desire to search for and ultimately reach meanings beyond the usual horizon of representation.

Like so many poems by Stevens, "The Comedian" starts by unsettling our confidence in the power of language to evoke images. This is mainly a consequence of sound dominance, but the sound does not only disturb the semantic solidity of the poem; it also offers the paradigm according to which meaning reconstitutes itself for the reader. Whether or not we notice that the words form a pattern as sounds do in music, we may easily become engaged in pursuing the relationships of which this pattern is composed. For instance, the poem's preestablished, traditional meter, which would not normally impress us as other than familiar, plays against the general effect of diction and rhetoric. For while the intelligibility of the story is perpetually threatened by the caprices of the language, which seems to claim an independent status, the regular, familiar iambic meter keeps us feeling that the text is homogeneous. The rhythm's regularity, although not always perfect, keeps us expecting further development, what Meyer calls continuation.

The importance of the rhythm in creating an expectation for continuation is noticeable in the opening, where a progressive disintegration of semantics is accompanied by the development of a sound pattern. The dry, vaguely academic sentence that opens the poem has a deceitful pretense of generality, which may lead one to believe that the poem is meant to be the demonstration of a thesis:

> Nota: man is the intelligence of his soil,
> The sovereign ghost. As such, the Socrates
> Of snails, musician of pears, principium
> And lex. Sed quaeritur: is this same wig
> Of things, this nincompated pedagogue,
> Preceptor to the sea? Crispin at sea
> Created, in his day, a touch of doubt.
>   [CP 27]

There is a philosophical flavor in the language of the first sentence, as "man" is used generically, and the metaphors "intelligence of his soil" and "sovereign ghost" are reminiscent of biblical style. By virtue of such associations, the statement may be read as a philosophical axiom of obvious grandiloquence. This quasi-theoretical formulation of the first sentence is followed by a reference to Socrates and by some Latin phrases that indicate the narrator's competence in philosophy and dead languages.

The contrast that Latin can strike in an Anglo-Saxon context is exploited by

Stevens in many ways. Latin words, or words of Latin and Romance origin, abound, and they usually appear in clusters whose variable density may have different effects.[12] First, the origin of these words impresses beyond their sense, because they are usually associated with Church language, legal vocabulary, or scientific terminology and suggest not only an esoteric quality but also an authority of a religious, legal, or didactic nature. Therefore, passages dominated by Latin words, or words of Latin origin, may remain slightly obscure, while the authority associated with them is conveyed directly and without difficulty. Even before or without understanding what the words represent, we can identify the contexts in which they usually function, and this recognition is meaningful in a nonsemantic way, for the precision with which they refer is secondary to their sound/sense. From a specifically acoustic point of view, such words also create sound dominance, given their greater number of vowels, whose sound offers itself to us before their meaning.

This grandiloquent, elaborate style may also create the impression of mockery, for "Socrates of snails" smacks of a parody, and the narrator's competence in grammar is used for the dubious task of transforming a trivial word like "nincompoop" into the strikingly odd but scholarly sounding "nincompated." Another indication of self-mocking intent from the narrator's part is the fact that "of his soil" is taken so literally as to be contrasted with "to the sea." As an ironic contrast for the more common metaphor of being "of the soil," "the sea" may appear as the most subtle stretching of the rhetoric so far, but it is, at the same time, the point where the parody becomes doubtful, because the phrase "Preceptor to the sea" is quickly succeeded by "Crispin at sea / Created, in his day, a touch of doubt." The repetition makes the word "sea" central, and its parodic potential dissolves together with its colloquial sense, opening the possibility of another sense as yet undefined.

Besides the complicated rhetoric, the Latinisms, and the unachieved parodic effect, another factor attracts attention to the significance of formal relations—the syntax. The two sentences of the opening, "Nota: man is the intelligence of his soil, / The sovereign ghost. As such, the Socrates" have the verb "to be" as a predicate. In most of its uses, "to be" is followed by a nominal phrase in order to fulfill a predicative function. Actually, most of the time, the verb "to be" is a copula, and the sentence is not perceived as finished until the nominal phrase appears. The balance of the sentence, as well as its meaningful integrity, is thus ensured by the symmetry between the subject and the nominal phrase, but here the imbalance in the usual pattern attracts attention. It creates semantic uncertainty because each verb is followed by not one but several nominal phrases. The speaker agglutinates one phrase after another, and every new phrase seems to be a correction or cancellation of the previous one. Such correction seems to be needed, for the phrases are metaphoric, sometimes cryptically so, but the replacements do nothing to enhance their semantic transparence. If we have been puzzled by "the intelligence of his soil," "the sovereign ghost" will not solve the puzzle. As for the series "The Socrates of snails, musician of pears, principium / And lex," its obscurity only culminates in the use of Latin words.

And while the meaning thus escapes, one cannot help but record, albeit unconsciously, the incremental repetition of the syntactic structure. If the first sentence has only two long nominal phrases following "to be," the second one, which is technically a fragment, has the verb eliminated and the number of phrases increased. Due to this augmentation, the nominal phrase acquires a special importance. It seems to be rather difficult, and probably important, to say *what is,* therefore *what is* may be the main question. There is the half expectation of a question, which forms itself gradually, as the nominal phrases succeed each other, and their succession may modify the sense as we first understood it, for the arrogant certainty readable in the first sentence has been diffused by the end of the second. With the nominal phrases following and canceling each other, predication becomes uncertain. The changes hardly touch the semantics of the first statement; however, the sentence's sense is considerably altered as it has become part of another context.

The process of reading, as it develops in time, includes a shift of our attention. Our interest lies in the meaning of the utterance, but as its semantic meaning is obscured by the extravagance of the diction, the syntactic relations become more salient. We are all aware that the syntactic relations between words are a component of meaning, but their full impact appears clearly only when semantics is set aside. Linguists are always ready to demonstrate that syntactic markers may give the impression of sense regardless of semantics by making up sentences out of invented words. In such a demonstration, Crispin's description as the "imperative haw / Of hum" (*CP* 28) could serve as an excellent example. Even though there is no meaning to the words, the syntactic structure is identifiable and the utterance "sounds" meaningful. Most of the meaning thus constitutes itself in a nonsemantic way and functions independently of the "reality," or the semblance of it, that language is supposed to represent.

The patterns that constitute themselves either syntactically or in the sound sequences absorb an increasing part of our concentration in the process of reading. We normally assume that our interest in a narrative is determined by the sequence of events, by the action referred to, which takes place in a "reality" that does not in any way depend on the language that tells about it. This is, of course, the "realistic" illusion that we can find in any well-told story. In many kinds of narrative, such an illusion is created by quasi-musical effects, and "The Comedian" is not different in this respect from other narrative poems or even some prose narratives. What makes it different is the extreme thinning of the story, which becomes a mere shadow of action. This dramatic absence of plot makes the illusory quality of the "real" all the more evident. The unveiling of the machinery that produces the illusion becomes, in itself, a spectacle of illusion. And as the story vanishes, so does the power of representation. The poem engages our memory of words in its temporal flow, as words evoke each other in repetitions and, because they have new associations, may make us reconsider their previous occurrences. For this reason, whatever configurations appear that we might find meaningful never seem final.

This story's intelligibility is hard to conceive of in conventional terms, because none of its patterns is fixed and liable to being mapped out. Most of its patterns fail or die out in the temporal development of the reading. When a pattern fails, it is replaced by another, which may have an altogether different nature, so that intelligibility is maintained but in another way. This kind of variable intelligibility does not help us form a total perception, but nonetheless, it maintains our total engagement in the process of perception. We are neither able nor free to perceive the whole, but our belief that there is a whole to be perceived is thoroughly sustained as our appetite for completion is permanently refreshed.

Most long narratives maintain our interest because they are based on such transitory patterns, but usually the "musical" development remains unnoticed and works rather toward a reinforcement of the realistic illusion. A story may appear more coherent and consequently more "real" because it is verbally patterned, and it returns to its verbal motifs. Stevens's poem looks deliberate that way, because it relies on repetition of words or syntactic constructions in an obvious manner and sheds all pretense of realistic accuracy. The fact that, in revising the poem, Stevens worked against its coherence proves that the realistic convention was to be mocked rather than obeyed. The realistic illusion is thus exposed and exploited as illusion. In its incessant and relentless play with our expectations, the telling displaces the story, and all the energy usually spent in our involvement with the action "spoken about" is channeled toward the perception of the language's own action. We get all the effects of a story—the interest in the drama, the tension of the suspense, the satisfaction in the resolution, the identification with the hero—without being able to attribute them to the story as such. The temporal flow of the telling produces these effects while it obscures the story's more usual scaffolding. The story makes sense mainly as a succession of delays, returns, and resolutions, which happen in the syntactic advance or in the pattern of the sound. The poem thus creates its own temporal territory and acquires a "reality" of its own. The reader must submit to its musical power in the same way Crispin himself surrenders to the tropical charm of his new home: by changing her notion of reality. For while "The affectionate emigrant found / A new reality in parrot-squawks" (CP 32), the reader must negotiate her own notion of the real in the poem's own terms.

The second section of the poem repeats some of the suspense-creating strategies found at the beginning, but it adds a few new twists to this syntactic manipulation. The result is the same detachment of the meaningful from the "real" doubled by a sort of decentering of the syntactic construction itself. The sentence starting with "Crispin" is especially interesting for the way it builds up suspense. We find, again, a postponement of the predicate achieved through the enumeration of a large number of appositions after the subject, which succeed each other with undaunted uniformity:

> Crispin,
> The lutanist of fleas, the knave, the thane,
> The ribboned stick, the bellowing breeches, cloak
> Of China, cap of Spain, imperative haw
> Of hum, inquisitorial botanist,
> And general lexicographer of mute
> And maidenly greenhorns, now beheld himself,
> A skinny sailor peering in the sea-glass.
>
> [CP 28]

Here suspense is created not only by the delay of the predicate, but also by the uniformity of this string of appositions, which may give us doubts about the possibility of a closure. It is true that one can always expect the string of appositions to end when the predicate occurs, but the expectation for the predicate could well be frustrated, and the sentence could remain a fragment. Actually, this sentence may well pass for a fragment, for its long-expected predicate has very little strength after so many appositions, and as if their weight was not enough, the verbal group itself is completed by another apposition. The length and structural uniformity of the secondary parts of the sentence may make us perceive them as much more important than its core: "Crispin . . . beheld himself" will seem of little significance by comparison with: "The lutanist of fleas, the knave, the thane, / The ribboned stick, the bellowing breeches, cloak / Of China, cap of Spain," and so forth. A lot of the communication's content appears to be on the margins rather than at the syntactic core of the sentence. We can infer this without actually considering the semantics of the utterance, for the impression is simply given by its grammatical structure, by the way it "sounds." By the time we arrive at the end, we have very little interest in the predicate, for the appositions seem enough to give a sense to the utterance. In a way, they predicàte more effectively than the predicate itself. Crispin is thus lost in his attributes as thoroughly as he is lost in the vastness of the sea, and the loss of a grammatical center makes evident his loss of identity.

In the process of understanding language, there is a formal design in whose perception we may put more energy than in the identification of individual words. The power of oratory, where syntax is heavily manipulated to arouse our emotions, proves that the unconscious focus on syntactic relations may be even stronger than the conscious pursuit of semantics. We may never be aware of the syntax as such, but our expectations are formed in relation to patterns that sentences usually follow. Such patterns are so strong that we may understand a sentence even when it is not finished, or we may catch its sense even though we do not understand all the words. Robert Frost illustrates this point with the situation when two people speak behind a closed door, and one can understand what they say even though the words are not distinguishable.[13] We do not have to be aware of the technical vocabulary that describes syntax in order to "hear" it, for it is part of the sound/sense.

The play on our expectations, which the manipulation of syntax can produce, is, in many ways, akin to the feeling we have when listening to music, for such feeling is also determined by the growth and frustration or fulfillment of expectations. As Leonard Meyer has pointed out, the "meaning" of music is generated by formal relationships, which engage both intellect and emotion. Such formal relationships come to our attention, because they touch upon a basic capacity of the human mind—that of perceiving a pattern, of subordinating the smaller units to the larger ones, that of expecting wholeness. These are basic cognitive impulses that do not need a material result in order to be satisfied. The perception of pattern can thus be meaningful simply by satisfying the desire for completion and closure.

In spite of the fact that musical development requires a permanent possibility of continuation, unless we are at the end of the piece, the wholeness of the pattern creates a feeling of cognitive satisfaction. Such satisfaction comes, in the poem, independently of its referential action, as subtly as if it were generated by an actual music. Sometimes the cognitive purpose of the verse is quite obvious, since the pattern takes the classic form of question and answer. But the cognitive satisfaction is produced by the syntactic pattern rather than by semantic resolution. The questions may remind us of the poem's opening, because they create the same kind of suspense—the predicate is delayed by a long nominal group, which is then balanced by an equally long verbal group—whereas the structure of a sentence gives us the pattern on which the answers will be structured. Not only are they delayed answers, answers that actually extend the question and lengthen the expectation, which mounts to suspense, but once they occur, they generate digression and lead to new questions. The end of the first section is only an example of this technique, which is used throughout the poem:

What word split up in clickering syllables
And storming under multitudinous tones
Was name for this short-shanks in all that brunt?
Crispin was washed away by magnitude.
The whole of life that still remained in him
Dwindled to one sound strumming in his ear,
Ubiquitous concussion, slap and sigh,
Polyphony beyond his baton's thrust.
    [CP 28]

Although the question is obviously rhetorical, the declarative, well-balanced sentence that follows it has the effect of an answer. But far from being final, this "answer" seems to require explanation: maybe because the syntax is here within normal limit, or maybe because we have been expecting it for a while, we feel that this sentence should be clear. The narrowing down of formal possibilities—the "right" form that the sentence assumes—attracts attention on its semantics, but the metaphoric vagueness and the semantic indirectness that accompany the established correct syntax create the contrary expectation for further development.

This development assumes also the form of a normally structured sentence but only up to a point, for a new series of appositions appears toward its end. Because of this new load of appositions, the sentence looks unbalanced, heavier in its second part, especially since the appositions modify not the subject but the object, thus pulling further and further away from the subject/predicate core: "Dwindled to one sound *strumming in his ear / Ubiquitous concussion, slap and sigh, / Polyphony beyond his baton's thrust.*" The dissolution of syntax generates also a certain amount of ambiguity, for the feeling that a unit has been completed, and the conviction that there should be some continuation occur both at the same time, and this simultaneity makes it hard to decide in favor of the one or of the other. The finality of the sentence that was supposed to complete the "answer" is thus impaired: the appositions suggest an unfinished, unbalanced thought that must continue in order to find its completion and balance. This can give us an indication about the development of Crispin's adventure, for although he is bodily and spiritually lost here, this is not the end but rather a beginning.

There is thus a pattern for our expectations: a question creates the expectation for the answer, while the apparent impossibility that the answer should be final creates digression and opens the utterance up toward other questions. We get thus the impression that we follow some ongoing events, the feeling that we are engaged in some action. The contradictory movements, toward closure and toward continuation, are perhaps the best illusion of reality that one can get from a narrative. And as the nature of this action is internal rather than external, we are not in the position of a passive observer of the action; on the contrary, it is our participation, our engagement with the language that gives the illusion that something is *happening* to Crispin.

As the sequence resolves in sound rather than finds its closure in syntax, the need to return to an earlier, more stable pattern underlies a desire for semantic clarification, which the verse satisfies in its own indirect ways. Because of its syntactic simplicity and precision, and because of its position after a sequence that raises doubts about closure, the sentence "Crispin / Became an introspective voyager" gives again the illusion that semantics is clear and the story advances. Our concentration on the sequence of events is minimal, for our mind is busy following the patterns that grow and then vanish, although not before having generated other patterns, as if we were listening to a piece of music. The illusion that the story is there, however, is maintained by the feeling that we make a temporal progress, that the time of our reading is consumed, as it were. A sequence of events, which we usually look for in a story, is replaced by a sequence of patterns. So that, at the point where the pattern gives us enough reassurance about its completion, we also experience the feeling that the story has completed one of its stages.

The section that follows ends the first part of the poem on a note of certainty, or rather with the promise of cognitive satisfaction, a promise that some answers will be given to the questions that motivated our advance so far. The attempt to close is clear, even if closure may occur through severance, since most of the sentences are short and declarative, cutting through irrelevancies:

> Severance
> Was clear. The last distortion of romance
> Forsook the insatiable egotist. The sea
> Severs not only lands but also selves.
> Here was no help before reality.
> Crispin beheld and Crispin was made new.
> The imagination, here, could not evade,
> In poems of plums, the strict austerity
> Of one vast, subjugating, final tone.
> The drenching of stale lives no more fell down.
> What was this gaudy, gusty panoply?
> Out of what swift destruction did it spring?
> It was caparison of wind and cloud
> And something given to make whole among
> The ruses that were shattered by the large.
> [CP 30]

Although the syntactic structure indicates a resolution, semantically, the statements are far from being satisfactory, as far as clarity is concerned. The sheer repetition of this structure, which looks like an attempt to reformulate an answer, gives a feeling of semantic uncertainty. The feeling is also increased by the fact that, at first, the sentences do not seem to fit into the meter: there are no fewer than three consecutive enjambments, disharmonies between syntax and meter that, in this particular context, may create anxiety about the fulfillment of meaning. The first three sentences in the quotation above seem to search for a balance, which is finally achieved in the sentence (line): "Here was no help before reality." And this balance is reinforced in the next line, where we find two coordinated clauses, both starting with Crispin's name: "*Crispin* beheld and *Crispin* was made new." The coordination, as well as the repetition of the name, creates a symmetry, which gives the line the look of coherence of a solid fact that can be known without difficulty or mediation.

The impression of coherence and stability is reinforced by a succession of questions and answers, which gives satisfaction not because the questions would actually be answered but because, formally, the answer recapitulates the question: "What was . . . it was . . . " This kind of recapitulation suggests that the answer is known, final, and without a doubt. Stevens makes use of such a pattern very successfully in another poem, "Sea Surface Full of Clouds," where self-containment is perceivable in the repetition of the pair question/answer at regular intervals. The self-containment of this pattern and its emptiness of significance solicit the reader's energy to supply the missing meaning.

As in other poems, repetition creates a space for certainties where certainty had been lost, and although satisfaction remains ambiguous—for this language is not easy to appropriate, as the sound intervals run across the divisions into lines, which form an equally strong sound pattern—the searching mind acquires a sense of identity or self-consciousness, determined by its participation in producing significance. As in some of the previous cases, in "The Comedian," repetition can give language onto-logical value. The patterns distinguishable in the poem's progress—some of them syn-tactical and some based on sound repetition—generate each other, every one spring-ing from a variation contained in its precedent. The generation of one pattern by another produces not only a conversion of our interest but a more profound change, which allows us to be ready for more than one shift in the focus of our attention. We do not simply give up semantics in order to follow the pattern of sound but become engaged with patterns of rhetoric, syntax, and sound in the same way. And as the pattern makes reality possible, it also generates the hero's reality.

The introduction of Crispin is performed within a pattern, and this gives his name a special status in the poem. Narrative expectations would prompt us to perceive him as the hero of the story, but such expectations are here frustrated, for we do not get any pertinent information about him, aside from his name, which may send us to medieval lore and indicate the parodic intent through its incongruity with heroism. But Crispin is so much less a hero that he hardly *is* at all. He appears mainly to be the illustration of the generalizing statement that opens the poem, his humanity subordinated to the function of proving some abstract truth. But once the formal connections begin to develop in the poem, the context, in which Crispin's name is first said, becomes all important. The name is made prominent against a constituted background, for "Crispin" is part of a self-contained sound unit—the line that is almost musically struc-tured by the symmetrical repetition of *sea:* "is this same wig / Of things, this nincom-pated pedagogue, / Preceptor to the *sea? Crispin at sea . . .* " As the name is a new element in this pattern, it may be perceived as a potential theme for what follows. So while the hero is not fleshed out, his name gains the status of a quasi-musical theme, of a sound unit, to which one may desire to return. The name's occurrence in a context so musically structured gives the impression that Crispin's identity is already known, and the repetitive context gives "Crispin" the value of a familiar phrase.

The musical framing thus fulfills the function of presenting the hero better than a more direct verbal introduction would. Normally, in a narrative, we come to know a character gradually, and we must let him grow into a hero. But Crispin, much like the heroes of ballads, becomes the hero as soon as the name is uttered, for this name is made to sound like that of an already known mythical personage, as if his exploits had been forever repeated in some national lore. From the point of view of realism, Crispin remains insubstantial, hardly a person at all, but as the play of the language engages the reader, and "Crispin" appears as a key element in this play, the name becomes (musically) thematic.

The pattern of repetition is, as expected, resumed in the description of Crispin's person. The interest in the hero from a realistic standpoint may be considerably diminished by this description, which makes indirection a virtue and conveys a more abstract idea about the center of the story:

> An *eye* most apt in gelatines and jupes,
> Berries of villages, a barber's *eye*,
> An *eye* of land, of simple salad-beds,
> Of honest quilts, the *eye* of Crispin, hung
> On *porpoises*, instead of apricots,
> And on silentious *porpoises*, whose snouts
> Dibbled in waves that were mustachios,
> *Inscrutable* hair in an *inscrutable* world.
>
> [CP 27, emphasis added]

The repetition of *eye* functions as a wordplay that not only presents Crispin in a synecdoche but, because of the obvious sound coincidence with "I," also creates a pun reminiscent of Emerson, and this device draws attention to selfhood in an abstract way. Its rhythmical repetition asserts not only the presence of the language but also its power, because it produces the impression of a refrain, which takes over a new narrative function. Our emotional participation in a narrative may depend on the identification of the hero as one of us. Here the perception of the hero as "I" is at once more literal and more subtle. For in a more realistic context, "I" would be perceived as the narrator, and the process of identification between the reader and the hero would go its long and mediated way through cultural and social constructs. But here the refrain erodes the meaning of eye/I in repetitions until the word acquires a material presence. Having lost transparency, the word is heard and stands ready to acquire meaning. The pun loses its balance, which is tipped now rather toward "I," the abstract idea of self. And in this way we read the "eye of Crispin" as Crispin's self, the self for which he is searching, as we may be searching for ours.

Crispin's awareness of himself is actually, if not the declared purpose, the result of the poem's progress, for what really happens to Crispin is an immaterial loss of self and its not less abstract recovery. This loss of self, with which the reader too must struggle when confronted with the poem's alienating language, as well as the search for its recovery, occurs nowhere else than in this language. Stevens can rival the greatest philosophical minds in working his way through grammar toward abstract conception, and as usual, the grammatical change takes place in repetition:

Crispin, merest minuscule in the gales,
Dejected his manner to the turbulence.
The salt hung on his spirit like a frost,
The dead brine melted in him like a dew
Of winter, until nothing of *himself*
Remained, except some starker, barer *self*
In a starker, barer world, in which the sun
Was not the sun because it never shone
With bland complaisance on pale parasols,
Beetled, in chapels, on the chaste bouquets.

[CP 29, emphasis added]

Again, the repeated element here is not, as one might expect, the syntactically salient word—the subject or predicate of the sentence—but always a marginal element, an object, or a qualifier. The first repetition in "until nothing of him*self* / Remained except some starker, barer *self* " is emphasized by the position of the word at the end of the line and the inevitable rhyme. When it is repeated, "self" also acquires a slightly higher syntactic function: the prepositional object becomes direct object. Moreover, it is also qualified by two adjectives. Normally, the presence of some qualifiers makes us perceive a noun as more important, as something that deserves attention. This emphasis makes us see the *self* detached from its possessor, an independent entity. The word *self* is also literally detached from the compound, in which it had the status of no more than a suffix, for *himself* is only a more emphatic variant of *he.*

These grammatical modifications give the "self" a certain independence and raise it to the status of a philosophical category. Like the "eye/I" in a previous section, the "self" becomes an abstract notion, and its usual referential capacity is reduced, as "self" ceases to be part of Crispin him*self,* and its situation places it in a void of meaning. As the more concrete and traceable reference becomes vague, we are prompted to fill its place with something much more speculative and slippery. Meaning here is clearly subject to negotiation with the reader. We are offered some kind of bargain, because free as it has become, the "self" can be appropriated by us and given any meaning we want it to have.

This void of sense mobilizes our interpretive energy, which we shall need in order to endow with meaning yet another quasi-musical development. The two adjectives that acted as separators of the "self" are used again to qualify "world," strongly suggesting an analogy between the two. But analogy does not succeed in clarifying the notion; on the contrary, semantic clarification remains a remote possibility. The move from the "self" to the "world" may seem to enlarge the notion, but its importance is only suggested by the addition of a whole adverbial clause, whose subject is the new element to be repeated: "In a starker, barer world, in which the *sun* / Was not the *sun*

. . . " The negation here is simply canceled by a repetition that makes the sentence sound more like a tautology and produces a reassuring effect while obscuring reference. The balance of sound thus achieved returns the sentence to the condition of music, of the empty sign.

The significant movement that we have been able to observe in this pattern is one of decentering the syntactical unit through repetitions. For the repetition, together with the change of grammatical function, makes us reconsider the role and significance of the repeated element. The center of meaning moves away from the syntactic center and creates doubts about its final fulfillment. This sequence, in which every marginal element of one unit can become central in the next, does not give us any clue about its possible closure. But if it cannot be resolved, the sequence somehow dissolves, for syntactically we get another weakening of shape: the subordinate clause is not only expanded, but its verbal group is lengthened, delaying the end and weakening the sentence's resolution. There is an aural compensation for this weakening, for the pattern of repetition is now perceivable as alliteration: "Was *n*ot the *s*un because it *n*ever *s*hone / With bland com*plai*sance on *pá*le *pá*rasols, / *B*eetled, in *ch*apels, on the *ch*aste *b*ouquets" (*CP* 29, emphasis added).

The decentering movement of the syntax may endanger the assurance with which we have been able to advance through the poem so far. The hero's presence, conditioned by our emotional engagement with the language, may seem to fade at this point of syntactic dissolution, for it was syntax that sustained our expectations, that both created and resolved the suspense. The excitement produced by suspenseful delay is replaced here by a more important and greater change, for in order to recover the certainty offered by the presence of a pattern, we shall have to direct more attention to sound proper. Sound has been implied in the syntactic pattern too, but now it forms an independent one and forces us to consider an even more abstract order. Such a dramatic change in the focus of our attention affects our sense of identity, because it modifies the whole configuration of our mental action. Like Crispin's, our "self" becomes "starker, barer" as it engages in the perception of abstraction. And it may seem paradoxical, but the abstraction becomes possible as language becomes more concrete and more sensual, and the words more closely approach the sounds of music.

The second half of the poem, marked by the reversal of the opening sentence, offers yet other interesting variations on the strategies employed in the first and constitutes, in a way, a symmetrical development. Such symmetry actually announces the poem's completion. The poem's very end (quoted at the beginning of this chapter) relies on the symmetry of two compound sentences to create the effect of a recapitulation of pattern, again of the kind that we find in some pieces of music. Closure is thus achieved, in one way at least, before the very last line, which has the aspect of an addition. This line, "So may the relation of each man be clipped," stands out not only because it is typographically separated from the rest but because it sounds different, its rhythm altered by an extra syllable. It is a firmly balanced declarative sentence that should certainly put an end to the "relation," if we had any doubts about it, but in spite of its length, which we would expect in a concluding line, it shocks us as an interruption, probably because of the frequent pauses, for most of the words here are monosyllabic. The last word especially gives this impression, which it reinforces semantically. The end comes thus as an interruption, and the poem is literally "clipped" here.

I have argued, from the beginning, that the dominance of sound and the general verbal extravagance of the poem obscure its intelligibility and direct our attention to the formal relations of words and sounds. But forms and sounds do not compete with meaning on account of being meaningless. The very vagueness of representation creates another kind of intelligibility in those forms that engages us powerfully and ensures our continued interest in reading. This is not to say that the poem does not make any sense in a more ordinary way. R. P. Blackmur remarked that, however extravagant, Stevens's vocabulary always fits the context and makes sense.[14] Stevens's rhetoric is equally meaningful: his wordplays are never gratuitous; his metaphors may seem outlandish, but they build upon each other with surprising consistency, even though they may not come to complete fruition; and there is a perfect orchestration of all devices so that the physics and the metaphysics of the poem become one. At a deeper level, however, they are all dependent on the "music" of the poem.

For at the level of "meaning," our interest may not be maintained for the duration of the poem, and the verbal extravagance makes the text too obscure for us to follow all its rhetorical strategies. Some analytical effort may yield the general design of the Comedian's adventure, but the difficulty of such an endeavor goes to prove the marginality of that design. Although we firmly believe that the apprehension of the total scheme is our purpose, what usually maintains our interest in a story is the way it advances step by step, the sustained promise of a totality rather than the actual possibility of perceiving the whole. And the extravagance of "The Comedian" does nothing but accentuate the difference between the two modes of perception, the one "visual," centered on representation, and the other aural, centered on patterns of sound.

Normally, language combines referentiality with pragmatic meaning and musicality, but Stevens seems to be willing to cleanse his verse of reference in order to accentuate the significance of the other two elements, especially of music. To a large extent, the music of the poem's language, which I have described above, aspires to displace and even replace the referential function, so that eventually all requirements of narrativity are fulfilled by its quasi-musical patterns. Nor are they ineffective in that direction, for we leave the poem with the illusion that we have listened to a story and have even learned something from it, although the source of that feeling is our own action.

The expectations that determine our perception of the poem's formal aspects are partly based on the conventions of a literary genre, but mostly they are determined by the grammatical structure of the sentences, whose variation produces effects similar to those of sound pattern in music. In our normal perception of language, we assume syntactical completeness, but there are numerous variations in the shape that a sentence can take. This syntactic flexibility, which Stevens exploits more interestingly than any other poet, permits the speaker to surprise us with unexpected delays or inversions, which may generate anxiety and suspense but also work to maintain our interest. Beyond the representational quality of the language lies a totally different kind of intelligibility of fluent, temporal patterns. The perception of patterns stimulates our intellect, but the variation upon them, which plays with our expectations, generates emotion. And since the perception of pattern is the very process in which expectations are delayed, betrayed, or fulfilled, meaning is as indistinguishable from emotion as it is in music. And the satisfaction with this meaning constituted in a patently intellectual exercise is paradoxically felt as an almost sensuous pleasure, again in a way similar to the understanding of music.

This "musicality" of the language enables the poem to transcend the impossibility of representing the ineffable. Situated in the inferential regions of thought as emotion, Crispin's adventure is as simultaneously concrete and abstract, bodily and spiritual, physical and metaphysical, as the exploits of a mythical hero. For in the fluctuations between semantic and musical intelligibility, there runs the flux of self-creation, the growth of a hero of uncommon yet familiar mind. The efforts to identify Crispin or to trace his spiritual voyage within the confines of semantics do not lead to a complete understanding of either hero or poem. For Crispin is so intensely lacking in physical substance as to seem real only somewhere in the metaphysical realm of abstract significance. His adventure is the adventure of the mind, which always starts somewhere in a provisional identity (as a citizen of Bordeaux, for instance) and searches for its self in the inscrutable realms of otherness (the sea, the jungle) only to find itself in its own repetition, in "the idea of a colony." And this is not only the story of the mind but also the mind's exercise in reading the story, actually listening to it and finding its satisfaction in a significant (because ontological) repetition.

"The Comedian as the Letter C," where the sounds of the letter C are supposed to be the center of the reader's attention, achieves more than this modest ambition of promoting the sound of language as a meaningful feature. It crowns the first phase of Stevens's career, when his purpose seems to have been to show the hidden powers of the language and its possibilities of creating significance in ways other than representational. He tends here toward a view of language that will enable him to unfold his antiphilosophical philosophy and to make poetry the very substance of thought. This view of language aligns his poetics with the musical theories of meaning that emphasize the role of the reader described by Kevin Barry: "As developments from ideas of music, we find in both linguistics and poetics an emphasis upon the power of suggestion, upon varying the figures of a discourse, upon the imaginative process of the reader/listener. This 'imperfection' or uncertainty of language becomes, therefore, its value: it shows how the mind can work."[15] Stevens's achievement is indeed not only to change the reader's view of language by downplaying representation and emphasizing the dependence of utterance on the listener's expectations but also to draw attention to uncertainty and mystery as positive values. With the musical handling of language, Stevens restores poetry's capacity to produce emotion in a way that does not separate it from significance or the workings of the mind.

9

The Poetics of Sound

SOUND, FOR STEVENS, proves to be one of the main instruments in transforming language into poetry. His poetry is aural in both the literal and the figurative senses, addressing the (mind's) ear rather than satisfying the (mind's) eye. This is probably why poetic discourse appears subversive of a whole tradition in philosophy, which had conceived of every mental activity in visual terms. The "metaphysics of sound" emerging as a result of Stevens's poetic experimentation changes, among others, the notion of philosophical poetry. For the poet does not philosophize in any ordinary sense, but since the technical aspect of his verse challenges assumptions about reality, truth, and knowledge that normally underlie philosophical discourse, his poetry engages philosophy in a special kind of rivalry. The poetic is, in Stevens, a particular use of language characterized by inclusion rather than exclusion of other types of usage, and this particularity enables poetry to undermine the assumptions on which other discourses rest.

As I have already emphasized, Stevens's experimentation takes place mainly in language. He works with language in order to create a language, for the changes he effects address the assumptions that govern language use and start on the surface of the language itself. The power of this surface linguistic pattern to touch deep-seated assumptions and, finally, to challenge the way we conceive of the world—a power usually coveted by philosophy—shows that language is not only an important component of culture but is also germane to the very substance of thought. And while this view of language presents a special challenge to tradition, it also situates Stevens in the contemporary trends of philosophy. Actually, the importance of Stevens's poetic experiment has become apparent in the context of a philosophical climate that places an increasing emphasis on the role of language in human affairs. One can even say that the displacement of philosophy by poetry, the subversion of its discourse by the poetic, starts with the philosophy's own self-subversion. The linguistic turn in European philosophy, starting with Nietzsche and Heidegger and continuing in poststructuralism and deconstruction, has offered, for many critics, not only a suitable context for Stevens but also a key to reading his poetry.

As I have shown, Stevens's experimentation with language has made him a serious candidate for deconstructive criticism,[1] if not a deconstructionist avant la lettre,[2] and his personal interest in Heidegger can only justify such opinions. One cannot deny that Stevens shares with Heidegger certain convictions about language and poetry, but his attraction to this European philosopher, as I have already suggested, has its roots in the earlier and more powerful influence exerted on him by American philosophers like William James and George Santayana. Here I shall conclude my argument about how the sound characteristics of Stevens's verse reflect a conception only partially similar to phenomenology and more thoroughly rooted in pragmatism. This point will become apparent when we look more closely at ideas about language and sound launched by Heidegger, James, and Santayana. A clarification of such affinities of Stevens's thought is important, I think, because the interpretation of his poetic gestures can be quite different according to the philosophical trend to which he is aligned. And the popularity of the opinion that phenomenology can be used to better understand Stevens makes it necessary that the demonstration of his closeness to pragmatism be done through fine discriminations between his practice and Heidegger's ideas.

Stevens manifested an uncommon interest in Heidegger, although he had only a limited acquaintance with the philosopher's work. A letter to Paule Vidal dated July 29, 1952, asks the latter anxiously about "a little work dealing with the poetry of the German poet Hölderlin" written by "Heidegger, the Swiss philosopher."[3] At a later date, another letter asks Peter H. Lee to look up Heidegger in Fribourg (*sic*): "If you attend any of his lectures, or even see him, tell me about him because it will help to make him real."[4] As Frank Kermode observed, "His knowledge of Heidegger seems scanty enough, more myth than reality. The only certain fact is that Stevens was mixing up the Swiss and German Freiburgs, which is why he used the French form of the name of the city and referred to Heidegger as Swiss. He can therefore have known nothing of the philosopher's brief tenure as the Nazi-appointed rector of Freiburg University. It is an odd mistake, if one reflects that Heidegger spent about as much time out of Germany as Stevens did out of the United States."[5]

Yet it is not difficult to guess why Stevens wanted Heidegger to be "real" to him, for in many ways, Stevens's poetry challenges the established notions of reality, knowledge, truth, and self/being as daringly as Heidegger's philosophy. The relation between the American poet and the German (not Swiss) philosopher has not been overlooked in criticism. Thomas Hines has used phenomenology as an essential instrument in analyzing Stevens's poetry.[6] Frank Kermode has drawn attention to the similarities between some of Stevens's theoretical formulations and Heidegger's philosophy, while Paul Bové has examined, in some detail, the parallels between Stevens's poetics and Heidegger's ideas about reality, knowledge, and self in *Being and Time*. Undoubtedly, Stevens has many affinities with Heidegger, and one could explore the similarity of their thinking, but since in the course of my argument the main emphasis has been on the action of the language, I shall focus here not on any philosophical ideas that may appear, in one form or another, in Stevens's poems but rather on the connection between certain conceptions about language developed by Heidegger, James, and

Santayana and Stevens's poetic practice, especially in those poems that may be considered philosophical.

The "little work" of Heidegger mentioned in the letter to Vidal was "Hölderlin and the Essence of Poetry," which was published in English translation in the collection *Existence and Being* in 1949. The essay starts with some questions about the nature of poetry. Through his characteristic hermeneutics, Heidegger proposes to reconcile two apparently contradictory remarks by Hölderlin—that poetry is the most innocent occupation and that language is man's most dangerous possession—and working toward that purpose, he evolves an original conception about language. Heidegger maintains that, contrary to general opinion, language is not just an instrument of communication and expression: "Language is a possession in a more fundamental sense. It is good for the fact that (i.e. it affords a guarantee that) man can *exist* historically. Language is not a tool at his disposal, rather it is that event which disposes of the supreme possibility of human existence."[7]

The notion of "historical" existence is developed in an extended comment on another line from Hölderlin that further reveals the nature of language. "Since we have been a conversation" means, in Heidegger's view, that human existence is dependent on speaking and listening to one another, and he argues that the possibility of perceiving time as present, past, and future arises against an idea of permanence that can be reached only in conversation. Historical existence means, for Heidegger, not only the connection to the past but also the ability to project oneself in the future. And it is language, as conversation, that makes existence possible and places being in history.

Since language seems to be the warrant of existence, one can legitimately ask who creates language. To this Heidegger's answer is, in Platonic fashion, the poet. As language becomes actual through the "harmless" occupation of the poet, poetry is revealed to be foundational of being: "The poet names the gods and names all things in that which they are. This naming does not consist merely in something already known being supplied with a name; it is rather that when the poet speaks the essential word, the existent is by this naming nominated as what it is. So it becomes known *as* existent. Poetry is the establishing of being by means of the word."[8] The claims Heidegger makes for poetry extend the meaning of that word from our common understanding of it as an aesthetic product to the larger sense of a general cultural activity—the building of a culture as opposed to an expression of it: "Poetry is the foundation which supports history, and therefore it is not a mere appearance of culture, and absolutely not the mere 'expression' of a 'culture-soul.'"[9]

The idea that poetry is foundational of being would appeal to any poet, but Stevens's affinity with Heidegger goes deeper than the satisfaction of having his profession validated on such high ground. The basis of that affinity lies in the way they both treat language. According to Heidegger's essay, language, being primarily a conversation, is directed not toward things, feelings, or ideas but toward other speakers.

The very being of mankind derives from the possibility of speaking to each other. The act of speaking is thus essential, because it brings human beings together. Since the conversation itself establishes existence, it cannot be said to reproduce or reflect something already existing. Consequently, when language is regarded as a conversation, the primary function habitually assigned to it—that of representing reality—becomes void, as reality originates in language itself. Such ideas—revolutionary in Heidegger's career—demolish with one stroke both the Platonic model of language, according to which the word corresponds to an idea, and the positivist one, according to which words represent things.

Most studies about Stevens and Heidegger have basically been concerned with the latter's philosophy of being and time, curiously leaving the question of language, which dominates his later work, aside.[10] To my mind, Stevens comes closest to the later Heidegger, who struggles to build up a conversational model of language. In Stevens's poems one can find a practical illustration of this conversational model, for his language seems to fail in what we consider to be its normal function: representation. The patterns of sound that dominate his verse, the numerous repetitions, and the musical path that meaning often takes in his poems are all part of a continuous struggle against the very concept of representation. And in many instances, the alternative to representation is indeed the dialogue, or conversation, as in "On the Road Home":

It was when I said,
"There is no such thing as the truth,"
That the grapes seemed fatter.
The fox ran out of his hole.

You . . . You said,
"There are many truths,
But they are not parts of a truth."
Then the tree, at night, began to change,

Smoking through green and smoking blue.
We were two figures in a wood.
We said we stood alone.

    [*CP* 203]

The very theme of this poem is the kind of debate about truth that would preoccupy a philosopher,[11] and it would seem that the participants in this conversation are as unsuccessful at representing their ideas as many of Stevens's speakers. Yet that failure does not rob the poem of significance, for as often happens in Stevens, the emphasis is transferred from what the two speak about to what their speech brings about. In this way, reality appears not to be found there, surrounding the speakers, but rather to result from the fact that they carry on their conversation. Their togetherness generates a reality in which their very existence becomes possible. Just as in Heidegger's argument, being *is* conversation.

In fact all Stevens's poems can be said to be conversational or dialogic to a large extent, for by discrediting the capacity of language to refer to a reality independent of the speakers' perceptions, they implicitly challenge the reader's expectation for a representation and thereby engage her in a dialogue. The poet carries on a conversation with his implied reader through a rhetoric that repeatedly elicits the reconsideration of the premises according to which a poem is perceived and understood. And through this "conversation" his poetry acquires originating powers and composes a new reality from a language that has been brought back to what looks like an origin. "The Glass of Water" (see analysis in the first chapter), for instance, demonstrates in an exemplary way how language, failing to refer precisely and objectively, can turn into a conversation and eventually become foundational of being.[12]

Naturally, the essay on Hölderlin is not the only work in which Heidegger's thought may seem inspiring for Stevens. A distrust of referential language surfaces also in the discussion of representation and poetry in "What Are Poets For?" Heidegger distinguishes there between a language used for the purpose of representation, which he connects with science, technology, and ultimately death, and the language of poetry. This differentiation should be interpreted, of course, in relation to his understanding of poetry as more than verse writing. In "The Origin of the Work of Art" poetry emerges as the essence of any creative and thoughtful activity, and every work of art can be considered, in that sense, poetry. Poetry is also the authentic state of language. While representational language obscures the thing and distances it from perception, the language of poetry remains authentic and is capable of disclosing truth. For Heidegger, the language of poetry does not mean a refinement of ordinary language; rather, ordinary language appears to be an overuse and a debasement of the poetic: "Everyday language is a forgotten and therefore used-up poem, from which there hardly resounds a call any longer."[13]

Authentic—that is, poetic—language is characterized by excess, for it does much more than signify: "Language is the precinct (*templum*), that is, the house of Being. The nature of language does not exhaust itself in signifying, nor is it merely something that has the character of sign or cipher. . . . This is why the return from the realm of objects and their representation into the innermost region of the heart's space can be accomplished, if anywhere, *only in this precinct*."[14] Language is again found to be essential to human existence, and its nonsignifying, nonrepresentational aspect appears to be the condition of being. As such, language acquires not only a certain independence from but also a kind of dominance over its speakers. "In its essence," says Heidegger, "language is neither expression nor an activity of man. Language speaks."[15]

The difference between the language of expression or representation and what Heidegger considers authentic language becomes evident in Stevens's poems, where language is often freed from its function of representing things or expressing feelings and can assert its independence. One could say that Stevens starts, most of the time, with a "used-up poem," which he eventually turns into genuine poetry in the sense Heidegger gives the word. "Of Mere Being" is a good example of such regeneration. The poem starts, like many others, with a failed representation, different perhaps only in that it is metaphorical from the start. The liberal use of metaphor proves that Stevens's quarrel is not with nonmetaphoric expression but with representational language in general, even when it is seemingly poetic:[16]

> The palm at the end of the mind,
> Beyond the last thought, rises
> In the bronze distance,
>
> A gold-feathered bird
> Sings in the palm, without human meaning,
> Without human feeling, a foreign song.[17]

This (somewhat narrative) beginning creates the expectation for a revelation of some moral that would increase our general knowledge. At the end of our mind is a palm, and in this palm a bird sings. This must have a meaning, must tell us something. Such expectation is even encouraged by a side commentary: "You know then that it is not the reason / That makes us happy or unhappy." Yet nothing is revealed in what follows. The image of the bird, on the other hand, becomes more convincing, more detailed, as does the image of the palm, which is no longer part of a metaphor but a plausible tree on the edge of something so vast that it must be called "space":

> The bird sings. Its feathers shine.
>
> The palm stands on the edge of space.
> The wind moves slowly in the branches.
> The bird's fire-fangled feathers dangle down.[18]

The purpose of creating a poetic, even philosophical, representation here is defeated by the language's movement toward its own fulfillment. The words seem to come back, asserting their own importance. They form an image already existing in language, for they are nothing but the usual way of speaking about palms or birds: the palm appears with its branches, because this is how we speak of palms; the bird with its feathers, because this is how we speak of birds. Such conventional associations subvert the speaker's intention to use the palm and the bird as metaphors. Language indeed speaks, and the poem's speaker simply listens, whether what is eventually spoken has meaning in the ordinary sense or not. For meaning results here from the tension between the accepted formulations and the speaker's desire for original ones, the latter being arrested and forced to return to the former but not without leaving the trace of their failing flight. This flight away from and return to the ordinary may be seen as a purification, through which language regains some of an original freshness. In Heidegger's terms, its estrangement is its way back to its origin.

Another Heideggerian way to look at such poetic gestures in Stevens would be to consider the speaker's relation to language. Language usually fails his speakers, who are normally confident in their mastery of it, and more than once, "the meaning escapes." The speaker's lack of control over meaning would seem to conform to Heidegger's idea that it is actually language that controls the speakers. According to Heidegger, the speakers' belief that they are in control destroys the authenticity, and therefore the poetry, of language:

> Man acts as though he were the shaper and master of language, while in fact language remains the master of man. When this relation of dominance gets inverted, man hits upon strange maneuvers. Language becomes the means of expression. As expression, language can decay into a mere medium for the printed word. That even in such employment of language we retain a concern for care in speaking is all to the good. But this alone will never help us to escape from the inversion of the true relation of dominance between language and man. For, strictly, it is language that speaks. Man first speaks when, and only when, he responds to language by listening to its appeal.[19]

Stevens's failed representations may appear as struggles between the speakers and language itself to establish dominance, and indeed their attempts at what Heidegger calls "expression" look like strange maneuvers. Yet eventually these speakers end by listening, and regardless of their manifest intention, language arranges itself in its own patterns of excess. To illustrate this apparent victory of language over the speaker, I will look at a poem whose title sounds as Heideggerian as "Of Mere Being": "Poetry Is a Destructive Force."[20]

That's what misery is,
Nothing to have at heart.
It is to have or nothing.

It is a thing to have,
A lion, an ox in his breast,
To feel it breathing there.

Corazon, stout dog,
Young ox, bow-legged bear,
He tastes its blood, not spit.

He is like a man
In the body of a violent beast.
Its muscles are his own . . .

The lion sleeps in the sun.
Its nose is on its paws.
It can kill a man.

[CP 192–93]

The initial statement has a decisive tone and momentarily seems clear: to have is the most important thing—misery means to have nothing. "At heart" poses some problems, however, because it modifies the meaning of "to have." "To have at heart" means to love, and if the speaker intends to talk about love, why does he then redefine his purpose by coming back to the sense of possession: "It is to have or nothing"? The speaker is here in a moment of crisis, since language clearly has escaped his control, while the literal and the figurative senses of his words have collapsed together in a rather contradictory statement. For barring the vulgarity of an equation between love and possession, which itself would clash with the poem's tone, one is left with no more than a contradiction.

As is usual for Stevens, the moment of crisis leads to the impulse to use metaphors in order to clarify expression. This may not be an especially poetic device, since even scientists resort to metaphors when things are hard to express, describe, or clarify. But even under such circumstances, Stevens's language takes an independent turn, for rather than clarifying the reference, the metaphors make it obscure, building upon each other in a maddening reversal of tenor and vehicle. Thus the man who wants to have the brave heart of a big animal becomes himself an animal, which in its turn is "like a man," and the significance of the image becomes at best ambiguous. The speaker is listening to language rather than trying to control it, but what does language say? Although it would be hard to define *what* it has revealed, the final image of the poem appears as clear as a revelation of truth of the kind Heidegger describes, the closer to his conception because it actually remains mysterious and strange.

It would thus seem that Heidegger's ideas about language and poetry can offer a means of interpreting Stevens's poetic gestures. But before deciding that his practice is genuinely Heideggerian, one must consider the importance that both James and Santayana gave language within a philosophy that was—radically in the case of James and more subtly in the case of Santayana—breaking with the rules of its own domain. Biographical details encourage us to believe that Stevens was much more familiar with their ideas than he was with the philosophy of Heidegger. Stevens was a student at Harvard while James and Santayana were teaching there. James's influence was felt, quite strongly, among all students interested in literature, and in spite of the fact that he never took a course with James, Stevens could not have been foreign to his ideas. In fact, in "*Harmonium* and William James" as well as in her book *Wallace Stevens and the Idealist Tradition*, Margaret Peterson[21] shows how James's plastic formulations of his pragmatic philosophy echo throughout Stevens's first volume of verse. According to her, one could use the texts by James as a gloss to the *Harmonium*. Stevens's indebtedness to pragmatism becomes evident in an article by Lyall Bush,[22] who demonstrates, against Leonard and Wharton, that Stevens's position is closer to James than to Nietzsche. Even more than William James, Santayana can be said to have been Stevens's mentor, since the two were personally acquainted and discussed matters concerning poetry. "To an Old Philosopher in Rome" is Stevens's expression of admiration for Santayana, and according to David P. Young, "Stevens owned everything that Santayana had published, and we may assume him capable of reading it closely."[23] It is no surprise, then, that both Santayana's ideas and his formulations echo in the later Stevens as often as James's do in the *Harmonium*. Margaret Peterson actually reveals his indebtedness to both philosophers but only insofar as the content of ideas is concerned.

The direct echoes seem to me less important, however, than the deeper formative influence that the innovative ideas about language promoted by James, and in different ways, by Santayana, exerted on the poet. In fact, the importance of Stevens's poetic experiment can become apparent only in this context, which allowed language to play a more and more important part among philosophical interests. The pragmatic perspective on reality, knowledge, and truth revealed some functions of language usually underplayed by classical philosophy. The view of language as appeal to the other and conversation with the other, which brings Stevens so close to Heidegger, may constitute a more direct inheritance from William James and George Santayana.

Unsystematic and largely polemic, James's remarks about knowledge, reality, and truth are still provocative today. James notes the transitional character of knowledge and the negotiable quality of "reality," and this subject leads him to the consideration of symbolic thought and language. The certainty of classic Western philosophical systems—relying either on a notion of reality as outstanding and independent of human perception or on a transcendental validation of the real and the true—is shattered by the necessity of verifying one's knowledge "against the neighbor's feeling," as James puts it, and by evidence that what is true is only what we all agree or believe is true. In such a context language, habitually considered only a means of representation, acquires a much more important role in the process of cognition. When he observes the lack of connection between the outstanding reality and our image of it, beyond a certain affinity with Heidegger, James sounds like an inspiration for the later Wittgenstein:

> In the whole field of symbolic thought we are universally held both to intend, to speak of, and to reach conclusions about—to know, in short—particular realities, without having in our subjective consciousness any mind-stuff that resembles them even in a remote degree. We are instructed about them by language which awakens no consciousness beyond its sound; and we know *which* realities they are by the faintest and most fragmentary glimpse of some remote context they may have and by no direct imagination of themselves.[24]

The importance of language in the process of cognition becomes clear here, as well as the fact that knowledge depends not on the language's relation to an outstanding reality but on context.

James's remarks on language may not attract much attention in his texts, which foreground the notions of knowledge, reality, and truth more than they speculate on the linguistic phenomenon. Yet they are essential to an understanding of his whole pragmatic enterprise. At the beginning of his career, James noticed how much the metaphysical systems rely on words—on a terminology that is actually taken for the answer to all the enigmas. Pragmatism was to do more than just invent a vocabulary; it was to verify its hypotheses in action and through practical results. In the later work, however, it becomes more and more apparent that the practical result depends on negotiations that take place in language, a nearly Heideggerian idea that, if not formulated by James himself, was to become attractive to Stevens.

But Stevens's way toward a theory of poetry as an essential activity of the mind goes through Santayana's inspirational passion for art. It should be noticed from the start that Santayana's aestheticism, which influenced Stevens's thought, is of a special kind, totally different from that of Pater or Arnold. As Frank Lentricchia observes, "For Santayana, aesthetic pleasure is a different kind of pleasure, and its difference lies in its teasing invitation to the very social being that Pater and genteel America had deliberately turned their backs on."[25] And it is to this relation between the aesthetic and the social that Wallace Stevens's poetics must be connected. For in rejecting a crude idea of direct involvement of poetry with social issues, Stevens writes in a language always positioned against current conventions or ideas, that is, always dependent on the reader's expectations. And his particular use of language responds, to a significant extent, to Santayana's view of language in general.

More than William James, Santayana concentrates his attention on language and its function. In *The Life of Reason,* he ascribes to language an evolution that originates in arbitrary but musically patterned sound. The relation between sounds and objects, feelings, or thoughts develops by association, language becoming attached to and enveloping its referent "as a cobweb might catch a fly, without destroying or changing it."[26] As if to pave the road for Foucault, Santayana distinguishes neatly between the "order of things" and the "order of discourse": "The object's quality passed to the word at the same time that the word's relations enveloped the object; and thus a new weight and significance was added to sound, previously nothing but a dull music. A conflict at once established itself between the drift proper to the verbal medium and that proper to the designated things; a conflict which the whole history of language and thought has exemplified and which continues to this day."[27]

The conflict that Santayana defines above fosters the independence of the two orders, and although language provides an organizational principle for the understanding and manipulation of reality, it remains mainly a means of exchange between people. For while language tends to be at odds with the continuous flux of things, it helps communication by imposing an order and by making the evanescent reality intelligible in human terms. Because they are always related to human activity, words make exchange possible between people and finally lead to an understanding of the "real" and the "true," which Santayana defines in terms that closely match the notions of William James and, in another anticipatory aspect, may also be related to Saussure: "What words add is not power of discernment or action, but a medium of intellectual exchange. Language is like money, without which specific relative values may well exist and be felt, but cannot be reduced to a common denominator. And as money should have a certain intrinsic value of its own in order that its relation to other values may be stable, so a word, by which a thing is represented in discourse, must be a part of that thing's contact with mankind."[28]

The emphasis that Santayana places on the "contact with mankind" relates to his discussion about sound. For him, the origin of language lies in what he describes as a kind of music. This "music" establishes relations between people on a primitive level, even before the relation between language and object (thing, feeling, thought) has been in any way developed. Sense grows out of music and appears as the fulfillment of a music, but that music does not desert language after sense has emerged; on the contrary, it always resides in language and accounts for its literary or poetic quality. Santayana thus sees the poetic not as the result of an evolution and sophistication of language but rather as the survival of its music. Both romantic and Heideggerian ideas about language's origins in poetry may fit in this picture, but Santayana insists less on the mythical origin of language, or on its strangeness, and more on the relations between speakers: music is transmissible, shared sound, arbitrary in relation to things, but conditioned by human interaction. This quality explains a certain excess in language, which often distances it from the objects it has to represent: "Language, while essentially significant viewed in its function, is indefinitely wasteful, being automatic and tentative in its origin. It overloads itself, and being primarily music, and a labyrinth of sounds, it develops an articulation and method of its own, which only in the end, and with much inexactness, reverts to its function of designation."[29]

Santayana's description of language could find no better practical illustration than the poems I have discussed above. For Stevens's language fails in its representational function because of excess, the overload of metaphors betraying its purpose. Stevens would often start his poems with a precise statement whose need of verification brings about this kind of overloading. Such excess works against an appetite for intelligibility and conclusiveness that language stimulates but cannot satisfy. Yet once the function of representation is abandoned, reality does not have to be renounced, since language can generate that which for us counts as real. Knowledge of reality is thus achieved in language, which, as William James described, "awakens no consciousness beyond its sound." To a certain extent, Santayana's ideas about the overloading of language correspond to Heidegger's description of its excess, and William James's notion that reality is given to us only in language may sound just like Heidegger's idea that existence starts in conversation.

Stevens's affinities with Heidegger result thus from some similarities with Heideggerian thought already present in James and Santayana, and such formative influences can also explain certain important differences. "The Glass of Water," which I fully analyzed in the first chapter, ends very far from where it began, saying something quite different from what it apparently intended to say. In Heidegger's terms, this amounts to an opening up of being: "in the centre of our lives, this time, this day." But the poem returns to concrete terms, to figural if not abstract representation: "this spring among the politicians / Playing cards." And while this sustains Santayana's view that language returns to its function of designation "with much inexactness," it seems to betray Heidegger. The image of politicians playing cards is, at best, a parody of the opening up of being that Heidegger imagines.

Equally puzzling for the Heideggerian interpretation of the poem is its last line: "One would continue to contend with one's ideas." The whole purpose of Heidegger's phenomenology is to put aside this kind of contention and to get at the "thingness of the thing." For by showing its conversational nature, Heidegger aims at attributing language a function of disclosure naturally superior to representation. That function is to bring forth the essence of being, since language has originating powers, whose strangeness makes it a "most dangerous possession." Stevens, on the other hand, like James and Santayana before him, is satisfied with the conversation, and that the contention with one's ideas is part of it becomes clear at the end of "The Poems of Our Climate," which debates the same questions as "The Glass of Water" but is more definitely community oriented:

> There would still remain the never-resting mind,
> So that one would want to escape, come back
> To what has been so long composed.
> The imperfect is our paradise.
> Note that, in this bitterness, delight,
> Since the imperfect is so hot in us,
> Lies in flawed words and stubborn sounds.
>
> [CP 194]

Stevens always comes back to what seemed to have been an imperfect language because *that* is the only language, *that* is the conversation. In most poems with a clear philosophical intent, what should be the poem's conclusion is a shared perception of reality, responding to William James's notion of knowledge and truth. "On the Road Home" insists on the presence of *two* speakers, which validates the reality growing out of their own speaking. The remarkable "Bouquet of Roses in Sunlight," a later and rather overlooked poem, explicitly defines reality as the product of shared perceptions. The poem centers, like many others that I have discussed before, on a description of things whose poignant reality seems to defeat the purpose of artistic representation. Leonard and Wharton[30] use it to demonstrate the dissolution of the dichotomy reality/

imagination, but I think that imagination is not the only issue here. The power of reality itself lies in a "sense" that is shared by the two people contemplating it:

> Our sense of these things changes and they change,
> Not as in metaphor, but in our sense
> Of them. So sense exceeds all metaphor.
>
> It exceeds the heavy changes of the light.
> It is like a flow of meanings with no speech
> And of as many meanings as of men.
>
> We are two that use these roses as we are,
> In seeing them. That is what makes them seem
> So far beyond the rhetorician's touch.
>
>   [CP 431]

There are many instances in Stevens's poetry when we have a sense of what Santayana means by saying that language overloads and "only in the end and with much inexactness reverts to its function of designation." Although the closeness to Heidegger is evident here, we can see that, in Santayana's view, the speaker can regain control. In fact, the very independence of language, the possibility that it should overload, derives from the fact that it is shared by many and not from Heideggerian strangeness. In "Poetry Is a Destructive Force" the overloading—the action of those forces latent in language but unattached to significance—works against the abstract expression, which suddenly becomes insufficient and evades its purpose in a kind of figuration, whose value as analogy is, at best, dubious. The intention to use analogy persists, in spite of the fact that its parallelism has been lost in the third stanza, where the metaphor's vehicle has obliterated its tenor altogether. But in a move characteristic of Stevens, the vehicle becomes the tenor and fulfills the desire for intelligibility on a totally different plane. Language reverts to sense indeed "with much inexactness," for the overwhelmingly clear image of the lion sleeping, with its pent-up violence ("It can kill a man"), has little if anything to do with the definition of misery attempted at the beginning. Yet it does fit the poem's apparently arbitrary title, for the poem indeed destructs its own statement and becomes possible only as an unexpected intelligence superior to the logic of the statement's initial formulation. The language behaves here in accord with Santayana's description, as it escapes the speaker's intention and does not attach itself to things but late and inadvertently. Language appears to act of its own accord, but although it disobeys the speaker's intentions, it preserves intentionality and the bond with other speakers. The similarity of the lion's image with that of the "fire-fangled" bird at the end of "Of Mere Being" shows that Stevens did not aspire to (or if he did, he never did reach) revelations of the essence of things. As Frank Kermode remarks, "Like Heidegger [Stevens] thought of poetry as a renovation of experience;

unlike him, he thought that the truth in the end did not matter."[31] What his poems do reveal is the fact that whatever is said in language is meaningful only when or if it is shared by others.

The Heideggerian illusion of the origin, too, is absent in Stevens. This absence may explain why Heidegger's ideal image of the poet as communicator with the gods does not quite fit Stevens, who is content to demonstrate that language has been overused and to show ways for its regeneration without seeking any absolute origin and without totally renouncing its everyday use. His attention to the reader's demands never flags, and this shows his awareness that without the participation of the reader his poems may lose their own reality. Stevens's emphasis is, therefore, not so much on language as on the *speaking* of the language, on the conversation between people. But conversation ceases to be important toward the end of Heidegger's argument in "Hölderlin and the Essence of Poetry," for instance, where his archetypal poet converses with the gods rather than with his fellow human beings. Actually, the emphasis on the "conversation of mankind" disappears altogether in Heidegger's later essays on language and poetry, whereas it remains consistent in Stevens. Stevens can thus be said to have some affinities with Heidegger only insofar as Heidegger had some affinities with the American philosophers.

The importance attached to language in the description of human interaction does indeed relate American thought to what may be called the linguistic turn in European philosophy—a series of arguments continuing with variations from Nietzsche, to Heidegger, to contemporary French theorists. But the American philosophers differ in essential ways from Nietzsche or Heidegger. As Richard Rorty explains: "They wrote, as Nietzsche and Heidegger did not, in a spirit of social hope. They asked us to liberate our new civilization by giving up the notion of 'grounding' our culture, our moral lives, our politics, our religious beliefs, upon 'philosophical bases.'"[32] Both James's frank reliance on the verification in practical results and Santayana's optimistic aestheticism lack the disappointment underlying the European culture's discovery that its foundations were constructed within itself and had no natural or transcendental warrant.

For the American philosophers, to discover the cultural (as opposed to natural or transcendental) foundation of values was a means of legitimation, in a relatively new culture still seeking to establish itself; whereas for the European philosophers, the same discovery meant a loss of legitimacy, in a traditional culture whose values had long been claimed as universal. Language acquired a special importance for all the philosophers who lost confidence in absolute values and discovered the culturally constructed basis of "reality." But while for the European philosophers language seems to become an independent force that both overwhelms and paralyzes human will, for the Americans language remains dependent on its speakers, and the emphasis on its working is an emphasis on community.

Although all his poetic endeavor is an experiment within the linguistic medium,

Stevens does not conceive of being as originating exclusively in language. In a letter to Delmore Schwartz dated April 6, 1948, Stevens clarifies, for the critic's benefit, his idea of poetic experiment, which he finds inextricable from experience: "The poet records his experience as poet in subjects and words which are part of that experience. . . . Experiment in respect to subjects and words is the effort on his part to record the truth of that experience."[33] In true pragmatic spirit, Stevens counts the experience of words as life experience responding to James's view that perception is always mediated by language. Santayana's special brand of aestheticism also surfaces in the same letter: "So, too, experiment in form is one of the constants of the spirit."[34] It is from James's pragmatism and through Santayana's aestheticism that Stevens progressed toward a concept of poetic language that contains the capacity to "make a profound difference in our sense of the world."[35] Seeing Stevens as a descendant of pragmatism rather than as a deconstructionist avant la lettre[36] may help us realize that his poems are not haunted by epistemological skepticism,[37] but they simply put epistemology aside to deal with the more important task of sharing the language and its beauty.

Stevens's experimentation embraces many aspects of language ranging from rhetoric to grammar, and to generic conventions, which have been duly addressed by criticism. His experimentation with sound, however, stands out not only because, in poetry, sound has always been considered a basic element but also because the "image of sound" is his main instrument in creating a discursive transformation that in itself promotes poetry's function in the community. Paradoxically, the alienating extravagance of his language mobilizes our reading energies toward a search for significance that ultimately leads to self-discovery. Instead of a conventionally constituted poetic discourse, Stevens offers his readers a discourse in the making, an exploratory language, in which sense is never settled but is permanently nascent and therefore subject to negotiation with the reader. Because the beauty of this discourse lies in its transitional quality, in its departure from what is established and conventional, it is rather difficult to imagine the final form it strives to attain. This language of tendencies cannot disclose that toward which it tends, whether that be a distillation projected in the future or the recovery of an unknown and unknowable past.

Because of its fluidity, his poetry generates ideas that would normally be considered philosophical, and it is indeed based on a philosophy, even if it is a nonconformist one and opposed to its own tradition. In this sense, all Stevens's poems are philosophical and not only the late, longer poems, which are usually recognized as such. It would be a mistake, I think, to consider Stevens's late poems as the achievement of the kind of poetry that he always struggled to write. Experimentation is, for Stevens, a permanent state of poetry, pertaining to its nature, and not an activity aiming at a certain result. Stevens's poetry, competing as it does with philosophy on the higher grounds of thought, does not mimic the work of a philosopher. His poetic work does not dash toward the fulfillment of a goal, and its total shape does not amount to a fully rounded body of ideas as a philosophical system would. For the challenge his poetics presents to philosophy is not of a systematic nature but is directed against the very idea of system. The pattern of his own early poems is the pattern of his entire oeuvre, and his work finds its fulfillment at the limit that will qualify it as "real"—in repetition.

Characteristic of his later work are the longer poems that, while offering a boon of aphoristic phrasings, are hard to interpret as unities. James Longenbach writes: "Stevens' longer poems were . . . successions of shorter poems; but over time, a sequence of poems became easier (and paradoxically less ambitious) for Stevens to write: endlessly elaborating a poetic donnée allowed Stevens the luxury of avoiding the question he first asked in "First Warmth"; it allowed him to sustain a hovering poetic vision that occluded the possibility of interrogating the vision's principles."[38]

Such poems obviously lack the narrative backbone that, although narrative convention is rejected and parodied, keeps together "The Comedian as the Letter C." Thematic unity may be discernible in some poems, like "Notes toward a Supreme Fiction," but basically the later long poems function as micro collections, in which slight similarities of pattern and a vague thematic resemblance are the only signs of unity. Such poems do not appear definitive, and they may seem conclusive of Stevens's work only in that they repeat his strategies in an exercise of intelligence, whose acceptance among readers the poet now feels entitled to take for granted.

The quality of exercise as opposed to experiment is evident in a poem that Stevens might have conceived beyond any desire to establish foundations. The title of this poem, "Description Without Place," is contrary to a notion inherited by Stevens from Santayana: that a culture defines itself through its place. And it is hard to believe that this poet, who constantly connects existence to places, real, imagined, or simply invented, could decide upon such a title. The title itself proclaims the independence of language and its power to create rather than represent the real, for it violates not only Stevens's own conviction that "a mythology reflects its region" but also the more commonly held belief that a description presupposes a place, that is, a space where there would be things to describe. But such initiative to violate convention is not new for Stevens, and the very defiance, which the title gestures, is muted by a sleight mannerism and self-pastiche.

The poem as a whole contains so many of Stevens's poetic devices, by now quite familiar, that it may disappoint his habitual readers. Helen Vendler, for instance, although she dedicates a substantial portion of *On Extended Wings* to the poem, finds it "childish and repetitive whether so intended or not."[39] Vendler's description of the first part of the poem actually matches some criticism of Stevens's early poems voiced by others, and indeed its repetitiveness, which Vendler finds less than desirable, bears Stevens's trademark:[40]

It is possible that to seem—it is to be,
As the sun is something seeming and it is.

The sun is an example. What it seems
It is and in such seeming all things are.

Thus things are like a seeming of the sun
Or like the seeming of the moon or night

Or sleep. It was a queen that made it seem
By the illustrious nothing of her name.

Her green mind made the world around her green.
The queen is an example . . . This green queen

In the seeming of the summer of her sun
By her own seeming made the summer change.

In the golden vacancy she came, and comes,
And seems to be on the saying of her name.

Her time becomes again, as it became,
The crown and week-day coronal of her fame.
        [CP 339]

Like many of Stevens's earlier poems, the first section starts with a quasi-theoretical statement, whose simplicity and clarity is gradually obscured by repetitions. Repetitions only attract attention to the fact that the simple statement is not simple to make.
In fact, under analysis the statement seems to be manipulated toward doubt rather than
certainty. For instance, in the opening, "to be" is directly opposed to "to seem," but
the opposition is governed by a condescending suspicion and by some doubt implied
in the cautious "it is possible." This pattern should be more than familiar to Stevens's
reader. The abstract discourse, which seems the poet's choice at the start, cannot be
sustained, and the argumentative stance is undermined by its very sources of evidence. As irrelevancies accumulate, they throw doubt on the very existence of the
essential. This is language overloading, as Santayana would say, a language that makes
one agree with Heidegger that its nature "does not exhaust itself in signifying, nor is it
merely something that has the character of sign or cipher."[41] And as the language reveals its nonsignificant aspect, the abstract becomes concrete, the logical degenerates
into the analogical, and metaphors begin to proliferate.

From the third couplet on, the thesis is lost in its own illustrations, for the examples
are more vivid than the principle they support, and their relevance becomes secondary
to their sheer presence. As usual in Stevens, the vividness of the concrete example, as
well as the pregnancy of the images, results from the pattern of sound, which establishes the limits necessary for foundations where there are none. In the second section
of the poem, it becomes evident that repetition is the only way of confining the dan-

gerous expansion to which exemplification can lead the poem. For it is repetition that on the one hand contains the irrelevancies and on the other endows the poem with an equivalent of conclusiveness.

From the third section on, there is a change of pace noticed by Vendler, a change that is determined, as I see it, not so much by the adoption of a different manner as by the fact that mannerism itself comes to some fruition here and achieves its purpose. Consolidated by repetition, the "argument" allows for more appropriate illustration here, and it is even permitted to advance in its own theoretical way. There are moments like this in Stevens when the poet earns his right to statement, and it is remarkable that in such instances, he describes, with uncanny accuracy, exactly what he is doing:

There might be, too, a change immenser than
A poet's metaphors in which being would

Come true, a point in the fire of music where
Dazzle yields to a clarity and we observe,

And observing is completing and we are content,
In a world that shrinks to an immediate whole,

That we do not need to understand, complete
Without secret arrangements of it in the mind.

[CP 341]

The poem, however, does not give up either its pattern or its mannerisms; it continues in the way it started, every section attempting to state things unequivocally and deflecting that attempt in an agglomeration of examples, concrete illustrations whose concreteness becomes a purpose in itself. The desire to approach the truth leads not toward but away from reality into the indefinite and infinite realm of fictions. Reality appears as a multitude of "seemings" changing with the change of its observers:

Things are as they seemed to Calvin or to Anne
Of England, to Pablo Neruda in Ceylon,

To Nietzsche in Basel, to Lenin by a lake.
But the integrations of the past are like

A *Museo Olimpico,* so much
So little, our affair, which is the affair

Of the possible: seemings that are to be,
Seemings that it is possible may be.

[CP 341–42]

As part of what is usually ascribed to the domain of the real, history presents a special challenge to Stevens. The use of history by modernist poets served the purpose of reviving a sense of cultural identity. In considering Santayana's influence on modernism, Frank Lentricchia notices his injunction to use history, which seems to have been obeyed by major modernists like Pound, Eliot, Williams: "The modernist poet of philosophical ambition will therefore need to revivify in his search for relevance what Santayana calls the topographical sense. His writing will need to 'swarm with proper names and allusion to history and fable.'"[42] Stevens is never so obvious in handling history, although he does have the topographical sense required by Santayana. His sense of place and character is, however, colored by an awareness that history, with its places and characters, is part of the fiction we believe in and live by, the fiction of which he spoke in "Adagia": "The final belief is to believe in a fiction, which you know to be a fiction, there being nothing else. The exquisite truth is to know that it is a fiction and that you believe in it willingly."[43] The way Stevens introduces historical figures in "Description Without Place" demonstrates his commitment to this fiction, the kind of fiction that fosters and justifies belief. For Nietzsche and Lenin appear in the poem neither as representations of their historical counterparts nor as fictional versions of themselves but as part of an ongoing fiction that contains them. They belong to a distinctly American consciousness that amalgamates an imagined Basel with half-understood philosophical statements ("Nietzsche in Basel studied the deep pool / Of these discolorations") and associates the rather obsessive image of the most famous revolutionist with the graceful image of the swans, obviously derived from Tchaikovsky's ballet ("Lenin on a bench beside a lake disturbed / The swans"). Nietzsche's Switzerland and Lenin's Russia, as they stand in the poem, are places in the American mind, designated by faded associations so obviously lacking in specific detail that the description seems indeed without place. Stevens does not have to fictionalize them, because they have already been fictionalized as they have penetrated the culture and the individual consciousness.

The fictionalizing process, which develops collectively, renders history a creation of the mind, and the beginning of the fifth section confirms the idea that everything in the poem belongs to "the spirit's universe." But besides this confirmation, the section revives the attempt to formulate the thesis of the poem, which is already contained in its title, in abstract terms. The attempt is sustained for a while and then deflected again in a movement characteristic of Stevens. The success in creating abstraction, however, may be greater here than in other poems, and this disappoints Helen Vendler: "'Description without Place' is Stevens at his most impersonal, his most logical, his most 'objective,' his most theoretical."[44]

The remark may seem rather curious, because the poem's logic is not at all apparent, and Vendler herself is not able to explain its theory. "Impersonal," "logical," "objective," and "theoretical" are adjectives more suitable for the poem's language, diction, and grammar than for its outcome. For the poem is not the argument, which does not quite achieve itself, but a demonstration of the futility of any abstract argument. Its thesis is indeed "the thesis of the plentifulest John," because it does not only state that reality is made of words but, against the reader's resistance to that eccentric statement, makes the words, the description, more powerful than the (missing) place. The poem thus deliberately deploys the decentering powers of the language and points to the significance of all that one habitually considers insignificant, and in that aspect it lives up to Stevens's standard.

While "Description Without Place" may not be Stevens's best among his later, longer poems, it fairly illustrates his development from an extravagant experimentalist to a more self-assured master who allows himself to fall back on his manner and to rely on the reader's full cooperation. In fact, the classification of the poems as early and late may create an excessively simplified image of Stevens's work. Toward the end of his career, he frequently returned to the short form and some of the later poems can be as fresh and exciting as the best of his early ones. One would perhaps be better advised to differentiate between poems that betray the reader's expectations and poems that are directed toward an expectation of such betrayal, poems where the sense of novelty prevails and poems that make us tolerate a certain mannerism based on that sense. In a way, if in the latter the poet is old, in the former he is new rather than young, a dubious characterization anyway for someone who started publishing so late in his life.

Throughout Stevens's career the preoccupation with the definition of his own art, based on inspiration from James and Santayana and conducted in a nearly Heideggerian spirit, found its expression in his technical innovations, and his use of sound pattern to give discourse its movement toward self-transcendence remains consistent. And while it is not the single technical aspect of his poetry intimately related to its meaning, the sound effect or sound image, as I have called it, reveals Stevens's thinking in one of its most important aspects, and

> It matters, because everything we say
> Of the past is a description without place, a cast
>
> Of the imagination, made in sound
> [CP 345–46]

The figure of sound looms large in Stevens's rhetoric, and its almost obsessive recurrence in both his poems and his essays or letters encourages one to believe that his manipulation of language away from referring or representing and toward "sounding" was as important to him as it is, or should be, to his readers. Without considering the metaphysics of sound, which my readings have, however partially, revealed, one may take his verbal actions for so many destructive, or rather deconstructive, gestures. But deconstruction—and I refer here to the philosophical concept as it has evolved since Derrida and not necessarily to a particular brand of criticism—can explain

Stevens's performance only halfway. For if he is indeed skeptical about the absolute truths and values of tradition, and if he tends to place all significance in the fluid domain of language, he also attracts attention to the shared quality of that domain. The excess of his language constitutes the medium in which the necessary chemistry, which produces the self from utter otherness and then returns it to the other, is allowed to perform its mysterious reactions. His poems may lead us to believe that everything exists in language indeed, but they also prove that language depends on the act of speaking, and above all, on its speakers.

Notes

Preface

1. In her book *Stanza My Stone: Wallace Stevens and the Hermetic Tradition* (West Lafayette, Ind.: Purdue University Press, 1983), Leonora Woodman suggests another definition of "harmonium" derived from the hermetic tradition. The suggestion is quite appealing and appropriate as a description of Stevens's opus; however, it does not disprove my point here, since her definition is even more esoteric and less available to anyone but a scholar of Stevens than the dictionary definition that describes a musical instrument.

2. Richard Poirier, *Poetry and Pragmatism* (Cambridge, Mass.: Harvard University Press, 1992), 148.

1. Sound and Language

1. Paul Fussell, *Poetic Meter and Poetic Form* (New York: Random House, 1966), 91 (my emphasis).

2. See Ann Goodman, "Phonological Aspects of Metaphor in Anglo-American Poetry," *Sigma: Revue du Centre d'Études Linguistiques d'Aix Montpellier* 6 (1982): 109–21, and Marie Borroff, *The Language and the Poet: Verbal Artistry in Frost, Stevens, and Moore* (Chicago: University of Chicago Press, 1979).

3. See Margaret Dickie, "Collections of Sound in Wallace Stevens," *Wallace Stevens Journal* 15(2) (Fall 1991): 133–43 and *Lyric Contingencies: Emily Dickinson and Wallace Stevens* (Philadelphia: University of Pennsylvania Press, 1991).

4. See Adelyn Dougherty, "Structures of Sound in Wallace Stevens's 'Farewell to Florida,'" *Texas Studies in Literature and Language* 16 (1975): 755–64.

5. See Diane Wakoski, "A Poet's Odyssey from Shakespearean Sonnets to Stevens' Not-So-Blank Verse," *Wallace Stevens Journal* 15(2) (Fall 1991): 126–32, and Dennis Taylor, "The Apparitional Meters of Wallace Stevens," *Wallace Stevens Journal* 15(2) (Fall 1991): 209–28.

6. See Harvey Gross, *Sound and Form in Modern Poetry* (Ann Arbor: University of Michigan Press, 1968).

7. See James Guetti, *Word-Music: The Aesthetic Aspect of Narrative Fiction* (New Brunswick, N.J.: Rutgers University Press, 1980).

8. See Roger Ramsey, "Sound and Music: Stevens' *Harmonium*," *Contemporary Poetry: A Journal of Criticism* 2(3) (1977): 67–74, and John Hollander, "The Sound of the Music of Music and Sound," in *Wallace Stevens: A Celebration*, ed. Frank Doggett and Robert Buttel (Princeton: Princeton University Press, 1980), 235–55.

9. See Alison Rieke, "Stevens' Armchair Travel: The Sound of the Foreign," *Wallace Stevens Journal* 15(2) (Fall 1991): 165–77, and *The Senses of Nonsense* (Iowa City: University of Iowa Press, 1992), 93–156.

10. See Marie Borroff, *Language and the Poet* (Chicago: University of Chicago Press, 1979), 42–79.

11. See Dougherty, "Structures of Sound," 755.

12. Charles Altieri, "Why Stevens Must Be Abstract; or, What a Poet Can Learn from Painting," in *Wallace Stevens: The Poetics of Modernism*, ed. Albert Gelpi (Cambridge: Cambridge University Press, 1985), 89–120, offers an analysis of some of Stevens's poems that discovers his philosophical thought

in grammar and stylistic devices. Sound is one of the devices that can change the meaning apparent in semantics.

13. Kevin Barry, *Language, Music, and the Sign: A Study in Aesthetics, Poetics, and Poetic Practice from Collins to Coleridge* (Cambridge: Cambridge University Press, 1987), 183.

14. Joseph Riddel, *The Clairvoyant Eye: The Poetry and Poetics of Wallace Stevens* (Baton Rouge: Louisiana State University Press, 1965).

15. Joseph Riddel, "Metaphoric Staging: Stevens' Beginning Again of 'The End of the Book,'" in Doggett and Buttel, *A Celebration*, 308–38; J. Hillis Miller, "Theoretical and Atheoretical Stevens," in Doggett and Buttel, *A Celebration*, 274–85; Paul A. Bové, *Destructive Poetics: Heidegger and American Poetry* (New York: Columbia University Press, 1980).

16. Frank Lentricchia, *Ariel and the Police: Michel Foucault, William James, Wallace Stevens* (Madison: University of Wisconsin Press, 1988). See also Alan Filreis, *Wallace Stevens and the Actual World* (Princeton: Princeton University Press, 1991), and James Longenbach, *Wallace Stevens and the Plain Sense of Things* (New York: Oxford University Press, 1991).

17. Jacqueline Vaught Brogan, *Stevens and Simile: A Theory of Language* (Princeton: Princeton University Press, 1986).

18. Ibid., ix.

19. Gerald L. Bruns, "Stevens Without Epistemology," in *Wallace Stevens: The Poetics of Modernism,* ed. Albert Gelpi (Cambridge: Cambridge University Press, 1985), 30.

20. Richard Rorty, *Consequences of Pragmatism* (Minneapolis: University of Minnesota Press, 1982), xvi.

21. Thomas Grey, *The Wallace Stevens Case: Law and the Practice of Poetry* (Cambridge, Mass.: Harvard University Press, 1991), 37.

22. Ludwig Wittgenstein, *Philosophical Investigations,* trans. G. E. M. Anscombe, 3d ed. (New York: Macmillan, 1966); John Searle, *Speech Acts: An Essay in the Philosophy of Language* (Cambridge: Cambridge University Press, 1969); Paul Grice, *Studies in the Way of Words* (Cambridge, Mass.: Harvard University Press, 1989); Richard Rorty, *Consequences of Pragmatism: Essays, 1972–1980* (Minneapolis: University of Minnesota Press, 1982).

23. Steven Levinson, *Pragmatics* (Cambridge: Cambridge University Press, 1984).

24. See Dominick LaCapra, *Rethinking Intellectual History: Texts, Contexts, Language* (Ithaca, N.Y.: Cornell University Press, 1983).

25. Michel Foucault, *The Order of Things: An Archeology of Human Sciences* (New York: Pantheon Books, 1971; reprint, New York: Vintage, 1973), 208.

26. Timothy J. Reiss, *The Uncertainty of Analysis: Problems in Truth, Meaning, and Culture* (Ithaca, N.Y.: Cornell University Press, 1988).

27. Grey, *The Wallace Stevens Case,* 37.

28. Foucault, *The Order of Things,* 300.

29. Mikhail Bakhtin, *The Dialogic Imagination,* ed. Michael Holquist, trans. Caryl Emerson and Michael Holquist (Austin: University of Texas Press, 1981), 271–72.

30. Ibid., 283.

31. Margaret Peterson, *Wallace Stevens and the Idealist Tradition* (Ann Arbor: UMI Research Press, 1983), 7–8.

32. Grey, *The Wallace Stevens Case.*

33. Thomas J. Hines, *The Later Poetry of Wallace Stevens: Phenomenological Parallels with Husserl and Heidegger* (Lewisburg, Pa.: Bucknell University Press, 1976).

34. Wallace Stevens, *The Collected Poems* (New York: Knopf, 1954; reprint, New York: Vintage, 1990), 392. All subsequent quotations from the poems in this edition will be indicated by the abbreviation *CP* throughout the book.

35. Recently, Glen MacLeod has discovered a possible literal meaning for the lion. His book *Wallace Stevens and Modern Art: From the Armory Show to Abstract Expressionism* (New Haven: Yale University Press, 1993), features photographs of two "Netherlandish, 17 century" goblets decorated

with drawings of lions (89). Stevens might have seen the pictures of the goblets in an art magazine. But if the goblets indeed occasioned Stevens's poem, one cannot reduce the poem's meaning to the source of the poet's inspiration. Stevens could not count on his readers' familiarity with the glasses—on the contrary, he seems to count on their ignorance, if the poem is to have any aesthetic value at all.

36. Leonard B. Meyer, *Emotion and Meaning in Music* (Chicago: University of Chicago Press, 1956); Wilson Coker, *Music and Meaning: A Theoretical Introduction to Musical Aesthetics* (New York: Macmillan, 1972).

37. Coker, *Music and Meaning*, 60.

38. See Meyer, *Emotion and Meaning in Music*, 22–42.

39. Lawrence Kramer, *Music as Cultural Practice, 1800–1900* (Berkeley: University of California Press, 1990).

40. Meyer, *Emotion and Meaning in Music*, 42.

41. Barry, *Language, Music, and the Sign*, 104.

42. Ibid., 2.

43. Ibid., 179.

44. See Roland Barthes, *Image, Music, Text,* trans. Stephen Heath (New York: Hill & Wang, 1977).

45. See Julia Kristeva, *The Revolution of Poetic Language,* trans. Margaret Waller (New York: Columbia University Press, 1984).

46. Garrett Stewart, *Reading Voices: Literature and the Phonotext* (Berkeley: University of California Press, 1990).

47. Milman Parry, *The Making of Homeric Verse: The Collected Papers of Milman Parry,* ed. Adam Parry (Oxford: Clarendon Press, 1971).

48. Albert Lord, *The Singer of Tales* (Cambridge, Mass.: Harvard University Press, 1960).

49. Walter J. Ong, *Orality and Literacy: The Technologizing of the Word* (New York: Methuen, 1982).

50. Ibid., 85.

2. Sound and Poetry

1. Jacques Derrida, *Of Grammatology,* trans. Gayatri Chakravorty Spivak (Baltimore: John Hopkins University Press, 1976).

2. Richard Poirier, *Poetry and Pragmatism* (Cambridge, Mass.: Harvard University Press, 1992), 150.

3. John Hollander, *Melodious Guile: Fictive Pattern in Poetic Language* (New Haven: Yale University Press, 1988).

4. Michel Foucault, *Language, Counter-Memory, Practice,* trans. Donald F. Bouchard and Sherry Simmons, ed. Donald F. Bouchard (Ithaca, N.Y.: Cornell University Press, 1977), 174.

5. Robert Frost, *Poetry and Prose,* ed. Edward Connery Lathem and Lawrence Thomson (New York: Holt, Rinehart & Winston, 1984), 256.

6. Wallace Stevens, *The Necessary Angel: Essays on Reality and the Imagination* (New York: Knopf, 1942; reprint, New York: Vintage, 1951), 32.

7. Richard Rodriguez, *Hunger of Memory: The Education of Richard Rodriguez: An Autobiography* (Boston: David R. Godine, 1983; reprint, New York: Bantam, 1988), 16.

8. Ibid., 22.

9. Poirier, *Poetry and Pragmatism*, 142.

10. Frost, *Poetry and Prose*, 257.

11. Ibid., 253.

12. Ludwig Wittgenstein, *Philosophical Investigations,* trans. G. E. M. Anscombe, 3d ed. (New York: Macmillan, 1966), #527.

13. Gerald Bruns, "Stevens Without Epistemology," in *Wallace Stevens: The Poetics of Modernism,* ed. Albert Gelpi (Cambridge: Cambridge University Press, 1985), 26.

14. Martin Heidegger, *Being and Time,* trans. John Macquarrie and Edward Robinson (New York: Harper & Row, 1962), 206.

15. Frost, *Poetry and Prose,* 253.

16. Wittgenstein, *Philosophical Investigations,* #337.

17. Frost, *Poetry and Prose,* 251.

18. Ibid., 251–52.

19. Margerie Sabin, "The Fate of the Frost Speaker," *Raritan* 2 (Fall 1982): 133.

20. See Eleanor Cook, "From Etymology to Paronomasia: Wallace Stevens, Elizabeth Bishop, and Others," *Connotations* 2(1) (1992): 34–51.

21. William Pritchard, *The Lives of the Modern Poets* (New York: Oxford University Press, 1980), 217.

22. Stevens, *The Necessary Angel,* 125–26.

23. Wallace Stevens, *Opus Posthumous* (New York: Knopf, 1980; reprint, New York: Vintage, 1982), 217.

24. Margaret Peterson in *Wallace Stevens and the Idealist Tradition* (Ann Arbor: UMI Research Press, 1983) comments that "by irrational, Stevens apparently means all that is subjective, and hence for Stevens inexplicable in poetry—the definition is typically vague" (10). This interpretation is hardly justified by the contents of the essay and would contradict Stevens's view of the subject/object dichotomy, which Peterson herself sees as being dissolved in Stevens.

25. Stevens, *Opus Posthumous,* 226.

26. Stevens, *The Necessary Angel,* 46.

27. Ibid., 45.

28. Ibid., 59.

29. See Peterson, *Wallace Stevens and the Idealist Tradition.*

30. See J. B. Leggett, *Wallace Stevens and Poetic Theory: Conceiving the Supreme Fiction* (Chapel Hill: University of North Carolina Press, 1987).

31. Stevens, *The Necessary Angel,* 165.

32. Ibid., 28.

33. Ibid., 150.

34. Stevens, *Opus Posthumous,* 183.

35. Ibid., 199.

36. Ibid., 200.

37. Ibid., 201.

38. Stevens, *The Necessary Angel,* 14.

39. Poirier, *Poetry and Pragmatism,* 159.

40. Stevens, *The Necessary Angel,* 32.

41. Ibid., 138.

42. Ibid., 32.

43. Ibid., 33.

44. Ibid., 163.

45. Ibid., 32.

46. Ibid.

47. Ibid.

48. See the discussion about the "femininity" of poetry in Frank Lentricchia, *Ariel and the Police: Michel Foucault, William James, Wallace Stevens* (Madison: University of Wisconsin Press, 1988).

49. Stevens, *The Necessary Angel,* 29.

3. Sense, Nonsense, and the Magic Word

1. Randall Jarrell, "Reflections on Wallace Stevens," *Partisan Review* 18 (1952), reprinted in *Wallace Stevens: A Critical Anthology,* ed. Irvin Ehrenpreis (Baltimore: Penguin Books, 1972), 199–210.

2. R. P. Blackmur, "Examples of Wallace Stevens," *Hound and Horn* 5 (1932), reprinted in *Wallace Stevens: A Critical Anthology*, ed. Ehrenpreis, 59–86.

3. J. Hillis Miller, *Poets of Reality: Six Twentieth Century Writers* (Forge Village, Mass.: Harvard University Press, 1965; reprint, New York: Atheneum, 1974), 252.

4. J. B. Leggett, *Wallace Stevens and Poetic Theory: Conceiving the Supreme Fiction* (Chapel Hill: University of North Carolina Press, 1987), 119–20.

5. Alison Rieke, *The Senses of Nonsense* (Iowa City: University of Iowa Press, 1992), 95.

6. Eleanor Cook, *Poetry, Word-Play, and Word-War in Wallace Stevens* (Princeton: Princeton University Press, 1988), 17.

7. Ibid., 16–17.

8. Jacqueline Brogan, *Stevens and Simile: A Theory of Language* (Princeton: Princeton University Press, 1986), 60.

9. Leonora Woodman, *Stanza My Stone: Wallace Stevens and the Hermetic Tradition* (West Lafayette, Ind.: Purdue University Press, 1983), 77.

10. Stevens's racism, of which there are proofs both in his poems and in the description of his behavior by contemporaries, is not of an aggressive nature—nothing resembling the attitude of extremists in his time. He does take the derogatory terms that designate African Americans for granted and never questions their effect on other people. Peter Brazeau in *Parts of a World: Wallace Stevens Remembered: An Oral Biography* (New York: Random House, 1983) collected testimony about Stevens's indifference to I. L. Salomon's remark that the title of "Like Decorations in a Nigger Cemetery" was offensive (133) as well as about the casualness with which the poet called Gwendolyn Brooks a "coon" (196). John Rogers (later a professor of black history at the University of Hartford), however, remembered Stevens as having behaved respectfully and deferentially to Rogers, who worked in the same office as a "manservant."

11. William H. Pritchard, *Lives of the Modern Poets* (New York: Oxford University Press, 1980), 216.

12. J. S. Leonard and C. E. Wharton, *The Fluent Mundo: Wallace Stevens and the Structure of Reality* (Athens: University of Georgia Press, 1988), 115.

13. Frank Kermode, "'Harmonium': Wallace Stevens," in *Wallace Stevens: A Critical Anthology*, ed. Ehrenpreis, 235.

14. Bronislaw Malinowski, *Argonauts of the Western Pacific* (New York: E. P. Dutton, 1961), 432.

15. See Susan Stewart, *Nonsense: Aspects of Intertextuality in Folklore and Literature* (Baltimore: Johns Hopkins University Press, 1979).

16. Samuel French Morse, *Wallace Stevens: Life as Poetry* (New York: Western Publishing, 1970), 90.

17. See Yvor Winters's criticism of Stanley P. Chase and Howard Baker in "Wallace Stevens; or, the Hedonist's Progress" (1943), reprinted in *Wallace Stevens: A Critical Anthology*, ed. Ehrenpreis, 120–42.

18. Roy Harvey Pearce, *The Continuity of American Poetry* (Princeton: Princeton University Press, 1961), 381. Pearce's intuition is confirmed by Glen MacLeod in *Wallace Stevens and Modern Art: From the Armory Show to Abstract Expressionism* (New Haven: Yale University Press, 1993), 22–23. MacLeod has traced the real jar and provides a picture of it with the word "Dominion" inscribed on the front.

19. Cook, *Poetry, Word-Play, and Word-War*, 17.

20. Frank Lentricchia, *Ariel and the Police: Michel Foucault, William James, Wallace Stevens* (Madison: University of Wisconsin Press, 1988), 7.

21. Lentricchia, *Ariel and the Police*, 11.

22. William W. Bevis, *Mind of Winter: Wallace Stevens, Meditation, and Literature* (Pittsburgh: University of Pittsburgh Press, 1988), 268.

23. Woodman, *Stanza My Stone*, 131–32.

24. Lentricchia, *Ariel and the Police*, 7.

25. Morse, *Wallace Stevens: Life as Poetry,* 92.

26. Malinowski, *Argonauts of the Western Pacific,* 451.

27. Morse, *Wallace Stevens: Life as Poetry,* 92.

28. Malinowski, *Argonauts of the Western Pacific,* 401.

29. Lentricchia, *Ariel and the Police,* 27.

30. Ibid., 20.

31. Margaret Peterson, *Wallace Stevens and the Idealist Tradition* (Ann Arbor: UMI Research Press, 1983), 102–103.

32. James Guetti, *Word-Music: The Aesthetic Aspect of Narrative Fiction* (New Brunswick, N.J.: Rutgers University Press, 1980), 38.

4. The Aural Foundations of the Real

1. J. Hillis Miller, *Poets of Reality: Six Twentieth Century Writers* (Forge Village, Mass.: Harvard University Press, 1965; reprint, New York: Atheneum, 1974); "Theoretical and Atheoretical Stevens," in *Wallace Stevens: A Celebration,* ed. Frank Doggett and Robert Buttel (Princeton: Princeton University Press, 1980), 274–85; Joseph Riddel, *The Clairvoyant Eye* (Baton Rouge: Louisiana State University Press, 1965); Roy Harvey Pearce, *The Continuity of American Poetry* (Princeton: Princeton University Press, 1961); "Toward Decreation: Stevens and the 'Theory of Poetry,'" in Doggett and Buttel, *A Celebration,* 286–307; Helen Regueiro, *The Limits of Imagination: Wordsworth, Yeats, and Stevens* (Ithaca, N.Y.: Cornell University Press, 1976); Paul Bové, *Destructive Poetics: Heidegger and Modern American Poetry* (New York: Columbia University Press, 1980); Frank Lentricchia, *After New Criticism* (Chicago: University of Chicago Press, 1980).

2. J. S. Leonard and C. E. Wharton, *The Fluent Mundo: Wallace Stevens and the Structure of Reality* (Athens: University of Georgia Press, 1988), ix.

3. The most important arguments about Stevens and phenomenology appear in Thomas Hines, *The Later Poetry of Wallace Stevens: Phenomenological Parallels with Husserl and Heidegger* (Lewisburg, Pa.: Bucknell University Press, 1976), which argues that the later poetry of Wallace Stevens shows a change in the poet's view of the reality/imagination complex and that it can profitably be explained by a comparison to phenomenological methods; and in Paul Bové, *Destructive Poetics* (above), which argues that Stevens's poetics closely resembles Heidegger's method of stripping off the culturally accumulated knowledge in order to reach an authentic knowledge of the thing itself. By extending the Heideggerian associations, Bové closely relates Stevens's method of writing to deconstruction.

4. See also J. B. Leggett, *Early Stevens: The Nietzschean Intertext* (Durham: Duke University Press, 1992).

5. Husserl's "reductions" were meant to avoid the interference of previous epistemological notions in the study of the phenomena given to consciousness. Heidegger applied the same method with the difference that he rejected the idea of "transcendental subjectivity" promoted by Husserl. For a complete explanation, see Hines, *The Later Poetry of Wallace Stevens,* 34–37, and Leonard and Wharton, *The Fluent Mundo,* 84–85.

6. Leonard and Wharton, *The Fluent Mundo,* 89.

7. J. B. Leggett, *Wallace Stevens and Literary Theory: Conceiving the Supreme Fiction* (Chapel Hill: University of North Carolina Press, 1987), 25.

8. Ibid., 5.

9. Margaret Peterson, *Wallace Stevens and the Idealist Tradition* (Ann Arbor: UMI Research Press, 1983). Peterson's argument covers most of the sources of Stevens's ideas about imagination in particular and is of a special interest for that topic.

10. Peterson, *Wallace Stevens and the Idealist Tradition,* 40.

11. Gerald Bruns, "Stevens Without Epistemology," in *Wallace Stevens: The Poetics of Modernism,* ed. Albert Gelpi (Cambridge: Cambridge University Press, 1985), 25.

12. Thomas Grey, *The Wallace Stevens Case: Law and the Practice of Poetry* (Cambridge, Mass.: Harvard University Press, 1991), 72.

13. Wallace Stevens, *The Necessary Angel: Essays on Reality and the Imagination* (New York: Knopf, 1942; reprint, New York: Vintage, 1951), 36.

14. See Hines, *The Later Poetry of Wallace Stevens;* Regueiro, *The Limits of Imagination;* Bové, *Destructive Poetics;* and so forth.

15. William James, *Pragmatism* and *The Meaning of Truth* (Cambridge, Mass.: Harvard University Press, 1981), 118.

16. Wallace Stevens, *Opus Posthumous* (New York: Knopf, 1980; reprint, New York: Vintage, 1982), 191.

17. Mark Halliday, *Stevens and the Interpersonal* (Princeton: Princeton University Press, 1991), 70.

18. See Glen MacLeod, *Wallace Stevens and Modern Art: From the Armory Show to Abstract Expressionism* (New Haven: Yale University Press, 1993).

19. James Longenbach, *Wallace Stevens: The Plain Sense of Things* (New York: Oxford University Press, 1991), 42.

20. Kenneth Burke, "A Dramatistic View of the Origins of Language and Postscripts on the Negative," in *Language as Symbolic Action* (Berkeley: University of California Press, 1966), 419–80.

21. Helen Vendler, *On Extended Wings* (Cambridge, Mass.: Harvard University Press, 1970).

22. Jacqueline Vaught Brogan, *Stevens and Simile: A Theory of Language* (Princeton: Princeton University Press, 1986), 132.

23. James, *Pragmatism,* 254–55.

24. Ibid., 119–20.

25. Richard Rorty, *Philosophy and the Mirror of Nature* (Princeton: Princeton University Press, 1979), 315.

26. George Santayana, *The Life of Reason* (London: Constable, 1954), 23.

27. Hayden White, *The Content of the Form: Narrative Discourse and the Historical Representation* (Baltimore: Johns Hopkins University Press, 1989), 24.

28. Hines, *The Later Poetry of Wallace Stevens,* 132–35.

29. Eleanor Cook, *Poetry, Word-Play, and Word-War in Wallace Stevens* (Princeton: Princeton University Press, 1988), 179.

30. White, *The Content of the Form,* 24.

31. Cook, *Poetry, Word-Play, and Word-War,* 179.

32. White, *The Content of the Form,* 4.

33. Bruns, "Stevens Without Epistemology," 26.

34. Stevens, *The Necessary Angel,* 36.

5. The Image of Sound

1. Thomas Hines, *The Later Poetry of Wallace Stevens: Phenomenological Parallels with Husserl and Heidegger* (Lewisburg, Pa.: Bucknell University Press, 1976), 87.

2. See Paul A. Bové, *Destructive Poetics: Heidegger and Modern American Poetry* (New York: Columbia University Press, 1980), 181–215.

3. Gerald Bruns, "Stevens Without Epistemology," in *Wallace Stevens: The Poetics of Modernism,* ed. Albert Gelpi (Cambridge: Cambridge University Press, 1985), 24.

4. Margaret Peterson, *Wallace Stevens and the Idealist Tradition* (Ann Arbor: UMI Research Press, 1983), 8.

5. Peterson, *Wallace Stevens and the Idealist Tradition,* 59–60.

6. Ibid., 80.

7. Ronald E. Martin, *American Literature and the Destruction of Knowledge: Innovative Writing in the Age of Epistemology* (Durham: Duke University Press, 1991), xii–xiii.

8. Martin, *American Literature,* 244–45.

9. Roger Ramsey, "Sound and Music: Stevens' *Harmonium,*" *Contemporary Poetry: A Journal of Criticism* 2(3) (1977): 67–74.

10. John Hollander, "The Sound of the Music of Music and Sound," in *Wallace Stevens: A Celebration*, ed. Frank Doggett and Robert Buttel (Princeton: Princeton University Press, 1980), 235–355.

11. Terrance King, " 'Certain Phenomena of Sound': An Illustration of Wallace Stevens's Poetry of Words," *Texas Studies in Literature and Language* 20 (1978): 599–614.

12. Lea Hamaoui, "Sound and Image in Stevens' 'Not Ideas About the Thing but the Thing Itself,'" *Comparative Literature Studies* 17 (1980): 251–59.

13. Harold Bloom, in *Wallace Stevens: The Poems of Our Climate* (Ithaca, N.Y.: Cornell University Press, 1976), 148, sees the overwhelming influence of Keats in "Autumn Refrain." John Hollander (see above) is disposed to hear both Keatsian and Miltonic echoes, and Eleanor Cook, in *Poetry, Word-Play, and Word-War in Wallace Stevens* (Princeton: Princeton University Press, 1988), 127, inclines more toward perceiving a Miltonic form of the sonnet.

14. Cook, *Poetry, Word-Play, and Word-War,* 126.

15. Ibid.

16. Ruth Finnegan, *Oral Poetry: Its Nature, Significance, and Social Context* (Cambridge: Cambridge University Press, 1977), 103.

17. The "disjunctive" philosophy of Gilles Deleuze probably offers as many parallels with Stevens's thought as Husserl's or Heidegger's phenomenology. That it does should come as no surprise, since, like Stevens, Deleuze was influenced by Bergson and the aesthetic of modernism. In a poststructuralist vein, Deleuze deconstructs traditional philosophy from the inside, by analyzing the work of its most prominent representatives. The subject/object dichotomy comes immediately under his attack, since in his view both notions have suffered erosion and dissolution because of developments in science and psychoanalysis and because of the subversion operated by modernist literary works. Equally suspicious of idealism and empiricism, Deleuze's philosophy proposes differentiation and repetition as basic modes of existence and at the same time as philosophical notions that can explain the world as we see it today. Traditional philosophy has always relied on the assumption that there is a basis, a center, a point of reference, whether an ideal essence or an empirical reality. Like Derrida and Heidegger before him, Deleuze proposes to do away with such grounding and to admit that reality, as we know it, comprises phenomena that either repeat or differentiate themselves from other phenomena. Since there is no central reality, all realities are either repetitions of or differentiations from other equally ungrounded realities. In fact, repetition and differentiation occur at the same time, since unless it is mechanical, repetition implies a difference (a spring repeats another spring, but it is not identical with it). To see the world as a process of repetition and differentiation means to admit that all realities are, in fact, simulacra—or as Stevens would say, fictions. The modern philosopher (or poet) looks upon the play of the simulacra as positive, not negative, and this, in Deleuze's terms, means that one liberates the difference.

Deleuze's theorizing about language is also useful in understanding Stevens. James Joyce's work is, in Deleuze's opinion, the best example and proof of the absence of a grounding for language. In Joyce, words refer not to a reality or an idea/concept but to other words—see the repetitions, nonsense words, and the portmanteau words. They are independent signifiers, free to play, and they generate sense exclusively through their play. What remains of the reference is only the suspicion of a "somber precursor" that a reader might hold onto. Deleuze's idea that words, in fact, gesture toward a mystery that has to be accepted as such could very well fit a description of Stevens's "magic" poems. According to Deleuze, the original word is always shrouded in mystery, an esoteric word, and, at the limit, a nonsense word.

A parallel study of Stevens and Deleuze would probably lead to the discovery of other remarkable similarities, but it is too vast to undertake in this book, which is concerned with Stevens's philosophical position only insofar as it affects his usage of sound. The distinction between naked and clothed repetitions is, however, useful here to explain how, in language, sense can crystallize beyond nonsense. As long as we see language as representation (either of empirical reality or of ideal concepts), we conceive of repetition only in a negative way, says Deleuze. Once we liberate the difference and begin to see that phenomena repeat each other under different guises, we can realize that repetition gives them meaning. In language, then, poetic devices like rhyme, rhythm, refrain, or simple word repetition have a sense—they send us to the mystery that generates all language. As I have suggested all along, in reading Stevens, we must, in order to make sense of his poems, renounce the representational frame of mind (as Deleuze is urging us to do) and adopt a different view of language and reality.

I shall return to Deleuze in chapter 6 when I analyze Stevens's ideas on ontology as they devolve from his use of sound. In the process I will explain the third kind of repetition, which is ontological.

18. Gilles Deleuze, *Différence et répétition*, 4th ed. (Paris: Presses Universitaires de France, 1981), 347 (translations mine).

19. Ibid., 373.

20. R. P. Blackmur, "Examples of Wallace Stevens," *Hound and Horn* 5 (1932), reprinted in *Wallace Stevens: A Critical Anthology*, ed. Irvin Ehrenpreis (Baltimore: Penguin Books, 1972), 63.

21. George A. Lensing, *Wallace Stevens: A Poet's Growth* (Baton Rouge: Louisiana State University Press, 1986), 299.

22. *Letters of Wallace Stevens*, ed. Holly Stevens (New York: Knopf, 1981), 251.

23. Steven C. Levinson, *Pragmatics* (Cambridge: Cambridge University Press, 1984), 101–102.

24. Jacqueline Brogan, *Stevens and Simile: A Theory of Language* (Princeton: Princeton University Press, 1986), 20.

25. Joseph N. Riddel, *The Clairvoyant Eye: The Poetry and Poetics of Wallace Stevens* (Baton Rouge: Louisiana University Press, 1967), 86.

26. Bloom, *The Poems of Our Climate*, 377.

27. Ibid.

28. Kenneth Burke, *A Grammar of Motives* (Berkeley: University of California Press, 1969), 225.

29. Timothy J. Reiss, *The Uncertainty of Analysis: Problems in Truth, Meaning, and Culture* (Ithaca, N.Y.: Cornell University Press, 1988). (See also my first chapter.)

30. Bruns, "Stevens Without Epistemology," 24.

6. Meaning and Repetition

1. Thomas Grey, *The Wallace Stevens Case: Law and the Practice of Poetry* (Cambridge, Mass.: Harvard University Press, 1991), 79.

2. J. S. Leonard and C. E. Wharton, *The Fluent Mundo: Wallace Stevens and the Structure of Reality* (Athens: University of Georgia Press, 1988), 59–82.

3. See William W. Bevis, *Mind of Winter: Wallace Stevens, Meditation, and Literature* (Pittsburgh: University of Pittsburgh Press, 1988).

4. Gerald Bruns, "Stevens Without Epistemology," in *Wallace Stevens: The Poetics of Modernism*, ed. Albert Gelpi (Cambridge: Cambridge University Press, 1985), 26.

5. Marius Bewley, "The Poetry of Wallace Stevens," *Partisan Review* 16 (1949), reprinted in *Wallace Stevens: A Critical Anthology*, ed. Irvin Ehrenpreis (Baltimore: Penguin Books, 1972), 165.

6. Martin Heidegger, *Being and Time*, trans. John Macquarrie and Edward Robinson (New York: Harper & Row, 1962), 280.

7. Robert Frost, "Education by Poetry," in *Poetry and Prose* (New York: Holt, Rinehart & Winston, 1984), 333.

8. Mircea Eliade, *The Myth of the Eternal Return; or, Cosmos and History*, 4th ed. (Princeton: Princeton University Press, 1974), 157. As a historian of religions, Mircea Eliade is interested in defining the main areas in which archaic/religious man differs from modern man. The main distinctions he makes are between the sacred mode of being of archaic cultures, and the profane, characteristic of modern cultures; and between cyclical and linear time. Unlike the profane mode in which events happen and things exist for no particular reason, the sacred mode of being gives every human activity, no matter how ordinary, a meaning. Such meaning derives from the perception of habitual acts like eating, having sex, or working, as repetitions or imitations of the acts of gods. Cyclical time also results from this conception. Archaic man perceives time not as a linear development whose beginning is unfathomable but as a repeated cycle of events that took place in the sacred time (eternity) of the gods.

Rituals are meant to reenact the beginning of time and thus to mark a new beginning. The cycle of vegetation provides a model for the archaic concept of time. Both the sacred mode of being and the concept of cyclical time reflect a worldview quite different from the modern one.

Eliade's views have been mentioned in connection with Stevens by Thomas Hines, *The Later Poetry of Wallace Stevens: Phenomenological Parallels with Husserl and Heidegger* (Lewisburg, Pa.: Bucknell University Press, 1976), 211, who finds Stevens's view of time to be close to the concept of cyclical time described by Eliade; and by Barbara Fisher, *Wallace Stevens: The Intensest Rendezvous* (Charlottesville: University Press of Virginia, 1990), 114–15, who thinks that Stevens has a notion of sacred space similar to Eliade's. Sacred space offers a grounding, a center, that is missing in the profane, and Fisher speculates that, when Stevens speaks about the center, he has in mind such a space. Fisher's speculation would encourage us to agree with Leonora Woodman, who argues that Stevens is a profoundly religious man. Eliade's ideas may also be useful in my argument here, since his description of archaic ontology comes to coincide to a large extent with the ontology emerging from Stevens's poems.

9. James Longenbach, *Wallace Stevens: The Plain Sense of Things* (New York: Oxford University Press, 1991), 70.

10. See Gilles Deleuze, *Différence et répétition,* 4th ed. (Paris: Presses Universitaires de France, 1981), 337–91.

11. After distinguishing between naked and clothed repetitions (see chapter 5, note 17), Deleuze proposes a synthesis of all repetitions in a third kind, which he calls ontological. Significantly, this repetition, which synthesizes all others, is the highest ambition of art, according to Deleuze. His example of such a synthesis is the work of Andy Warhol in which a picture becomes unique (and therefore meaningful) because it repeats the very repeated image, the stereotype. What Deleuze fails to notice is that the power of repetition to give meaning is not exclusively the discovery of modernism. Folkloric productions use the repetition of words in language to the same effect. Malinowski's descriptions of magic language, as well as the work of Parry, Lord, and Havelock, show it.

12. Longenbach, *The Plain Sense of Things,* 69–72, 79–82.

13. Paul Fussell, *The Great War and Modern Memory* (New York: Oxford University Press, 1975).

14. Eric A. Havelock, *Preface to Plato* (Cambridge, Mass.: Harvard University Press, 1982), 123.

15. Leonard Meyer, *Emotion and Meaning in Music,* 3d ed. (Chicago: The University of Chicago Press, 1957), 152.

16. Meyer, *Emotion and Meaning in Music,* 53.

17. Deleuze, *Différence et répétition,* 370 (my translation).

18. Eliade, *The Myth of the Eternal Return,* 34.

19. Ibid.

20. Wallace Stevens, *Opus Posthumous* (New York: Knopf, 1980; reprint, New York: Vintage, 1982), 163.

21. See Lyall Bush, "'Satisfactions of Belief': Stevens' Poetry in a Pragmatic World," *Wallace Stevens Journal* 1(14) (Spring 1990): 3–20.

7. The Metaphysics of Sound

1. Margaret Peterson, "*Harmonium* and William James," *Southern Review* 7(3) (1971): 657–82.

2. Gerald L. Bruns, "Stevens Without Epistemology," in *Wallace Stevens: The Poetics of Modernism,* ed. Albert Gelpi (Cambridge: Cambridge University Press, 1985), 28.

3. Frank Lentricchia, *Ariel and the Police: Michel Foucault, William James, Wallace Stevens* (Madison: University of Wisconsin Press, 1988), 149.

4. James Longenbach, *Wallace Stevens: The Plain Sense of Things* (New York: Oxford University Press, 1991), 73.

5. See Yvor Winters, "Wallace Stevens; or, The Hedonist's Progress" (1943), reprinted in *Wallace Stevens: A Critical Anthology,* ed. Irvin Ehrenpreis, 120–42; J. V. Cunningham, "The Poetry of Wallace Stevens," *Poetry* 75 (1949), reprinted in Ehrenpreis, 182–98.

6. See Joseph Riddel, *The Clairvoyant Eye: The Poetry and Poetics of Wallace Stevens* (Baton

Rouge: Louisiana State University Press, 1965), 79–86; Harold Bloom, *Wallace Stevens: The Poems of Our Climate* (Ithaca, N.Y.: Cornell University Press, 1977), 23–35.

7. Timothy J. Reiss, *The Uncertainty of Analysis: Problems in Truth, Meaning, and Culture* (Ithaca, N.Y.: Cornell University Press, 1988), 148.

8. Mikhail Bakhtin, *The Dialogic Imagination,* trans. Caryl Emerson and Michael Holquist, ed. Michael Holquist (Austin: University of Texas Press, 1981), 276.

9. Jacqueline Brogan, " 'Sister of the Minotaur': Sexism and Stevens," in *Stevens and the Feminine,* ed. Melita Schaum (Tuscaloosa: The University of Alabama Press, 1993), 12.

10. *Letters of Wallace Stevens,* ed. Holly Stevens (New York: Knopf, 1981), 250.

11. Frank Lentricchia, "Philosophers of Modernism at Harvard circa 1900," *South Atlantic Quarterly* 89(4) (1990): 792–93.

12. Longenbach, *The Plain Sense of Things,* 78.

13. Bakhtin, *The Dialogic Imagination,* 298.

14. See Bloom, *The Poems of Our Climate,* 29; Riddel, *The Clairvoyant Eye,* 81.

15. Lentricchia, *Ariel and the Police,* 156.

16. Stevens, *Letters,* 250.

17. Bloom, *The Poems of Our Climate,* 35.

18. Stevens, *Letters,* 183.

19. Ibid., 590.

20. Julia Kristeva, *The Revolution of Poetic Language,* trans. Margaret Waller (New York: Columbia University Press, 1984).

21. Bloom, *The Poems of Our Climate,* 141.

22. Glen MacLeod, *Wallace Stevens and Modern Art: From the Armory Show to Abstract Expressionism* (New Haven: Yale University Press, 1993), 94.

23. Longenbach, *The Plain Sense of Things,* 256.

24. Thomas Hines, *The Later Poetry of Wallace Stevens: Phenomenological Parallels with Husserl and Heidegger* (Lewisburg, Pa.: Bucknell University Press, 1976), 93–94.

25. J. S. Leonard and C. E. Wharton, *The Fluent Mundo: Wallace Stevens and the Structure of Reality* (Athens: University of Georgia Press, 1988), 112.

26. Stevens's familiarity with Dante is detailed by Barbara Fisher, *Wallace Stevens: The Intensest Rendezvous* (Charlottesville: University of Virginia Press, 1990), 96–106.

27. Margaret Peterson, "*Harmonium* and William James," 661.

28. For a reading of "The House Was Quiet and the World Was Calm" that is quite germane to this study, refer to Charles Altieri's "Why Stevens Must be Abstract," in *Wallace Stevens: The Poetries of Modernism,* ed. Albert Gelpi (Cambridge: Cambridge University Press, 1985), 114–15. Altieri, who also reads "Crude Foyer," identifies "here" and "there" as the scene and the projected reader. Consistent with my conclusions that Stevens uses sound to achieve visibility, Altieri concludes his essay by stating: "The words themselves create an abstract space of such elemental sounds that one feels reading given the same concrete presence in the work and in the world that color and line give to sight. Reading poetry there provides a substantial theory for living here" (115–16).

29. Leonard and Wharton, *The Fluent Mundo,* 113.

30. Ralph Waldo Emerson, *Essays and Lectures,* ed. Joel Porte (New York: Literary Classics of the United States, 1983), 271.

8. "And if the music sticks"

1. Harold Bloom, *Wallace Stevens: The Poems of Our Climate* (Ithaca, N.Y.: Cornell University Press, 1976), 70.

2. Helen Vendler, *On Extended Wings: Wallace Stevens' Longer Poems* (Cambridge, Mass.: Harvard University Press, 1969); Joseph Riddel, *The Clairvoyant Eye: The Poetry and Poetics of Wallace Stevens* (Baton Rouge: Louisiana State University Press, 1965); Paul Bové, *Destructive Poetics: Heidegger and Modern American Poetry* (New York: Columbia University Press, 1980).

3. Kevin Barry, *Language, Music, and the Sign: A Study in Aesthetics, Poetics, and Poetic Practice from Collins to Coleridge* (Cambridge: Cambridge University Press, 1987).

4. Barry, *Language, Music, and the Sign,* 16.

5. Ibid., 65.

6. Leonard B. Meyer, *Emotion and Meaning in Music* (Chicago: University of Chicago Press, 1956), 140.

7. *Letters of Wallace Stevens,* ed. Holly Stevens (New York: Knopf, 1981), 351–52.

8. Bloom, *The Poems of Our Climate,* 71.

9. Gerald L. Bruns, "Stevens Without Epistemology," in *Wallace Stevens: The Poetics of Modernism,* ed. Albert Gelpi (Cambridge: Cambridge University Press, 1985), 24–40; Jacqueline Vaught Brogan, *Stevens and Simile: A Theory of Language* (Princeton: Princeton University Press, 1986); Eleanor Cook, *Poetry, Word-Play, and Word-War in Wallace Stevens* (Princeton: Princeton University Press, 1988).

10. Cook, *Poetry, Word-Play, and Word-War,* 82.

11. Frank Kermode, *Wallace Stevens* (Edinburgh: Oliver & Boyd, 1960), 45.

12. See Marie Borroff, *Language and the Poet: Verbal Artistry in Frost, Stevens, and Moore* (Chicago: University of Chicago Press, 1979), 42–60.

13. Robert Frost, *Poetry and Prose,* ed. Edward Connery Lathem and Lawrence Thompson (New York: Holt, Rinehart & Winston, 1981), 261.

14. R. P. Blackmur, "Examples of Wallace Stevens," *Hound and Horn* 5 (1932), reprinted in *Wallace Stevens: A Critical Anthology,* ed. Irvin Ehrenpreis (Baltimore: Penguin Books, 1972), 59–86.

15. Barry, *Language, Music, and the Sign,* 182.

9. The Poetics of Sound

1. See J. Hillis Miller, "Stevens' Rock and Criticism as Cure," *Georgia Review* 30(1) (1976): 5–31; and Joseph Riddel, "Metaphoric Staging: Stevens' Beginning Again of the 'End of the Book,'" in *Wallace Stevens: A Celebration,* ed. Frank Doggett and Robert Buttel (Princeton: Princeton University Press, 1980), 308–38.

2. Paul A. Bové, *Destructive Poetics: Heidegger and Modern American Poetry* (New York: Columbia University Press, 1980).

3. *Letters of Wallace Stevens,* ed. Holly Stevens (New York: Knopf, 1981), 758.

4. Stevens, *Letters,* 839.

5. Frank Kermode, "Dwelling Poetically in Connecticut," in Doggett and Buttel, *A Celebration,* 259.

6. Thomas J. Hines, *The Later Poetry of Wallace Stevens: Phenomenological Parallels with Husserl and Heidegger* (Lewisburg, Pa.: Bucknell University Press, 1976).

7. Martin Heidegger, *Existence and Being* (South Bend, Ind.: Gateway Editions, 1949), 276.

8. Ibid., 281.

9. Ibid., 283.

10. Gerald Bruns, who has written about Stevens elsewhere, mentions the poet several times in his book *Heidegger's Estrangements: Language, Truth, and Poetry in the Later Writings* (New Haven: Yale University Press, 1981). His remarks show both similarities and differences between the poet and the philosopher. Bruns also mentions the efforts of Michael Murray in *Modern Critical Theory: A Phenomenological Introduction* (The Hague: Martinus Nijhoff, 1975) to show how Stevens and Heidegger are similar in their "orphic" conception of language.

11. Both Margaret Peterson, *Wallace Stevens and the Idealist Tradition* (Ann Arbor: UMI Research Press, 1983), 141, and Thomas Grey, *The Wallace Stevens Case: Law and the Practice of Poetry* (Cambridge, Mass.: Harvard University Press, 1991), 98, think the poem was inspired by William James. J. B. Leggett, *Wallace Stevens and Poetic Theory: Conceiving the Supreme Fiction* (Chapel Hill: University of North Carolina Press, 1967), 75–76, on the other hand, suggests that it might have been inspired by the aesthetic ruminations of Charles Mauron, whose work Stevens read in order to compose his lectures

on poetry. Leggett's suggestion changes the meaning of the poem from a philosophical to an aesthetic debate, but one must not forget that for Stevens the line between the two was not so clearly marked. My conclusions will bring Stevens back to William James, but I will also show that the view of language that emerges in the poem's performance is, up to a certain point, Heideggerian.

12. Thomas Hines in *The Later Poetry of Wallace Stevens,* 96–99, analyzes this poem from a phenomenological perspective but with a total disregard for the reality of its language. For Hines, the poet simply philosophizes, as anyone would, in prose. This attitude is rather curious, in the Heideggerian context, where language occupies such a central place.

13. Martin Heidegger, *Poetry, Language, Thought,* trans. Albert Hofstadter (New York: Harper & Row, 1971), 208.

14. Ibid., 132.

15. Ibid., 197.

16. This particular poem has been discussed by too many critics for a review of the criticism to be possible here. J. S. Leonard and C. E. Wharton, *The Fluent Mundo: Wallace Stevens and the Structure of Reality* (Athens: University of Georgia Press, 1988), 75–78, offers a useful summary of most interpretations. None of these interpretations, however, considers the discourse in the poem or the possibilities of meaning beyond representation. A reading of the poem that is closer to mine is that of James Guetti, *Word Music: The Aesthetic Aspect of Narrative Fiction* (New Brunswick, N.J.: Rutgers University Press, 1980), 45–47, which argues that this, as well as other poems by Stevens, brings cognitive images to exhaustion and ultimately promotes noncognitive images.

17. Wallace Stevens, *Opus Posthumous: Poems, Plays, Prose,* ed. Samuel French Morse (New York: Knopf, 1980; reprint, New York: Vintage, 1982), 117.

18. Stevens, *Opus Posthumous,* 118.

19. Heidegger, *Poetry, Language, Thought,* 215–16.

20. This poem received some attention from Leonard and Wharton, in *The Fluent Mundo,* who use it to support their thesis about Stevens's Nietzschean rather than Heideggerian inclination.

21. Margaret Peterson, "*Harmonium* and William James," *Southern Review* 7 (1971): 658–82.

22. See Lyall Bush, "'Satisfactions of Belief': Stevens' Poetry in a Pragmatic World," *Wallace Stevens Journal* 14(1) (1990): 3–20.

23. David P. Young, "A Skeptical Music: Stevens and Santayana," *Criticism* 7 (1965), reprinted in *Wallace Stevens: A Critical Anthology,* ed. Irvin Ehrenpreis (Baltimore: Penguin Books, 1972), 254.

24. William James, *Pragmatism* and *The Meaning of Truth* (Cambridge, Mass.: Harvard University Press, 1981), 193.

25. Frank Lentricchia, "Philosophers of Modernism at Harvard circa 1900," *South Atlantic Quarterly* 89(4) (1990): 791.

26. George Santayana, *The Life of Reason* (London: Constable, 1954), 326.

27. Santayana, *The Life of Reason,* 326.

28. Ibid., 327.

29. Ibid., 331.

30. Leonard and Wharton, *The Fluent Mundo,* 15.

31. Doggett and Buttel, *A Celebration,* 257.

32. Richard Rorty, *Consequences of Pragmatism: Essays, 1972–1980* (Minneapolis: University of Minnesota Press, 1982), 161.

33. Stevens, *Letters,* 589.

34. Ibid., 590.

35. Ibid.

36. See Bové, *Destructive Poetics.*

37. See J. Hillis Miller, "Stevens' Rock and Criticism as Cure."

38. James Longenbach, *Wallace Stevens: The Plain Sense of Things* (New York: Oxford University Press, 1991), 294.

39. Helen Vendler, *On Extended Wings: Wallace Stevens' Longer Poems* (Cambridge, Mass.: Harvard University Press, 1969), 219.

40. Again, I will not refer here to interpretations of the poem that consider its ideas. Hines, *The Later Poetry of Wallace Stevens,* 156–57, uses the poem as another example of phenomenological reduction, while Longenbach in *The Plain Sense of Things,* 282, sees it as firmly rooted in history. Naturally, Leonard and Wharton in *The Fluent Mundo,* 122, use it for the references to Nietzsche. None of them considers the effects of sound and repetition that have been my interest throughout this book.

41. Heidegger, *Poetry, Language, Thought,* 132.

42. Lentricchia, "Philosophers of Modernism at Harvard circa 1900," 799.

43. Stevens, *Opus Posthumous,* 163.

44. Vendler, *On Extended Wings,* 229.

Bibliography

Primary Sources

Stevens, Wallace. *The Collected Poems.* New York: Knopf, 1954. Reprint. New York: Vintage, 1982.

———. *Letters of Wallace Stevens.* Ed. Holly Stevens. 1966. Reprint. New York. Knopf, 1981.

———. *The Necessary Angel.* New York: Knopf, 1942. Reprint. New York: Vintage, 1951.

———. *Opus Posthumous.* New York: Knopf, 1980. Reprint. New York: Vintage, 1982.

———. *The Palm at the End of the Mind: Selected Poems and a Play.* Ed. Holly Stevens. New York: Knopf, 1971. Reprint. New York: Vintage, 1972.

Secondary Sources

Baird, James. *The Dome and the Rock: Structure in the Poetry of Wallace Stevens.* Baltimore: Johns Hopkins University Press, 1968.

Bakhtin, Mikhail. *The Dialogic Imagination.* Trans. Caryl Emerson and Michael Holquist. Ed. Michael Holquist. Austin: University of Texas Press, 1981.

Barry, Kevin. *Language, Music and the Sign: A Study in Aesthetics, Poetics, and Poetic Practice from Collins to Coleridge.* Cambridge: Cambridge University Press, 1987.

Barthes, Roland. *Image, Music, Text.* Trans. Stephen Heath. New York: Hill and Wang, 1977.

Bauman, Richard. *Verbal Art as Performance.* Rowley, Mass.: Newbury House, 1977.

Ben Amos, Dan, ed. *Folklore Genres.* Austin: University of Texas Press, 1976.

Benamou, Michel. *Wallace Stevens and the Symbolist Imagination.* Princeton: Princeton University Press, 1972.

Bergson, Henri. *Oeuvres.* Paris: Presses Universitaires de France, 1963.

Bevis, William W. *Mind of Winter: Wallace Stevens, Meditation, and Literature.* Pittsburgh: University of Pittsburgh Press, 1988.

Bloom, Harold. *Wallace Stevens: The Poems of Our Climate.* Ithaca, N.Y.: Cornell University Press, 1977.

Borroff, Marie. *The Language and the Poet: Verbal Artistry in Frost, Stevens, and Moore.* Chicago: University of Chicago Press, 1979.

———. "Sound Symbolism as Drama in the Poetry of Wallace Stevens." *ELH* 48(4) (Winter 1981): 914–34.

———, ed. *Wallace Stevens: A Collection of Essays.* Englewood Cliffs, N.J.: Prentice-Hall, 1963.

Bové, Paul A. *Destructive Poetics: Heidegger and American Poetry.* New York: Columbia University Press, 1980.

Brazeau, Peter. *Parts of a World: Wallace Stevens Remembered: An Aural Biography.* New York: Random House, 1983.

Brogan, Jacqueline Vaught. *Part of the Climate: American Cubist Poetry.* Berkeley: University of California Press, 1991.

––––––. *Stevens and Simile: A Theory of Language.* Princeton: Princeton University Press, 1986.

Brown, Merle Elliot. *Wallace Stevens: The Poem as Act.* Detroit: Wayne State University Press, 1970.

Bruns, Gerald. *Heidegger's Estrangements: Language, Truth, and Poetry in the Later Writings.* New Haven: Yale University Press, 1989.

Burke, Kenneth. *A Grammar of Motives.* Berkeley: University of California Press, 1969.

––––––. *Language as Symbolic Action.* Berkeley: University of California Press, 1966.

Bush, Lyall. "'Satisfactions of Belief': Stevens' Poetry in a Pragmatic World." *Wallace Stevens Journal* 14(1) (1990): 3–20.

Coker, Wilson. *Music and Meaning: A Theoretical Introduction to Musical Aesthetics.* New York: Macmillan, 1972.

Cook, Eleanor. "From Etymology to Paronomasia: Wallace Stevens, Elizabeth Bishop, and Others." *Connotations: A Journal for Critical Debate* 2(1) (1992): 34–51.

––––––. *Poetry, Word-Play, and Word-War in Wallace Stevens.* Princeton: Princeton University Press, 1988.

Deleuze, Gilles. *Différence et répétition.* 4th ed. Paris: Presses Universitaires de France, 1981.

Derrida, Jacques. *Of Grammatology.* Trans. Gayatri Chakravorty Spivak. Baltimore: Johns Hopkins University Press, 1976.

Dickie, Margaret. "Collections of Sound in Stevens." *Wallace Stevens Journal* 15(2) (1991): 133–43.

––––––. *Lyric Contingencies: Emily Dickinson and Wallace Stevens.* Philadelphia: University of Pennsylvania Press, 1991.

Doggett, Frank, and Robert Buttel, eds. *Wallace Stevens: A Celebration.* Princeton: Princeton University Press, 1980.

Dougherty, Adelyn. "Structures of Sound in Wallace Stevens' 'Farewell to Florida.'" *Texas Studies in Literature and Language* 16 (1975): 755–64.

Ehrenpreis, Irvin, ed. *Wallace Stevens: A Critical Anthology.* Baltimore: Penguin Books, 1972.

Eliade, Mircea. *The Myth of the Eternal Return; or, Cosmos and History.* Trans. Willard R. Trask. Bollingen Series XLVI. 4th ed. Princeton: Princeton University Press, 1974.

––––––. *The Sacred and the Profane: The Nature of Religion.* Trans. Willard R. Trask. New York: Harcourt, Brace & World, 1959.

Emerson, Ralph Waldo. *Essays and Lectures.* Ed. Joel Porte. New York: Literary Classics of the United States, 1983.

Filreis, Alan. *Wallace Stevens and the Actual World.* Princeton: Princeton University Press, 1991.

Finnegan, Ruth. *Oral Poetry: Its Nature, Significance, and Social Context.* Cambridge: Cambridge University Press, 1977.

Fisher, Barbara M. *Wallace Stevens: The Intensest Rendezvous.* Charlottesville: University Press of Virginia, 1990.

Foucault, Michel. *Language, Counter-Memory, Practice.* Trans. Donald F. Bouchard and Sherry Simmons. Ed. Donald F. Bouchard. Ithaca, N.Y.: Cornell University Press, 1977.

————. *The Order of Things: An Archeology of Human Sciences* (Translation of *Les mots et les choses*). New York: Pantheon Books, 1971. Reprint. New York: Vintage, 1973.

Frost, Robert. *Poetry and Prose*. Ed. Edward Connery Lathem and Lawrence Thomson. New York: Holt, Rinehart & Winston, 1984.

Fussell, Paul. *Poetic Meter and Poetic Form*. New York: Random House, 1966.

Gelpi, Albert. Ed. *Wallace Stevens: The Poetics of Modernism*. Cambridge: Cambridge University Press, 1985.

Goodman, Ann. "Phonological Aspects of Metaphor in Anglo-American Poetry." *Sigma: Revue du Centre d'Etudes Linguistiques d'Aix Montpellier* 6 (1982): 109–21.

Grey, Thomas C. *The Wallace Stevens Case: Law and the Practice of Poetry*. Cambridge, Mass.: Harvard University Press, 1991.

Grice, Paul. *Studies in the Way of Words*. Cambridge, Mass.: Harvard University Press, 1989.

Gross, Harvey. *Sound and Form in Modern Poetry*. Ann Arbor: University of Michigan Press, 1968.

Guetti, James. *Word/Music: The Aesthetic Aspect of Narrative Fiction*. New Brunswick, N.J.: Rutgers University Press, 1980.

Halliday, Mark. *Stevens and the Interpersonal*. Princeton: Princeton University Press, 1991.

Hamaoui, Lea. "Sound and Image in Stevens' 'Not Ideas About the Thing but the Thing Itself.'" *Comparative Literature Studies* 17 (1980): 251–59.

Havelock, Eric A. *Preface to Plato*. Cambridge, Mass.: Harvard University Press, 1982.

Heidegger, Martin. *Being and Time*. Trans. John Macquarrie and Edward Robinson. New York: Harper & Row, 1962.

————. *Existence and Being*. South Bend, Ind.: Gateway Editions, 1949.

————. *Poetry, Language, Thought*. Trans. Albert Hofstadter. New York: Harper & Row, 1971.

Hines, Thomas J. *The Later Poetry of Wallace Stevens: Phenomenological Parallels with Husserl and Heidegger*. Lewisburg, Pa.: Bucknell University Press, 1976.

Hollander, John. *Melodious Guile: Fictive Pattern in Poetic Language*. New Haven: Yale University Press, 1988.

————. "The Metrical Emblem." *Kenyon Review* 21 (1959): 279–96.

Ihde, Don. *Listening and Voice: A Phenomenology of Sound*. Athens: Ohio University Press, 1976.

James, William. *Pragmatism* and *The Meaning of Truth*. Cambridge, Mass.: Harvard University Press, 1981.

Kermode, Frank. *Wallace Stevens*. Edinburgh: Oliver & Boyd, 1960.

King, Terrance. "'Certain Phenomena of Sound': An Illustration of Wallace Stevens's Poetry of Words." *Texas Studies in Literature and Language* 20 (1978): 599–614.

Kramer, Lawrence. *Music as Cultural Practice, 1800–1900*. Berkeley: University of California Press, 1990.

Kristeva, Julia. *The Revolution of Poetic Language*. Trans. Margaret Waller. New York: Columbia University Press, 1984.

LaCapra, Dominick. *Rethinking Intellectual History: Texts, Contexts, Language*. Ithaca, N.Y.: Cornell University Press, 1983.

La Guardia, David M. *Advance on Chaos: The Sanctifying Imagination of Wallace Stevens*. Hanover, N.H.: University Press of New England, 1983.

Langer, Susanne K., ed. *Reflections on Art.* New York: Arno Press, 1979.

Leggett, J. B. *Early Stevens: The Nietzschean Intertext.* Durham: Duke University Press, 1992.

———. *Wallace Stevens and Poetic Theory.* Chapel Hill: University of North Carolina Press, 1987.

Lensing, George S. *Wallace Stevens: A Poet's Growth.* Baton Rouge: Louisiana State Universtiy Press, 1986.

Lentricchia, Frank. *After New Criticism.* Chicago: University of Chicago Press, 1980.

———. *Ariel and the Police: Michel Foucault, William James, Wallace Stevens.* Madison: University of Wisconsin Press, 1988.

———. *The Gaiety of Language: An Essay on the Radical Poetics of W. B. Yeats and Wallace Stevens.* Berkeley: University of California Press, 1968.

———. "Philosophers of Modernism at Harvard circa 1900." *South Atlantic Quarterly* 89(4) (1990): 787–834.

Leonard, J. S., and C. E. Wharton. *The Fluent Mundo: Wallace Stevens and the Structure of Reality.* Athens: University of Georgia Press, 1988.

Levinson, Steven C. *Pragmatics.* Cambridge: Cambridge University Press, 1984.

Litz, A. Walton. *Introspective Voyager: The Poetic Development of Wallace Stevens.* New York: Oxford University Press, 1972.

Longenbach, James. *Wallace Stevens: The Plain Sense of Things.* New York: Oxford University Press, 1991.

Lord, Albert. *The Singer of Tales.* Cambridge, Mass.: Harvard University Press, 1960.

MacLeod, Glen. *Wallace Stevens and Modern Art: From the Armory Show to Abstract Expressionism.* New Haven: Yale University Press, 1993.

Malinowski, Bronislaw. *Argonauts of the Western Pacific.* New York: E. P. Dutton, 1961.

Martin, Ronald E. *American Literature and the Destruction of Knowledge: Innovative Writing in the Age of Epistemology.* Durham: Duke University Press, 1991.

Meyer, Leonard B. *Emotion and Meaning in Music.* Chicago: University of Chicago Press, 1956.

Miller, Hillis J. *Poets of Reality: Six Twentieth Century Writers.* Forge Village, Mass.: Harvard University Press, 1965. Reprint. New York: Atheneum, 1974.

———. "Stevens' Rock and Criticism as Cure." *Georgia Review* 30(1) (1976): 5–31.

Mitchell, W. J. T. *Iconology: Image, Text, Ideology.* Chicago: University of Chicago Press, 1986.

Morse, Samuel French. *Wallace Stevens: Life as Poetry.* New York: Western Publishing, 1970.

Nassar, Eugene Paul. *Wallace Stevens: An Anatomy of Figuration.* Philadelphia: University of Pennsylvania Press, 1965.

Ong, Walter J. *The Barbarian Within.* New York: Macmillan, 1962.

———. *The Presence of the Word.* New Haven: Yale University Press, 1967.

———. *Orality and Literacy: The Technologizing of the Word.* New York: Methuen, 1982.

———. *Rhetoric, Romance, and Technology.* Ithaca, N.Y.: Cornell University Press, 1971.

Paredes, Américo. "Some Aspects of Folk Poetry." *Texas Studies in Literature and Language* 6 (1964): 213–25.

Parry, Milman. *The Making of Homeric Verse: The Collected Papers of Milman Parry.* Ed. Adam Parry. Oxford: Clarendon Press, 1971.

Pearce, Roy Harvey. *The Continuity of American Poetry.* Princeton: Princeton University Press, 1961.

Peckham, Morse. *Man's Rage for Chaos: Biology, Behavior, and the Arts.* New York: Chilton Books, 1965.

Perlis, Alan. *Wallace Stevens: A World of Transforming Shapes.* Lewisburg, Pa.: Bucknell University Press, 1976.

Peterson, Margaret. "*Harmonium* and William James." *Southern Review* 7(3) (1971): 657–82.

———. *Wallace Stevens and the Idealist Tradition.* Studies in Modern Literature, ed. A. Walton Litz. Ann Arbor: UMI Research Press, 1983.

Poirier, Richard. *Poetry and Pragmatism.* Cambridge, Mass.: Harvard University Press, 1992.

Pritchard, William H. *Lives of the Modern Poets.* New York: Oxford University Press, 1980.

Ramsey, Roger. "Sound and Music: Stevens' *Harmonium.*" *Contemporary Poetry: A Journal of Criticism* 2(3) (1977): 67–74.

Regueiro, Helen. *The Limits of Imagination: Wordsworth, Yeats, and Stevens.* Ithaca, N.Y.: Cornell University Press, 1976.

Reiss, Timothy J. *The Uncertainty of Analysis: Problems in Truth, Meaning, and Culture.* Ithaca, N.Y.: Cornell University Press, 1988.

Riddel, Joseph N. *The Clairvoyant Eye: The Poetry and Poetics of Wallace Stevens.* Baton Rouge: Louisiana State University Press, 1965.

Rieke, Alison. *The Senses of Nonsense.* Iowa City: University of Iowa Press, 1992.

———. "Stevens' Armchair Travel: The Sound of the Foreign." *Wallace Stevens Journal* 15(2) (1991): 165–77.

Rodgers, Lise. "Stevens' 'Certain Phenomena of Sound.'" *Explicator* 39(4) (Summer 1981): 39–41.

Rodriguez, Richard. *Hunger of Memory: The Education of Richard Rodriguez: An Autobiography.* New York: David R. Godine, 1983. Reprint. New York: Bantam, 1988.

Rorty, Richard. *Consequences of Pragmatism: Essays, 1972–1980.* Minneapolis: University of Minnesota Press, 1982.

———. *Philosophy and the Mirror of Nature.* Princeton: Princeton University Press, 1979.

Sabin, Margerie. "The Fate of the Frost Speaker." *Raritan* 2 (Fall 1982): 128–39.

Santayana, George. *The Life of Reason.* London: Constable, 1954.

Schaum, Melita. *Wallace Stevens and the Critical Schools.* Tuscaloosa: University of Alabama Press, 1988.

———, ed. *Wallace Stevens and the Feminine.* Tuscaloosa: University of Alabama Press, 1993.

Searle, John. *Speech Acts: An Essay in the Philosophy of Language.* Cambridge: Cambridge University Press, 1969.

Springer, Mary Doyle. "Repetition and 'Going Round' with Wallace Stevens." *Wallace Stevens Journal* 15(2) (1991): 191–208.

Stewart, Garrett. *Reading Voices: Literature and the Phonotext.* Berkeley: University of California Press, 1990.

Stewart, Susan. *Nonsense: Aspects of Intertextuality in Folklore and Literature.* Baltimore: Johns Hopkins University Press, 1979.

Taylor, Dennis. "The Apparitional Meters of Wallace Stevens." *Wallace Stevens Journal* 15(2) (1991): 209–28.

Vendler, Helen. *On Extended Wings.* Cambridge, Mass.: Harvard University Press, 1970.

Wakoski, Diane. "A Poet's Odyssey from Shakespearean Sonnets to Stevens' Not-So-Blank Verse." *Wallace Stevens Journal* 15(2) (1991): 126–32.

White, Hayden. *The Content of the Form: Narrative Discourse and the Historical Representation.* Baltimore: Johns Hopkins University Press, 1989.

Willard, Abbie F. *Wallace Stevens: The Poet and His Critics.* Chicago: American Library Association, 1978.

Wittgenstein, Ludwig. *Philosophical Investigations.* Trans. G. E. M. Anscombe. 3d ed. New York: Macmillan, 1966.

Woodman, Leonora. *Stanza My Stone: Wallace Stevens and the Hermetic Tradition.* West Lafayette, Ind.: Purdue University Press, 1983.

Index

About the Author

Anca Rosu teaches in the English Department at Rutgers University. She received her master's degree in English at the University of Bucharest and her doctorate in American Literature at Rutgers. After being awarded the Republic's Fellowship, Romania, 1970–1971, she has gone on to teach at universities in Romania, Madagascar, and the United States. Her other publications include a translation of *Emma* by Jane Austin (1977) and articles about John Donne, T. S. Eliot, and Wallace Stevens.